The President as Statesman

American Political Thought

Edited by

Wilson Carey McWilliams & Lance Banning

The President as Statesman

Woodrow Wilson and the Constitution

Daniel D. Stid

University Press of Kansas

Published by the University Press of Kansas (Lawrence, Kansas 66049), which was organized by the Kansas Board of Regents and is operated and funded by Emporia State University, Fort Hays State University, Kansas State University, Pittsburg State University, the University of Kansas, and Wichita State University

Library of Congress Cataloging-in-Publication Data

Stid, Daniel D.
      The president as statesman : Woodrow Wilson and the Constitution /
   Daniel D. Stid.
         p.   cm. — (American political thought)
      Includes bibliographical references and index.
      ISBN 0–7006–0884–2 (alk. paper)
         1. Wilson, Woodrow, 1856–1924—Views on the Constitution.
   2. United States—Politics and government—1913–1921.   3. Separation
   of powers—United States.   I. Title.   II. Series.
   E766.S85   1998
   973.91′3′092—dc21   97–50019

British Library Cataloguing in Publication Data is available.

Printed in the United States of America

10 9 8 7 6 5 4 3 2 1

The paper used in this publication meets the minimum requirements of the American National Standard for Permanence of Paper for Printed Library Materials Z39.48-1984.

✿ Contents

❦ Preface

By the late 1980s, many political scientists were bringing a new sense of urgency to their discipline's perennial concern about problems of governance in the United States. They had their reasons. The 1970s had witnessed Watergate, the Vietnam debacle, stagflation, and the Iranian hostage crisis; the 1980s, ballooning budget deficits, the Iran-Contra scandal, and nearly a decade of sniping and gridlock between Republican chief executives and Democratic legislators. The extent and variety of the problems suggested that something was fundamentally wrong with the political system. Leading scholars contributed essays to volumes published by Washington think tanks whose titles asked blunt questions such as *Separation of Powers—Does It Still Work?* (American Enterprise Institute, 1986) and even *Can the Government Govern?* (Brookings Institution, 1989). To explore these questions and develop the systemic reforms that seemed necessary, James MacGregor Burns and several other political scientists banded together with J. William Fulbright, Robert McNamara, Daniel Patrick Moynihan, and other prominent citizens to form the Committee on the Constitutional System. Even *Time* magazine got into the act. The cover of its October 23, 1989, issue depicted George Washington shedding a fat tear and asked, "Is Government Dead?"

Whether or not the nation is undergoing a crisis of governability is the kind of big, messy question that beginning graduate students love to take up, much to the chagrin of their teachers. I was no exception to this pattern. Fortunately, my adviser, Paul Peterson, was. With his encouragement, I set out to get some historical perspective on the issue by doing a seminar paper on Woodrow Wilson. Reformers usually cited Wilson's writings as the starting point for concerns about governance in the United States, and I reasoned that since Wilson, unlike most reform-minded political scientists, came to hold real power, his teachings and experience would make a useful contribution to the contemporary debate about governance.

I soon discovered, however, that it would take more than a quick study to bring the lessons of Wilson's theory and practice to bear on the debate, as scholars disagreed sharply about the nature and effects of his program. Many of his biographers and an earlier generation of political scientists who focused on his travails and accomplishments as president saw him as an innovative and effective leader. But more recent work by political scientists concentrated on Wilson's political theory and led to the conclusion that he had established an unstable form of democratic leadership. This scholarly impasse raised a number of intriguing questions. What was Wilson attempting to do with his theoretical program and how well did he do it? Should he be cast as a constructive master or a destructive idealist in the drama of American political development—or, as increasingly seemed likely to me, in another role entirely? I concluded that the way to resolve these questions was to pursue them in an interdisciplinary fashion—fully exploring the logic and importance of Wilson's ideas about leadership and governance but in the appropriate historical context and with an eye as to how he developed and applied them.

I had one other goal in undertaking this book that deserves mention. Early on, I believed that Woodrow Wilson's attempt to establish responsible government in the United States would be highly useful in determining the potential influence of ideas and leadership on the American polity. If ever a statesman was in position to bring about the sort of fundamental change that reformers in the 1980s were claiming was necessary to solve the nation's quandaries, it was Woodrow Wilson, not simply because of the power of his ideas and his office, but also because he led the nation at a time when its politics and government were, in a sense, up for grabs. To determine the methods and extent of his influence amid the tumult of the Progressive Era was indeed an exciting prospect. I was thus somewhat taken aback when the evidence increasingly suggested that while Wilson's program had reshaped some of the basic features of the U.S. polity, those features had far greater impact on the shape of his program. This idea seemed a depressing commentary on the power of democratic statesmanship, but two lines of thought led me to conclude otherwise.

One was elaborated in James March and Johan Olsen's seminal essay "The New Institutionalism" (*American Political Science Review* 78 [March 1984]), in which they observed that leadership, even in its most compelling form, consists of an interplay. Leaders seek to transform the institutional and political circumstances in which they operate—and are transformed in the process. "Leaders interact with other leaders and are co-opted into new beliefs and commitments. The leadership role is that of an educator, stimulating and accepting changing world views, redefining meanings, stimulating commitments" (p. 739). This discussion led me to appreciate that Wilson's adaptations were just as much a part of his statesmanship as his innovations, not simply because he deemed them necessary, but also because, once made, they were integral to his program and shaped his thought and actions.

The second line of thought was that Wilson's difficulty in remaking key features of the Founders' regime, and his substantial accommodation of their constitutional logic in his own program, did not mean that human agency was losing out to impersonal structure or that statesmanship did not matter. For the Founders were statesmen too. They had sought to create a constitutional system that would be resistant to the changes Wilson wanted to bring about, and as Wilson struggled to transform the separation of powers and the diversity of the extended republic, he was struggling with the legacies of their statesmanship. Insofar as it was not Wilson's program but rather the constitutional legacies that prevailed, it was because history and the wisdom those legacies embodied, whatever their shortcomings, had given them the advantage.

I HAD invaluable help in completing this book. Generous financial assistance came at key points from the Government Department at Harvard University, the Mellon Foundation, the Intercollegiate Studies Institute, and the Faculty Development Committee at Wabash College.

It was my good fortune to be a graduate student in the Government Department at the same time as several thoughtful and good-natured colleagues who shared and enlightened my interest in American political thought and history: Gordon Silverstein, Matthew Dickinson, Robert Lieberman, Patrick Wolf, and Jessica Korn. I was lucky to catch up with Jessica several years later, during the year of our congressional fellowships, when we solved many of the problems I had in writing this book during lunchtime walks on the Mall in Washington, D.C.

Many teachers, colleagues, and friends have kindly read papers, chapters, and drafts of this book over the years and offered much help in the way of constructive criticism. In this regard, I want to thank Sidney Milkis, Michael Nelson, James Ceaser, Stephen Skowronek, Harvey C. Mansfield, Jr., Richard Ellis, Mark Peterson, Shep Melnick, Jeffrey Sedgwick, Jeffrey Tulis, Terri Bimes, Lauren Osborne, Jerry Mileur, and the late H. Douglas Price. My greatest intellectual debt is to Paul Peterson. From the outset, he combined enthusiastic support for this project with incisive criticism, bolstering me and improving the work at the same time. I could not have asked for more in an adviser.

I received generous support in other ways as well. Jerry Mileur was so kind as to present me with a signed first edition of Wilson's *Congressional Government*, which I took special pleasure in using while writing this book. Arthur Link extended another wonderful gift when, as he was closing up shop in Princeton, having edited the last volume of the monumental *Papers of Woodrow Wilson*, he hosted me for a day, answered a whole notebook full of questions, and took me to lunch at Prospect House, Wilson's home while he was president at the university. I would be remiss if I did not thank Christine, Teddy, John, and the rest of the early morning crew at Bella's Diner in Tarrytown, New York. The hearty ambiance they provided nurtured many an insight at a critical stage in this study, while the bad coffee they served made certain that, sooner or later each morning, I would return home and get to work.

My colleagues and students in the Department of Political Science at Wabash College provided a most collegial and stimulating setting in which to teach and to refine and test the propositions that are presented here. I am especially indebted to Phil Mikesell, Chair of the Social Sciences Division, and Melissa Butler, Chair of the Department, for many professional and personal kindnesses.

The Congressional Fellowship Program of the American Political Science Association and its administrator, Kay Sterling, gave me the great opportunity to serve as a participant-observer for a year on Capitol Hill. I will always appreciate the welcome extended to me by the Honorable Richard Armey, his chief of staff, Kerry Knott, and the other staff members in the Office of the Majority Leader. Spending a year working alongside them in the 104th Congress gave me a real Ph.D. in politics and, in the process, improved many of the arguments in this book.

Fred Woodward, director of the University Press of Kansas, is the kind of publisher everyone should wish for: patient but persistent, insightful as a critic, and quick with a joke for an anxious author. I also appreciate the careful readings that Wilson Carey McWilliams and Lance Banning, coeditors of the American Political Thought series, gave the manuscript. I am proud indeed to have my book deemed worthy of inclusion in their series. I am especially indebted for the thoroughgoing review of the manuscript that Kendrick Clements did for the press; he saved me from many problems of historical interpretation.

The book you are about to read has been improved dramatically because of the critical readings provided by the colleagues noted above. Insofar as faults remain, I alone am responsible for them.

One final note: my family has contributed much—no doubt too much—to the completion of this work. I am grateful to my father, Peter Stid, for teaching me the meaning of workmanship, and to my mother, Sara, for her benevolent overestimation of my potential. My in-laws, Alain and Rosemary Enthoven, gave me the downstairs study and a Stanford Library card and their house over to my family for several summers in a row. The twins, Noah and Sophia, have endured far too many weekends with me at the office—although, given my mood when writing, they might well have been better off. As for my wife, Martha, she has been wonderful, in this and so many other things.

Introduction

Toward the end of the evening on September 29, 1914, Woodrow Wilson settled down in his study at the White House for a talk with his closest friend and adviser, Colonel Edward House. It was their custom in such meetings to review the various conundrums of politics and policy facing the administration, and on this night, the two men spent most of their time hashing out plans for a diplomatic overture to the British Foreign Office concerning the war that had just engulfed Europe. Before retiring, though, Wilson and House turned to a less troublesome, more familiar topic, one they could discuss in broader strokes. "We talked much of leadership and its importance in government," House recorded in his diary. "He has demonstrated this to an unusual degree. He thinks our form of government can be changed by personal leadership." For his part, though, the normally obsequious Colonel House had reservations. He told Wilson that "no matter how great a leader a man was, I could see situations that would block him unless the Constitution was modified. He does not feel as strongly about this as I do."[1]

At that point in his presidency, Wilson had every reason for confidence in the power of his personal leadership. His program for establishing what he termed responsible government, developed during his three decades as a political scientist, appeared to be working. The crux of the program was to have a wise and visionary leader, supported by a principled political party, draw together the executive and legislative branches that Wilson believed the Founders had impractically separated in the Constitution. The resulting integration of the separated powers would provide for responsible government by giving the leader and his party the power they needed to govern and by enabling voters to reward or punish them for what they did or failed to do. Upon becoming president, Wilson put his plan into practice. He reached out to lead the disciplined Democratic majorities in Congress in several innovative, even audacious ways. The result was the New Freedom, a sweeping set of reform bills that lowered tariff rates, stiffened the antitrust laws, and established the Federal Reserve Board and Federal Trade Commission.

In his diary entry for September 29, 1914, Colonel House also made note of Wilson's intention, after leaving the presidency, to write a book entitled *Statesmanship,* in which he would explore the "essence of government."[2] Had Wilson ever managed to write this study, he might well have accepted House's point about the need for constitutional reform, not least because of Wilson's eventual failure to secure Senate ratification of the Versailles Treaty and the League of Nations Covenant contained within it. But Wilson was in no shape to undertake his magnum opus at the end of his presidency. During his disastrous confrontation with Henry Cabot Lodge and the Senate, Wilson exhausted himself and suffered a crippling stroke. The separation of powers, which Wilson had bridged with such drama and effect during the New Freedom, ultimately gave rise to a struggle that left his dearest policy, his presidency, and the man himself in ruins.

The irony—or rather the tragedy—of Wilson's overwhelming defeat is that he could have predicted it himself. At the outset of his career as a political scientist, Wilson had been convinced that constitutional amendments that would fuse the separated executive and legislative powers were necessary preconditions for the establishment of responsible government. But the political prospects for Wilson's amendments were dim at best. "How to bring the country to adopt the new system?" he asked in one of his early essays. "There's the rub." Wilson concluded that the situation called out for "a contest of reason, a mission of statesmanship."[3]

Wilson's "mission of statesmanship" is the subject of this book. It can be noted here, to preview the argument elaborated below, that Wilson's mission took a fateful turn with a decision he made shortly after embarking on it. In order to widen the audience for his reform tracts, he decided to drop his calls for constitutional amendments and instead began advocating, to use his phrase and emphasis, "responsible government *under* the Constitution."[4] The change in tack cleared the way for his remarkable achievements as a political scientist and leader. But—as the ambivalent Wilson realized—the change also left his plan for responsible government vulnerable to the countervailing and constitutionally entrenched logic of the Founders' separation of powers. This logic ultimately confounded his efforts to lead as the prime minister of a responsible party. And it meant that Wilson had both the means and the inclination to lead as an independent and energetic president, which further jeopardized his parliamentary ideal.

In approaching Wilson, this book sets out to understand him as he understood himself throughout his public life, as a statesman, i.e., a leader endeavoring to coordinate political theory and practice in order to improve the health of the polity.[5] This approach might seem presumptuous. The inclination of realistic if not cynical political scientists and citizens—and these days there are not many other kinds—is to see the ideas of political leaders as fancy cover for underlying ambitions or compulsions. Several studies of Woodrow Wilson do just this; indeed, he has become something of a poster boy for the field of psychobiography.[6] It will be shown here, however, that Wilson's ideas about responsible government need to be taken seriously, both in their own right and as a key to understanding his leadership. His program had a coherence and consistency of its own, as he developed and applied it, that cannot easily be explained by his personality.

Although Wilson's program cannot be reduced to a mere rationalization of the drives of his complex personality, neither can it be elevated to the realm of political philosophy. Some thoughtful interpreters of the broad sweep of Wilson's political, social, and religious thought have cordoned off the cigar smoke and compromises that clouded his political career and concentrated instead on his thinking as it matured, in a presumably more pristine setting, during his academic years.[7] When studying Wilson's program for responsible government, though, it is neither possible nor desirable to sustain this intellectual quarantine. In 1883, when Wilson decided to opt out of his fledgling legal practice and commence graduate study in history and political science at Johns Hopkins University, he was not giving up on his long-standing desire to be a statesman. Indeed, he decided on an academic career because he believed it was the best outlet for his ambitions, that he could maximize his impact by serving as an "outside force" in politics.[8] Right from the start of his academic career, Wilson began pulling theoretical punches in order to make his program more practical and appealing to politicians and reformers. He did not view his accommodation of political reality as a compromise of his intellectual integrity; rather, he saw it as a form of statesmanship. In 1886, in his first year as a professor, Wilson proposed that the ideal professor of politics "should bridge over the gulf between closet doctrine and rough, everyday practice" and "be no less a scholar for being studiously a man of the world."[9]

Later, in Wilson's 1910 presidential address to the American Political Science Association, he spoke of "the statesmanship of thought" and "the statesmanship of action," and had this to say about the connection between them: "The man who has the time, the discrimination, and the sagacity to collect and comprehend the principal facts and the man who must act upon them must draw near to one another and feel that they are engaged in a common enterprise. . . . Know your people and you can lead them; study your people and you may know them."[10]

By this point in his career, Wilson believed that the American people could be best known and led, and his program for responsible government best implemented, from the presidency. If Wilson is to be judged as he would have judged himself, the analysis of his theoretical program needs to be measured by the practical test he put it to during his presidency.

Wilson himself struggled to come to terms with the preliminary results of this test, and as he did so he continued to modify his program. In the crucible of the White House, he came back to and reaffirmed the teachings of his early, "immature" writings on relations between Congress and the president. As president, Wilson also changed his mind and concluded that, in some instances, the constitutional separation of the executive and legislative powers was preferable to a parliamentary fusion of them. Examining these significant but heretofore unappreciated modifications in Wilson's program dissolves the common notion that it had assumed a final, mature formulation by the end of his academic career.

My aim, then, is to study Wilson's statesmanship of thought and his statesmanship of action as a piece, to look over Professor and then President Wilson's shoulder as he grappled with the separation of powers. But Wilson's statesmanship also needs to be situated in the appropriate historical context. He was profoundly influenced and animated by the unsettling political developments and controversies in which he was engaged, remaining convinced throughout his life that he lived amid a critical conjuncture in American history. Historians and political scientists have since borne him out. Dramatic industrial growth, the closing of the frontier, the swelling of American cities with newcomers from the farmlands and abroad, the emergence of the United States as a world and colonial power—these and other developments were overwhelming the patterns of leadership and party politics that had prevailed for most of the nineteenth century. As a result, American reformers began what Robert Wiebe has termed a "search for order."[11] Woodrow Wilson was in the thick of the search, and his program for responsible government was his unique contribution to it.

The nature of Wilson's program left him no choice but to fight on two fronts in the debate over what direction the search should take. Wilson took on defenders of the constitutional status quo and the traditional parties that thirsted for its offices. At the same time, he opposed radicals wanting to empower heroic executives and expert administrators by eradicating party politics altogether. Wilson generally gave as good as he got in these debates, but they also shaped and constrained the evolution of his program.

Approaching Wilson in this manner yields a perspective that challenges both the traditional and revisionist schools of thought on his statesmanship.[12] The traditional interpretation appears in the work of biographers and political scientists who are sympathetic to (if not outright supporters of) Wilson, his progressive policies, and the office of the presidency. These scholars hold their subject up as an inspiring exemplar for contemporary presidents. Arthur Link summarizes the conclusions of this school of thought when he argues that during the New Freedom, Wilson was able to "demonstrate conclusively" that the president could serve as "the chief spokesman of the American people" and "destroy the wall between the executive and legislative branches." As a result, "historians a century hence will probably rate his expansion and perfection of the powers of the presidency as his most lasting contribution."[13]

The revisionist view of Wilson appears in the work of conservative political theorists sympathetic to the constitutional design of the Founders. These scholars criticize Wilson for tearing down the obstacles that the creators of both the Constitution and the nineteenth-century party system placed athwart the presidential leadership of public opinion. Even though the popular appeals that Wilson made over the heads of his Senate opponents in the Treaty fight backfired, his "rhetorical presidency" left a permanent mark on the polity. As a result of Wilson's dangerously naive theory and practice, James Ceaser and his coauthors contend, we are led more and more "to neglect our principles for our hopes and to ignore the benefits and needs of our institutions for a fleeting sense of oneness with our leaders."[14]

As divergent as these interpretations are, scholars in both camps depict a theorist and leader who boldly confronted and profoundly changed the separation of powers. The following account, in contrast, pays due homage to the moderation of Wilson's statesmanship, his persistent ambivalence regarding his program for "responsible government *under* the Constitution," and the resilience of the separation of powers. It also finds Wilson's program implicated in both his successes and his failures, in the New Freedom and the treaty debacle. This reconsideration will not support the sharply divergent and unabashed conclusions regarding Wilson and the separation of powers in the traditional and revisionist interpretations, but it may be useful in discerning what, if anything, might be done to meet better the challenges of leadership and governance that Wilson confronted and that continue to face the United States.

✦ ONE

Toward "Power and Strict Accountability for Its Use"

"Our patriotism seems of late to have been exchanging its wonted tone of confident hope for one of desponding solicitude. Anxiety about the future of our institutions seems to be daily becoming stronger in the minds of thoughtful Americans." Thus began Woodrow Wilson's quest to bring responsible government to the United States. These sentences, leading up to a warning about "a marked and alarming decline in statesmanship," introduced an essay that he wrote in 1879, at the age of twenty-two, during his senior year at Princeton.[1] Entitled "Cabinet Government in the United States," the essay appeared in the *International Review* (the editor of which, it is worth noting, was a young Harvard scholar named Henry Cabot Lodge). Over the next six years, as Wilson studied law at the University of Virginia, practiced it for a short time in Atlanta, then undertook graduate study in political science at Johns Hopkins University, he expanded and refined the argument of "Cabinet Government" in a series of essays and unpublished manuscripts. The series culminated in Wilson's doctoral dissertation, better known as *Congressional Government*.

In his thesis, the young political scientist had the audacity to criticize the separation of powers—deemed "the sacred maxim of free government" in *The Federalist*[2]—as instead a "radical defect" in the Constitution, the root cause of the sorry statesmanship, political skulduggery, and governmental drift that was then bedeviling the nation. Wilson acknowledged that given the prevailing "blind worship" of the Constitution, this proposition made him something of a heretic.[3] In spite of his heresy—or perhaps because of it—he quickly became a nationally prominent voice for political reform. Before analyzing Wilson's argument and the way he managed to achieve such prominence, it will be helpful to consider what prompted him to become a heretic in the first place.

6

I

In large part the answer lies with the historical conditions in which Wilson came of political age during the 1870s. Though each generation of Americans hears charges of unmatched corruption in Washington, at this point the accusations might well have been true. The 1870s witnessed the apex of the fabled "great barbecue," in Vernon Parrington's apt phrase, in which the ruling bands of politicians liberally passed out favors to their benefactors in the form of favorable tariff rates, jobs, land grants, veterans' pensions, and so forth. The distinction between business deals and political agreements, often ambiguous in the United States, became a distinction without a difference. The corrupt reign of the Tweed Ring and the Credit Mobilier, Whiskey Ring, and congressional salary grab scandals marked the first part of the decade. So did the final, more dubious stages of what Wilson would subsequently term the "damnable cruelty and folly of Reconstruction."[4]

All of this was no doubt made more intolerable to the young Woodrow Wilson because it was presided over by the hapless Ulysses S. Grant, the conqueror of his boyhood homeland. Though Wilson's father, the Reverend Joseph Ruggles Wilson, was an Ohioan, he had moved his family to the South and was a leader of the proslavery wing of the Presbyterian Church. During the war, the boy saw his father's church in Augusta, Georgia, serve as a hospital for Confederate wounded and as a makeshift prison for captured Union soldiers. Although Wilson was only nine when the war ended and would say as an adult that he had always considered himself a "Federalist," his rearing in the South gave his allegiance to the national government a well-honed critical edge.[5]

Wilson's unique perspective shows up clearly in a draft of one of his earliest public speeches, entitled "The Union," which he gave to his fellow students at Princeton in November 1876. He proposed that "no American can think of the Union and the principles upon which it is founded without a flush of pride and thrill of patriotism," and proceeded to rely chiefly on the words of Yankee Daniel Webster to flesh out these principles. However, Wilson left no doubt about his views on Reconstruction. He condemned "the fanatical partisans who enrage the people by their frantic wavings of the bloody shirt" and the "traitors who have crept into favor in certain parts of the country by the miserable ambition of petty politicians." The greatest danger to the Union, though, was "the sad lack of great men. . . . of guiding genius." Were statesmen like Webster to reappear, there would be hope for healing "the lesions of all parts of the country" laid open by the war, for promoting "that union of hearts for which the Southern people are so eager if their Northern brethren will only meet them half way."[6]

It was no coincidence that Wilson made his appeal for integrating statesmanship in the anxious weeks following the election of 1876, in which the ultimate victor in the presidential contest had yet to be decided. The campaign had excited and drawn out Wilson's formative political sentiments, which he recorded in his journal. He viewed the Democratic candidate, Samuel Tilden, as the sort of "good and prominent man" the riven nation had lacked for too long. Tilden's battles with Tammany Hall and his allegiance to the economic principles of sound money and free trade also convinced Wilson that he was just the right man for the Democratic Party. While Wilson's southern upbringing had placed him firmly in the Democratic fold, he believed that his party, too, had the tendency to stray from principle and indulge in the jobbery and corruption that were then prevalent. The tendency was especially disturbing because, to Wilson's mind, the Democratic Party was the only hope for initiating a new age of reform politics, one in which great issues, especially the march toward freer trade, would replace retrograde, bloody-shirt politics. If this was to happen, the leadership of a statesman like Tilden was essential. Indeed, the night before the election Wilson remarked in his journal that "the salvation of the country from frauds and the reviving of trade depends upon his election."[7]

Such convictions led Wilson to immerse himself in the political rallies, bonfires, and debates held at Princeton in the suspenseful time that followed the popular vote. His mother, writing from North Carolina, described the "intense anxiety" that gripped southerners as they waited for the outcome of the election. She admonished her son not to get in fights with Republican students on campus—he evidently had come close. In this context, the eventual elevation of Hayes, "that weak instrument of the corrupt Republicans," as Wilson saw him, notwithstanding Tilden's winning the popular vote, no doubt worsened the young man's disillusionment with his nation's politics.[8]

A set of more diffuse influences interacted with the particulars of Woodrow Wilson's time and place to sharpen further the young man's political views. Prominent among them, as John Mulder has documented, was the Covenanter tradition of Calvinism espoused by Joseph Wilson. This tradition carried a profound sense of both the difficulty and the necessity of the struggle for moral progress, upon which all social progress rested. At the same time, Woodrow Wilson's personal faith included an optimism about the possibility of progress, an outlook that made him all the more impatient with politicians who did not foster it.[9] He held political leaders to a moral standard that the bosses of the Gilded Age could not begin to meet. Notwith-standing the corruption in Washington, in 1876 he proposed that a "Chris-tian statesman," one committed, like a minister, to a determined "search for the truth," was not a contradiction in terms but rather an attainable ideal.[10]

The connection between Woodrow Wilson's moral and political views was reinforced by two political journals that Joseph Wilson subscribed to, the *Nation* and the *Edinburgh Review.* In the former, edited by the moralistic Scots-Irish liberal E. L. Godkin, the young Woodrow Wilson read frequent castigations of Grant and the spoilsmen. Through the latter, Wilson followed the golden age of Victorian liberalism, particularly the speeches and exploits of his heroes, John Bright and—especially—William Gladstone, whose por-trait hung over the schoolboy's desk.[11]

As a young man, Woodrow Wilson proposed that there was not a states-man "whose character is worthier of the study and imitation of the young men of a free country than is Mr. Gladstone's." Wilson held Bright in high esteem for the constancy with which the great radical had adhered to his reform principles over the years. Paradoxically, Wilson's even greater admi-ration for Gladstone stemmed in large part from his famous shifts on the grand issues of his time as he struggled, both in and outside of the cabinet, to come to terms with the best sentiments of public opinion, the logic of reform ideas, and the lessons from his experience in governing. Thus it was, Wilson argued, that Gladstone dropped the defense of the corn laws and the Church of England that had marked his days as an elitist young Tory to become a champion of free trade, religious toleration, and democratic re-form. Implicitly comparing this embodiment of the "Christian Statesman" with the sorry types that he saw ruling in Washington, Wilson declared that "[Gladstone's] life has been one continuous advance, not towards power only—fools may be powerful; knaves sometimes rule by the knack of their knavery—but towards truth also the while."[12]

The capacity of Bright and Gladstone to move men with speech, which Wilson believed ultimately came from their "earnestness and sincere con-viction," was also responsible for his high estimation of their leadership.[13] Rhetorical power clearly impressed the preacher's son. Wilson would listen to his father's sermons on the Sabbath, then return later in the week and hold forth before the empty pews to hone his own voice with the great speeches of Gladstone and Bright, Patrick Henry and Daniel Webster. After leav-ing home for college, he continued to solicit and receive guidance from his father on the art of speaking. At Princeton he was not only a frequent public speaker but an unceasing advocate for rigorous training of the student body in oratory and elocution so that its members might later be more effective in public life. Wilson declared to his peers in a speech entitled "The Ideal Statesmen" that such a leader must "possess an orator's soul, an orator's words, an orator's actions. To nobleness of thought he must add nobleness of word and conduct."[14]

In Wilson's mind, the crucial setting for the development and demonstration of mastery in oratory came in formal debate. He was an avid participant in debating societies at every school he attended and paid great attention to the constitutional forms of these groups, seeing a relationship between a group's formal structure and the quality of its debates. The constitution he drafted in early 1877 for the Liberal Debating Club at Princeton illustrated his belief in the supremacy of parliamentary forms that pitted two speakers against each other in a truth-winnowing debate, the hearts and minds of the audience and ultimately the power and authority of the antagonists hanging in the balance. A few months later, Wilson presented a debate resolution to his fellow members that called for establishing in the federal government parliamentary forms akin to those he had instituted in their club.[15]

Wilson's activities in the Liberal Debating Club demonstrated his growing conviction that the stark contrast he detected between the likes of Gladstone and Bright and their American counterparts was not merely the result of personal virtue or the lack thereof. The different forms of government in Great Britain and the United States now appeared to him to be eliciting virtuous and vice-ridden leadership, respectively. The "severe and unintermitted training" that the English leaders had undergone while rising up through the ranks in Parliament was what had ultimately enabled them "to command with effect and success." The American polity, with its diffusion of governing power and responsibility, had no such revealing proving ground for aspiring statesmen.[16] Initially, this realization had driven Wilson to despair. Witness his diary entry on July 4, 1876: "One hundred years ago America conquered England in an unequal struggle and this year she glories over it. How much happier she would be now if she had England's form of government instead of this miserable delusion of a republic."[17] But instead of wallowing in pessimism and Anglophilia, Wilson fixed upon the idea of saving the "miserable" government of his own country by establishing English forms in it.

During his senior year at Princeton, Wilson began to frame his argument for such a change. He did so primarily with the aid of Walter Bagehot's *The English Constitution*. In this essay, first published in 1867, Bagehot had sought to probe beneath the "dignified parts" of the English Constitution, i.e., the triune balance of the Crown, Lords, and Commons, in order to reveal its "efficient secret," namely, the fusion of executive, legislative, and party leadership in the cabinet. In a comparison of the British and American systems, Bagehot praised cabinet government for producing—and criticized the separation of powers for thwarting—responsible legislation, sound administration, and an edifying public debate over the means and ends of policy.[18]

Bagehot's highly stylized treatment of parliamentary and presidential government resonated with and organized Wilson's impressions of the two regimes. In the process, Bagehot whetted the young man's desire for political reform in the United States. Bagehot also provided Wilson with a method for proceeding. As Wilson began working on *Congressional Government* a few years later, he reread Bagehot's book and confided to Ellen Axson, his fiancée, that it "has inspired my whole study of our government." Wilson wanted to rest his analysis, as had Bagehot, on interpretive insight and literary flourish, forsaking the systematic empirical research and objective presentation advocated by his graduate advisers at Johns Hopkins University. Wilson believed that his alternative approach, "if it could be successfully applied to the exposition of our federal constitution, would result in something like a revelation to those who are still reading *The Federalist* as an authoritative constitutional manual."[19]

Yet on one point, Wilson's purposes diverged from those of Bagehot and paralleled those of the authors of *The Federalist*. Bagehot had laid bare the workings of the English Constitution so that his countrymen could better understand it and hold back from reforms that might jeopardize the political benefits that they were accruing under it.[20] In contrast, Hamilton, Madison, and Jay sought to expose the shortcomings of the government of the United States under the Articles of Confederation in order to support their efforts to transform it. Wilson likewise wanted to reveal what he saw as the real nature of the American regime and the pathologies of power within it in order to bring about fundamental change. As Wilson confided to a friend soon after *Congressional Government* was published, the book's "mission was to *stir* thought and to carry irresistible practical suggestions . . . and set reform a-going in a very definite direction."[21]

II

As Wilson explored the troublesome ramifications of the separation of powers in his book, he argued that they were ironic in two key respects. One irony was the curious staying power of this "radical defect." When the Founders framed the Constitution, Wilson argued, they had sought above all else to prevent the dangerous concentration of power that had occurred when King George III, Lord Bute, and the "King's Friends" had corrupted and dominated Parliament. Toward this end, the Founders decided that seated members of the legislative branch could not hold executive offices, lest they trade their votes for a place in the administration. The resulting "absolute separation" of powers, Wilson argued, was an improvement over the British system under George III, but it was unnecessary. For at that very moment, Britain's unwritten constitution was already evolving toward the more responsible system of government that emerged there in the mid-nineteenth century, a system in which the executive power was lodged in a cabinet elected by and accountable to the legislature. This form of government not only checked executive machinations but also allowed for more efficient policy-making through its fusion of executive and legislative power. The American separation of powers, however, had not undergone a similar progressive evolution because its growth had been "hindered or destroyed by the too tight ligaments of a written fundamental law."[22] By overreacting to a temporary perversion of the British Constitution, the American Founders had prevented their nation from subsequently experiencing its eventual perfection.

What is more, for all of their precautions, the Founders had still failed to prevent a dangerous concentration of power with their Constitution. Indeed, their design had brought one about, which was the second irony. Publius may have warned against the "impetuous vortex" of the legislature, yet in Wilson's view the Founders' constitutional design, by formally insulating Congress from executive control, effectively transferred all power to that vortex.[23] Bereft of sustained direction, Congress had, with time, met the invariable need for such guidance from within, setting up a complex internal structure of committees to organize its activities. As Congress's institutional capacity to act increased, it involved itself in more and more spheres of governmental activity. With this increased involvement came a distortion of the legislative function and a confounding of the separation of powers. Congress maladroitly sought to perform functions that Wilson held to be properly executive in nature, namely, framing legislation and supervising administration. Thus preoccupied, Congress became, at the same time, much less suited for what he saw as the appropriate legislative functions of debating the policies prepared and administered by the executive. Yet there was no stopping the congressional monolith once it had organized itself to govern. Hence the unpleasant but nonetheless efficient secret of the American regime, according to Woodrow Wilson: "The balances of the Constitution are for the most part only ideal. For all practical purposes the national government is supreme over the state governments, and Congress predominant over its so-called coordinate branches."[24]

For all of its ostensible power, the American presidency had proven to be an ineffectual counterbalance to congressional government. Wilson observed that there had once been signs of hope in this regard, in the early days of the republic, before Congress had blindly organized itself to take the initiative. The priority of foreign affairs in this period and the special responsibilities of the presidency for them had elevated the position of the office, not least by attracting great statesmen who felt called to wield its power. However, over the course of the nineteenth century, with Congress attempting more and more to govern on its own and with the growing importance of domestic affairs, the power and prestige of the presidency had gone into a downward spiral. The diminished office, Wilson argued, had become a creature of the parties. The brokering that party officials engaged in during the nominating conventions was geared to select not the best statesmen but the least controversial candidates—the latter would give the party the best chance of controlling the spoils that came with winning the presidential contest. "The shoals of candidacy," Wilson lamented, "can be passed only by a light boat which carries little freight and can be turned readily about to suit the intricacies of the passage" (*Congressional Government*, pp. 41–45; subsequent parenthetical citations in this section are to this book).

Wilson's critical analysis of the Gilded Age presidency anticipated the more famous observations offered three years later by James Bryce in *The American Commonwealth* on "why great men are not chosen presidents." But while Bryce criticized the debasement of the presidency by the party organizations, he nonetheless appreciated the safety and stability that all the politicking brought to the presidency. He also detected a rough-hewn administrative effectiveness in the workings of the office. More recently, James Ceaser has likewise concluded that although the party brokering undermined the independence of the office, it mitigated against factionalism and demagoguery, fostered the development of broad national coalitions, and preserved at least some energy in the executive.[25] Unlike these observers of the nineteenth-century presidency, Wilson could not temper his criticism of it. He believed the nation needed more in the way of commanding statesmanship, and it was not going to come from an executive office that had been bowled over by the legislature and the parties.

In his extended critique of congressional government, Wilson laid out its dire implications for public policy. Bills whose support came from logrolling between and among the multifarious committees in the House and Senate, and which leaders pushed through in the normal course of congressional business with little or no debate, were destined to lack coherence and often to work against the public interest.[26] And once the legislation was passed, the congressional capacity to intervene in the details and staffing of administration, while sufficient to generate inefficiency and corruption, was insufficient to produce the wisdom and information needed to frame laws successfully or to hold administrators fully accountable (270–82). "Nobody stands sponsor for the policy of the government," Wilson complained. "A dozen men originate it; a dozen compromises twist and alter it; a dozen offices whose names are scarcely known outside of Washington put it into execution" (318). Although this situation was generally intolerable, Wilson believed it to be urgently so at a time when, in the face of accelerating social and economic change, "the sphere and influence of national administration and national legislation are widening rapidly" (316).

Congressional government also perverted party politics. In the absence of a conspicuous and sustained debate between the party controlling the government and the party opposing it, the electorate was neither in a position nor prompted to pass judgment on either party (101–2). As a result, Wilson argued, the parties did not feel compelled to work toward the passage of a systematic legislative program or even collectively subscribe to a coherent set of principles. "They are like armies without officers," he observed, "engaged upon a campaign which has no great cause at its back. Their names and traditions, not their hopes and policy, keep them together" (324). Getting into power and keeping hold of it, rather than using it, was the imperative. The unhealthy power of the patronage-fed organizations was geared largely toward these more mundane ends (98–99). Although a necessary antidote to the committee system, the sole mechanism providing for concerted party action—the legislative caucus—was an unsatisfactory instrument, for it operated secretly, providing a haven in which compromises of principles and the squelching of dissenting views could occur in secret (326–31).

The policy and political perversions of congressional government produced a dearth of statesmanship in the United States. So long as the game was played in such an unseemly manner and for relatively insignificant prizes in terms of the power one might ultimately exercise, good men and prospective leaders held back from public life, leaving the field to less admirable types. To make things worse, without the revealing and repeated tests of oratory and public leadership that characterized the parliamentary arena, these types had little difficulty in ascending to the highest echelons in the congressional government (205–6).

What did Wilson propose to do about the problem of congressional government? His solution was to galvanize the political power that had been first divided by the separation of powers and then dispersed by the rise of the committee system in Congress: "*Power and strict accountability for its use are the essential constituents of good government.* A sense of highest responsibility, a dignifying and elevating sense of being trusted, together with a consciousness of being in an official station so conspicuous that no faithful discharge of duty can go unacknowledged and unrewarded, and no breach of trust undiscovered and unpunished,—these are the influences, the only influences, which foster practical, energetic, and trustworthy statesmanship" (284; Wilson's emphasis).

Wilson demurred from explicitly stating how the "power and strict accountability for its use" that he was calling for might be established in the United States, claiming, "I am pointing out facts,—diagnosing, not prescribing remedies" (315). But he left little doubt that the remedy was cabinet government, the British version of which he openly admired in the book. To tease out his prescription, it is necessary to leave behind the comprehensive diagnosis of *Congressional Government,* which Wilson proposed was the culminating work in his series, and delve into his previous studies.

In both of the essays that Wilson published prior to his book, he had called for a constitutional amendment to Article 1, Section 6's proscription on members of Congress holding offices in the executive branch. Wilson's amendment instead would have enabled and effectively required the president to select his cabinet secretaries from among seated members of the legislature. This change was the linchpin of his program for responsible government at this point in time. It meant that "power and strict accountability for its use" would be concentrated in the cabinet—a single committee of congressional leaders who would retain their legislative positions and, at the same time, administer the executive departments. Wilson believed that the president would have to select the leaders of the majority party on Capitol Hill, for a combination of pride and necessity would quickly force the resignation of cabinets that were unable to maintain the support of Congress. Wilson's plan thereby envisioned a de facto system of Westminster-style ministerial responsibility operating on Capitol Hill, one that would produce a multitude of benefits.[27]

Prominent among those benefits was more effective government. Holding the leadership positions in both branches—and in a party clearly accountable to the electorate—the cabinet would have both the drive and the capacity to frame, pass, and administer, with coherence and efficiency, the policy proposals upon which their party had stood before the electorate. Wilson argued that the ensuing debate between the counterpoised government and opposition parties in Congress over the merits and execution of these policies would winnow and improve, not thwart or pervert, legislation and administration. "The educational influence of such discussion . . . op-erates in two directions,—upon the members of the legislature themselves, and upon the people whom they represent."[28]

With the immense political fortunes riding on the outcome of this de-bate, principles and oratory would replace the dispensation of patronage and pork-barrel legislation as the unifying forces of party action. Given the pressing need for them, men of principle and rhetorical power would be attracted into politics and rise to the forefront of the party organizations, taking over the leadership positions held by the backroom politicos. At elec-tion time, with so much power destined to fall into the hands of the major-ity party, party leaders would have to propose concrete and compelling pro-posals to the voters—and hold to them after the election. In this sense, public opinion, brought into focus by an ongoing debate over principles and pro-grammatic mandates, would replace the caucus leader as the true "boss" of the party in power.[29]

III

Such was the basic logic of Wilson's program to establish responsible gov-ernment in the form of cabinet government. To appreciate it fully and to understand the ways in which Wilson elaborated it, his writings need to be juxtaposed with the proposals of other reformers then at work. Wilson formed and honed his program so that it might win out over them. By far the most widely advocated of the alternatives was civil service reform. Lib-eral and mugwump reformers such as E. L. Godkin and Carl Schurz insisted that if government jobs were not handed out as rewards for political service but rather filled on the basis of merit with "the best men," in the phrase of the time, the political, economic, social, and moral health of the nation would be set aright.[30] Woodrow Wilson likewise believed that the spoils system had to go. As he put it in 1887 in "The Study of Administration"—a seminal essay in the founding of the discipline of public administration—"although politics sets the tasks for administration, it should not be suffered to manipu-late its offices."[31]

But Wilson also held that putting a stop to inappropriate political involve-ment in administration had to await the establishment of responsible gov-ernment. In *Congressional Government*, Wilson proposed that this priority was inadvertently borne out by Dorman Eaton's *Civil Service in Great Britain: A History of Abuses and Their Bearing upon American Politics*, the bible of American advocates of civil service reform. Only after responsible govern-ment was established in Britain, Wilson argued, did the ministry feel com-pelled to make the service of the government professional and neutral, lest it be called to account for incompetent or political administration of the laws. In the United States, civil service reform had come later and was incomplete because the separation of powers did not allow for such a compelling responsibility—no institution or leader had both the power and the incentive to clean up the spoils.[32] Hence the priority of establishing responsible government.

Although Wilson offered counsel to advocates of civil service reform, he took sharp issue with the reform plan of Albert Stickney, who wanted to do away with politics altogether. A New York lawyer and the most prominent of the beleaguered antipartisan reformers of the Gilded Age, Stickney became convinced during his battles with Tammany Hall that parties were inherently corrupt. "In order to get anything which really deserves the name of republican government," Stickney argued, "one must destroy party altogether." In 1879, Stickney presented a scheme for doing this in *A True Republic,* calling for the end of regular elections—legislative and executive officers alike would hold their positions during good behavior—and for the establishment of a hierarchical, professional administration of "the best men" under the control of the chief executive.[33] It would be hard to overestimate the alarm in Wilson's reaction to Stickney's plan, which he read in late 1879 during his first semester in law school. Wilson spent much of that autumn, and more time thereafter, rebutting Stickney. Four years later, when a publisher thought that his extensive criticism of Stickney's plan weighed down a manuscript that Wilson had submitted for review, the author responded by arguing that "mine is necessarily a *rival scheme.* To fortify my positions I must destroy his."[34]

Wilson felt compelled to disagree primarily because Stickney proposed doing away with the very institution—the political party—that played the central role in his own plan for cabinet government. Wilson was convinced that antipartisanship was inherently impractical. Given human nature and the issues at stake in politics, parties arose as a matter of course: individuals would invariably band together to pursue the political ends that they held in common. Citing the reasoning of Edmund Burke, Wilson also contended that political parties were necessary and beneficial institutions; indeed, they made representative government possible. Only through concerted party action could good men work effectively to achieve their ends. What is more, partisanship refined the views and behavior of individual politicians by bringing political connections out into the open and by generating a public, shared commitment to principles. The trick, then, Wilson insisted, was not to attempt the impossible and misguided task of eradicating partisanship but rather to create the conditions in which it had these positive effects.[35]

Wilson's advocacy of party government differed from Burke's in some key respects. Harvey C. Mansfield, Jr., has shown that Burke offered his argument for party government in large part to constrain the discretion of individual statesmen, discretion that, as the reign of George III led Burke to believe, too often resulted in corruption if not tyranny. Party government was a safer, less arbitrary form of rule than reliance on individual statesmen.[36] Wilson, in contrast, advocated sharpening party responsibility not to restrain but to foster statesmanship in the United States. The concentration in the cabinet of "power and strict accountability for its use" would attract the ambitions of men of talent and principle. And while the path toward power in the new system still would be arduous, it would be a path that such men could endure, even thrive upon. To Wilson, party government, properly understood, would result in much needed innovation and discernment in policy; it was more constructive than preventive in aim.

Wilson believed better statesmanship and more responsible partisanship were compatible because of an additional departure from Burke's argument. When Burke had worked to legitimize party "connexions" in the age of George III, he had done so over and against the traditional, ostensible norm of political independence among members of Parliament, a norm that members should stand for "not men, but measures," in Chatham's phrase. In Burke's estimation, this rationale simply allowed members "to get loose from every honourable engagement" in order to serve their own ambitions. Burke emphasized the possibility of and need for men of principle, once they had joined together, to maintain their political connections. Party was the bulwark against the temptations of individual ambition; straying from the fold, in Burke's mind, was inherently suspect.[37]

Wilson's time and challenge were different. Intense party solidarity was the norm—and a ripe target for critics such as Stickney who wanted to do away with parties altogether in order to enable "the best men" to govern. To Wilson's mind, though, the question of whether the party or the individual within it was to predominate was poorly framed. "Is it the *party* . . . which men of thought owe and pay allegiance?" Wilson asked in an essay on John Bright. "No. It is to the *principles,* of which party is the embodiment."[38] If the statesman was not free from obligation, in Wilson's thinking, at least he was free from the need to uphold the axiom of "party, right or wrong" that then prevailed. The obligation took a much different form: to discern and elucidate the principles of the party and to set it aright when it strayed.

Wilson's efforts to create more room and responsibility for principled statesmanship in the American polity did not mean that he was willing to hand everything over to a great statesman. Indeed, in addition to Stickney's antipartisanship, Wilson sought to combat the total concentration of power and responsibility in the executive leader called for in *A True Republic*. Stickney's executive could hire and fire his department heads as he saw fit; he alone was responsible for the entire branch (and it was only by means of a two-thirds majority that the legislature could turn him out of office). The chief executive also held the legislative initiative: the legislature would simply ratify (or not) his proposals. A collectively responsible executive of the sort that Wilson called for, Stickney argued, confounded the chain of individual responsibility that was necessary to secure an administration of "the best men" doing "their best work for the people."[39]

In 1882, in an outline for an unpublished, book-length manuscript entitled "Government by Debate," Wilson took issue with Stickney on this point: "Why subordinate the President to his Cabinet? Why not make the *President* responsible—somewhat as *Stickney* suggests? Because no one man can be equal to all the responsibilities of all the offices of executive government. His supervision can at best be but very superficial."[40] To avoid the problem of overreliance on one man, Wilson maintained that the department heads should stand together as a collectively responsible political link between the legislature and the executive branches. The president, nominally the chief executive, would take on an essentially symbolic role, much like the British monarch, presiding over the administration and formally recognizing the executive ministers.

The other major reform that Wilson grappled with as he formulated his program for responsible government involved sending members of the president's cabinet into Congress, where they might introduce legislation, field questions, and take part in debates. Gamaliel Bradford and E. L. Godkin's *Nation* were persistent advocates of this idea. So was Senator George Pendleton, who in 1879 introduced a bill to institutionalize such cabinet appearances in both houses of Congress. Their idea was very similar to Wilson's cabinet government design, and Arthur Link has even suggested that Wilson cribbed his plan from Bradford and Pendleton without attribution.[41]

No doubt Wilson was influenced by these proposals, but he did acknowledge if not directly cite them when formulating his own. More important, Wilson's plan differed in a fundamental respect. Bradford and Pendleton explicitly rejected formal amendment of the separation of powers, in essence calling for the informal imposition of the president's authority upon an incorrigible Congress. Wilson's plan, in contrast, hinged on a formal amendment that would have left the president no choice but to select the cabinet from among seated leaders of the majority party in Congress. This change would effectively transfer the executive power to the legislature.[42] After

Wilson made his initial pitch for this constitutional amendment, he realized that at least three more amendments were required before the potential benefits of a parliamentary system could be fully realized in the United States. In 1882, he spelled them out in "Government by Debate." In doing so, Wilson further differentiated his reform plan from that of Bradford and Pendleton.

The first additional change involved the political status of the president. In Wilson's plan, the president would serve as the symbolic chief of state and the first administrator in "the line of non-partisan permanent officials."[43] Except for selecting the leaders of the majority party to serve in the cabinet, the president had no political role to play, and this remaining role was essentially a formality. Even his use of the veto would have to subside. Were the president to indulge in politics, e.g., by refusing to name to the cabinet the leaders of a congressional majority with which he disagreed or by vetoing bills passed by such a majority, Wilson's plan for cabinet government was at risk. And certainly a political president could not symbolize the state or lead a nonpartisan administration with compelling authority. Yet as long as the president was elected and nominated by partisans, he would be tempted by politics. Wilson knew that Albert Stickney had a point here. So, borrowing and modifying a page from Stickney's book, Wilson proposed that the president hold office permanently during good behavior. The presidency was to become a nonhereditary throne. Removing the office from politics in this way would leave those filling it in a better position to discharge their remaining duties (*The Papers of Woodrow Wilson [PWW]*, 2:227–28, 244–46).

Wilson also faced the difficult task of reconciling responsible government with a bicameral legislature. A cabinet could not be readily accountable to two houses, especially if they were controlled by opposite parties. Which legislative body would the cabinet be drawn from and responsible to? Wilson proposed that this was "the most awkward question" he faced; the weakness of his answer certainly indicated as much. In formulating it, Wilson compared the Senate to the British upper house. When it came to controlling the cabinet, the Senate's "claims, like those of the Lords, would necessarily be postponed to the claims of the popular chamber." The lower house's democratic legitimacy and control of the federal purse made it the natural repository of a responsible cabinet. As a result, the Senate, indirectly elected by the states, would find its political power, though not its prestige and authority, diminished. How exactly this transition in legislative power might occur, however, Wilson did not say (*PWW*, 2:246–47).

Assuming that the Senate's power could be diminished and the House of Representatives would come to host the cabinet, there remained the problems arising from the biennial, fixed terms of House members. The short time span would regularly generate campaigns of excitement and detract from serious political debate. The fixed intervals between elections also raised the prospect of a serious impasse if a cabinet were to be voted out in midterm by the majority that elected it and the majority then refused to support a new cabinet drawn from the opposition party. To get around these difficulties, Wilson proposed that House members' terms be lengthened to six or eight years. He also argued that the cabinet ministers should be able to have the American monarch, i.e., the president, dissolve the legislature and call for new elections in case of a deadlock, a power without which "there would be no having Cabinet government" (*PWW*, 2:223–24, 247–49).

IV

With the sweeping constitutional changes that Wilson proposed in "Government by Debate," he demonstrated an astute grasp of what it would take for American politics and government to work like British politics and government. But his theoretical insight was effectively denying him a voice in the ongoing debates over political reform. Harper refused to publish the manuscript because an editor deemed Wilson's proposed constitutional changes too radical. The editor saw the Bradford-Pendleton plan for a cabinet presence in Congress as a much more realistic option. Wilson, though, saw this option as a flight from the truth. Complaining to a friend who worked at the publishing house, Wilson acknowledged that the changes he proposed were radical, "perhaps they are *too* radical; but if one goes one step with me, he cannot, as it seems to me, escape going all the way. To stop short of the length to which I carry the argument would be simply to be afraid of the legitimate and logical conclusions towards which it inclines with an inevitable tendency." Wilson vowed he would hold to what he emphasized were his "*deliberate* convictions" regarding the necessity of constitutional amendments—and his manuscript remained unpublished.[44]

However, the longer Wilson faced the hard choice between theoretical rigor and political relevance, the more he was convinced that as a man embarked on "a mission of statesmanship," he had to opt for the latter. A few months later, when Wilson began writing *Congressional Government,* he decided to "leave out all advocacy of Cabinet Government—all advocacy, indeed, of any specific reform—and devote myself to a careful analysis of Congressional government." Wilson decided that such an analysis, especially one that relied on the British system for comparative leverage, would lead his readers indirectly but just as inevitably to the imperative of establishing cabinet government in the United States. And, of course, by abandoning "the evangelical for the exegetical," Wilson could avoid the rejections and criticism that an author proposing impossible constitutional changes was destined to receive.[45] Wilson now understood that if he was to become "one of the guides of public thought" that he aspired to be, he would have "to stand apart from advocacy of radical measures for which the public mind may not be ripe."[46]

But Wilson could not stand back from his own logic so easily. Much to his chagrin, Gamaliel Bradford reminded him of it in a positive review of *Congressional Government* that appeared in the *Nation*. Bradford opened by stating that "we have no hesitation in saying that this is one of the most important books, dealing with political subjects, which has ever issued from the American press" and went on to compare the book favorably with Bagehot's *The English Constitution*. Subsequently, though, Bradford referred to one of Wilson's previously published articles in which the young reformer had called for constitutional amendments. The reviewer noted that even though amendments were not discussed in the book, the nature of Wilson's argument indicated that the author still believed they were necessary.[47] Of course, Wilson still did. Nevertheless, the reference to his earlier call for amendments upset Wilson—he regarded it as "a slap in the face"—for it undermined the image of a tough-minded realist, diagnosing problems, not prescribing remedies, that he had worked so hard to project in his book.[48]

Wilson overreacted. It was the praise of Bradford's review, and not the tweak about Wilson's unlikely amendments, that resonated with the reception of *Congressional Government* in most circles. Wilson soon came around. At the first indications that his book was drawing favorable notices in Washington and in reform circles generally, he reaffirmed his choice to serve as an "outside force" in politics. "I have—almost unwittingly—taken the lead in a very great work," he wrote to his fiancée, Ellen Axson. "My book succeeds because I have taken the lead: and now, the opening having been made, I must come up to my opportunities and be worthy of them."[49]

V

Wilson met with his first opportunity to defend the arguments of *Congressional Government* shortly thereafter. The challenge did not come from the reformers Wilson had argued with as he formulated his program for responsible government. Instead, two defenders of the constitutional status quo, Sir Henry Maine, the English jurist, and A. Lawrence Lowell, then a young instructor in government at Harvard, cast doubt on Wilson's criticism of the constitutional separation of powers and the independent executive office it established. The indirect criticism of *Congressional Government* in Maine's

Popular Government, published in 1885, and the direct and sustained criticism of it in Lowell's "Ministerial Responsibility and the Constitution," which appeared in the *Atlantic* the following year, clearly got to Wilson. He responded with an essay in the same magazine two months later. In his response, Wilson incorporated new arguments on behalf of responsible government that he would increasingly rely on in the years ahead. He also took the fateful step, signaled by his title, of advocating "Responsible Government Under the Constitution."

Maine and Lowell rejected Wilson's view that the presidency had been subordinated by Congress and the political parties. While Maine saluted the lawmaking power and independence of Congress, he also praised the persistent autonomy of the president. Unlike the monarchs after George III, he argued, the constitutional position of American presidents meant that they did not have to hand their power over to legislative leaders.[50] Lowell, for his part, after acknowledging that the balance of power along Pennsylvania Avenue often shifted, emphasized the resilience of the American chief executive. Among other things, the ongoing use of the veto by presidents both demonstrated and protected their constitutional independence. Moreover, Lowell argued, the administrative tools and prerogatives at the president's disposal enabled him to exercise leadership in his own right, as Lincoln had done during the Civil War.[51] Like neo-Federalist critics of the rhetorical presidency in the late twentieth century, then, Lowell and Maine understood the presidency to be grounded in the Constitution. It could and should, therefore, refine and even resist, rather than excite or submit to, public opinion.

Wilson could not yet see the considerable constitutional power that inhered in the presidency. His difficulties here may well have originated in his misreading of the Founders' purposes regarding the separation of powers: in his belief that they had established it solely to prevent the abuse of executive power.[52] Wilson acknowledged that during the high stakes diplomacy conducted by the first few presidents, during Andrew Jackson's administration, and then again during the Civil War, the American chief executive had had "Congress at his beck." But Wilson did not see these temporary interruptions in the general pattern of congressional dominance as having much to do with constitutional provisions for an independent, energetic executive.[53]

Nor did Wilson accept the argument that the president's veto was a suitable means of leadership, and here he had a point. Unlike Lowell and Maine, he was looking for constructive legislative leadership. "Government *lives* in the origination, not in the defeat, of measures of government," he argued. "The President obstructs by means of his 'No'; the houses govern by means of their 'Yes'" (*PWW,* 5:116–19; Wilson's emphasis).

Wilson was also on sturdier ground with his essential point about the dispersion of political power and governmental authority in the United States. Congress may not have been as dominant, nor the president as subordinate, as he insisted. Still, nowhere within the two branches were the power and authority necessary to govern in the hands of a group capable of doing so in a consistent, concerted fashion.

Wilson had his sharpest disagreement with Maine and Lowell on the question of whether a responsible focal point for governing should be established. If it were, a disciplined legislative party would be in a sense unstoppable—at least until the next election—once it was given a majority of seats by the voters. Giving unchecked sway to democratic forces was a recipe for disaster in Maine's estimation; democracy was only feasible when constrained by the checks and balances that distinguished the American Constitution. Arguing from similar premises, Lowell proposed that a responsible ministry in the United States would endanger individual and minority rights as it made policy on the basis of a "popular feeling" caused by "temporary excitement" rather than "a mature and lasting opinion."[54]

Lowell's argument was particularly challenging to Wilson because it was based on the assumption that there was a fundamental difference between the British and American political systems. Lowell held that this difference originated in the divergent governing values of the two nations, and that it was manifested in the provisions in the U.S. system for checking power and preserving minority rights for which there were no counterparts in Britain. Hence Lowell argued that "a responsible ministry cannot be grafted into our institutions without entirely changing their nature, and destroying those features of our government which we have been in the habit of contemplating with the most pride."[55]

Wilson's first response to criticism of the democratic aspects of responsible government was to extol the stability invested in both the British and American regimes by public opinion. Wilson argued that the British and their more rough-hewn but nonetheless politically mature brethren in America were the inheritors of a unique political tradition that had instilled in them a tremendous respect for law—indeed, a "constitutional morality." This tradition also carried a healthy pragmatism and a corresponding disdain for the abstract theories and revolutionary action that had plagued France's political development. It was the stability of Anglo-American public opinion that ultimately made the government of both nations constitutional. "Parliament dare not go faster than the public thought," Wilson argued. "There are vast barriers of conservative public opinion to be overrun before a ruinous speed in revolutionary change can be attained. In the last analysis, our own Constitution has no better safeguard."[56]

Wilson also moved to rebut Maine and Lowell by insisting that counter to their arguments, responsible government reconciled majority rule with authoritative leadership and the capacity to govern.[57] Wilson's program would temper the popular will by making its focal point a cabinet of "men of first rate powers" whose administrative responsibilities enabled them to "see the problems of government at first hand" and to recognize the trade-offs, imperatives, and limitations accompanying various policies. The executive officers could then use their congressional and party leadership status to school the legislators and the nation at large in the necessities of government (*PWW,* 5:122).

Bringing the point about governability home, Wilson drew attention to the "grave social and economic problems" that were beginning to arise with urbanization and industrialization. Since Wilson had written *Congressional Government,* the nation had experienced mounting labor strife. In the face of the serious economic turbulence, "any clumsiness, looseness, or irresponsibility in governmental action must prove a source of grave and increasing peril." The spreading "commercial heats and political distempers" called for "a carefully prescribed physic" (*PWW,* 5:123).

However, Wilson hesitated at the moment when he might have prescribed a specific change in the Constitution. He "fully admitted" that he had called for constitutional change elsewhere and that he was "strongly of the opinion that such changes would not be too great a price to pay for the advantages secured." But Wilson then bowed to the difficulty of bringing them about and suggested that a more realistic aim would be the erection of a leadership committee in each house. The committees would be charged with preparing and initiating legislation, thereby providing a modicum of integration and system on the congressional side of policy-making. This centralization on Capitol Hill could then perhaps be supplemented, Wilson observed, by more public consultation on the floors of the houses between the new steering committees and the executive department heads. These developments might find the secretaries answering questions, taking part in debate, and generally serving as representatives of the executive branch. "Such arrangements," he argued, "would constitute responsible government *under* the Constitution" (*PWW,* 5:121–22; Wilson's emphasis).

At the same time, though, such arrangements, while more feasible, amounted to far less than the fusion of the executive and legislative branches that Wilson had explicitly called for earlier and that, according to his own

logic, was still the solution to the nation's problem of governance. His de-
murral was his way of resolving the conflict between the callings of the academic student of politics and the statesman. Wilson saw himself as a statesman first; he was quite frank in professing that he was studying politics
ultimately to bring about political changes. Therefore, it is not surprising that
he muted the implications of his analysis to offer a more palatable prescription. Given the dire situation, he believed "some measure of legislative reform is clearly indispensable." It would not do to hold out for the as yet un-
realizable ideal of "ministerial responsibility in its fullness" (*PWW,* 5:123).

Wilson thus took another step in keeping with a political value that he
would come to admire more and more over the years—political expediency.
Reform, to be plausible and effective, had to build on structures already in
existence, on values that were already intimated in a nation's political development.[58] As he came to embrace the need for expediency in his statesmanship, his program became, on the face of it, more plausible. However, Wilson
had to pay for his greater hearing and relevance by subduing the more pene-
trating insights of his own political analysis concerning the constitutional
preconditions of responsible government, to the point where he himself
risked losing sight of them.

爨 TWO

Political Development,
Interpretive Leadership,
and the Presidency

The impact of *Congressional Government,* published in 1885, Wilson's first year as a college instructor, propelled him on to an increasingly prominent academic career. In 1888, Wesleyan University in Connecticut hired the young scholar away from his initial teaching position at Bryn Mawr. That same year he accepted an invitation to give a short series of lectures in public administration at Johns Hopkins University, an engagement that became an annual affair over the next decade. Then, in 1890, he returned to Princeton as professor of jurisprudence and political economy.

During this rewarding period, Wilson opened a new line of inquiry in which he explored the origins and development of what he termed, in the first installment of this research project, "the modern democratic state."[1] The project was broader in scope than Wilson's previous work. Nevertheless, it was closely related to his writings on the virtues of responsible government and the need to institute it in the United States. Among other things, he wanted "to answer Sir Henry Maine's 'Popular Government' by treating modern democratic tendencies from a much more truly historical point of view." By presenting such a viewpoint, Wilson could better substantiate his claims about the political maturity of the English-speaking peoples and the English origins of U.S. political institutions, thereby buttressing his case against the separation of powers. Hence Wilson's observation that it was into his new line of research that "all my previous schemes have merged drawn by a centripetal force unmistakably natural."[2] This intellectual force field, in turn, substantially altered the dynamics of Wilson's program for responsible government. His new studies prompted him to reconsider the dynamics of constitutional change, to reaffirm the catalytic role of visionary leaders in bringing it about, and, ultimately, to discover the need for and possibility of presidential leadership in the United States.

I

In 1889, Wilson published his comprehensive analysis of political development in *The State: Elements of Historical and Practical Politics*.[3] Wilson's analysis drew on the theories of social Darwinism that were then coming to the fore in the United States. His instructors at Johns Hopkins had familiarized him with the organic, evolutionary view of historical development that predominated in Germany, where many of them had been trained, as well as the theories of Herbert Spencer. But the primary influence on Wilson's thinking in this regard was Walter Bagehot's *Physics and Politics, or Thoughts on the Application of the Principles of "Natural Selection" and "Inheritance" to Political Society*.[4]

Bagehot's account of national political development emphasized the importance of social cohesion and commanding authority in the initial stages, when military threats and war were the primary challenge. Over time, however, the "cake of custom" needed to be broken to provide a suitable range of material for the "natural selection" of the best leaders and behaviors along with technological advancement. Likewise, traditional authority had to give way to government by discussion. "Progress is only possible in those happy cases where the force of legality has gone far enough to bind the nation together, but not far enough to kill out all varieties and destroy nature's perpetual tendency to change." The "happy cases" that Bagehot referred to were limited to a few Anglo-Saxon nations, including the United States. For all of Bagehot's criticism of the American form of government in his prior work, he did not see the Americans as less evolved than the British. Indeed the "difficulty of struggling with the wilderness" was in some ways an advantage in that it imparted "the eager restlessness, the high-strung nervous organization" to the American character, which, in turn, speeded along the nation's development.[5]

Arguing along similar lines in *The State,* Wilson likened societies to organisms that adapted to their environment and the changes brought on by war, migration, economic development, technological change, and so on (22–29). Government was "merely the executive organ of society, the organ through which its habit acts, through which its will becomes operative, through which it adapts itself to its environment and works out for itself a more effective life." The medium through which this change occurred was the melange of habits, meanings, prejudices, beliefs, sentiments, fears, and aspirations that Wilson sometimes subsumed under the concept of national character but more often than not referred to as public opinion (597–99).

Against those who argued that constitutions were the fundamental political facts that determined nations' fates, Wilson maintained that opinion was "a controlling fact; in political development it is the fact of facts."[6] As public opinion changed with historical circumstances, new institutions and policies became conceivable. So long as political innovation emerged from and was legitimate in terms of the prevailing public opinion, it would contribute to progressive development. If, however, leaders and reformers pursued drastic or anomalous changes, then the outcome would be regressive. "Every nation must constantly keep in touch with its past: it cannot run towards its ends around sharp corners."[7]

The secret to the well-advanced political evolution of the English-speaking peoples, Wilson argued, was the gradualism and pragmatism that over time had marked the adaptation of their institutions, practices, and policies. This slow but steady evolution had taken place on both sides of the Atlantic. In a revealing new tone, Wilson was now less inclined to compare the U.S. polity unfavorably with that of Great Britain. Americans, too, he suggested, had manifested in their institutions the English genius for politics. Indeed, Wilson argued in *The State* that American political institutions were "in all their main features simply the political institutions of England, as transplanted by English colonists . . . [and] worked out through a fresh development to new and characteristic forms" (449–69).

Wilson was now prepared to argue that the government of the United States had developed progressively over the years. It had overcome the systemic weaknesses of the Articles of Confederation; survived the War of 1812 and then was victorious in Mexico; adjusted to the rapid expansion of the railroads and the tremendous internal migration westward; and, finally, through the painful national catharsis of the Civil War, resolved the sectional crisis and eradicated the increasingly obsolete institution of slavery. Social change, economic development, and international challenges had produced in American public opinion the growth of what Wilson termed "the national idea." In turn, Wilson argued, this ascendent ethos had transformed the Constitution, creating an effectively national government where one had not previously existed (469–80).

To be sure, Wilson noted in *The State* that there were some persistent aberrations in American political development, namely, the estrangement of the executive from the legislature and the intrusion of politics into administration that resulted. These problems were not in keeping with U.S. status as an otherwise well-evolved polity of English lineage (565–66, 591–92). Wilson continued to reject A. Lawrence Lowell's argument that the separation of powers reflected a fundamental difference in the principles underlying the American and British polities. Instead, Wilson believed that the arrangement was a historical artifact that had managed thus far to resist progressive development because of its "peculiar legal status."[8]

If the separation of powers thus remained an anomaly in Wilson's theory of political development in the United States, it was one that he predicted would disappear soon enough. In 1889, in a review of James Bryce's *American Commonwealth,* Wilson observed: "America is now sauntering through her resources and through the mazes of her politics with easy nonchalance; but presently there will come a time when she will be surprised to find herself grown old,—a country crowded, strained, perplexed,—when she will be obliged to fall back upon her conservatism, obliged to pull herself together, adopt a new regimen of life, husband her resources, concentrate her strength, steady her methods, sober her views, restrict her vagaries, trust her best, not her average members. That will be the time of change."[9] That America would soon "concentrate her strength" and "trust her best, not her average members" in order to respond to the changing environment was an overriding implication of Wilson's Darwinian theory of political development, in which, "tested by history's long measurements, the lines of advance are seen to be singularly straight."[10] This historical optimism marked a considerable shift from Wilson's earlier writings, in which he foresaw with some pessimism the continued degradation of the U.S. polity unless reformers actively intervened to overhaul the Constitution.[11]

Traces of the pessimism remained, however. Wilson continued to be discomforted by what he believed were the anachronistic limits on responsible government in the United States. Although his theory of political development predicted progress over time, the dearth of leadership in the United States at this critical juncture in its history needed to be resolved soon. By 1889, the same year in which *The State* was published, Wilson indicated that he was ready to pull back from his more assertive theses about the primacy of broad socioeconomic and international forces, and corresponding adjustments in public opinion, as the fundamental variables in political development. Wilson wrote in a set of personal notes that "the formula of evolution is easy, we know; but it is not wholly safe, we suspect." He did not want to lose sight of the role "that human choice and originating thought" played in political development. Therefore, Wilson concluded that "we need a fresh formulation of the principles [of] political change, and a somewhat shifted point of view."[12]

II

Wilson offered such a "fresh formulation" in "Leaders of Men," which he wrote in December 1889 and gave as a popular lecture several times in the 1890s. In this lecture, Wilson celebrated the transformative power of leaders such as William Gladstone, his boyhood hero. This power began to figure more prominently in Wilson's theory of political development; visionary leaders, he concluded, had to play a catalytic role in bringing it about.[13]

To his audiences, Wilson proposed that "leadership, for the statesman, is *interpretation*. He must read the common thought: he must test and calculate very circumspectly the *preparation* of the nation for the next move in the progress of politics" (*PWW,* 6:659; Wilson's emphasis). Given the subtleties of this task, the statesman clearly needed to possess a special insight into the vectors of history. At the same time, though, he also had to be a man of the people, capable of establishing a rhetorical rapport with them. In this regard, the nuanced reasoning of an Edmund Burke could not bring about the same political movement as the straightforward, resounding oratory of a John Bright (*PWW,* 6:650–56).

For James Ceaser, Jeffrey Tulis, and other adherents of the Hamiltonian vision of political leadership, in which the executive's power is best grounded in the formal Constitution, leaving him independent of and in a position to refine or even act contrary to public opinion, the Wilsonian leader threatens to become either too weak or too strong. If the leader merely caters to public opinion, the former occurs; if the leader manipulates public opinion and through his demagoguery acquires an irresistible power, the latter.[14]

Wilson recognized that suggesting that the power of leaders depended in large part on their popular support was a controversial step, but in "Leaders of Men," he defined it as a realistic and necessary one. He noted that the world had changed considerably since the era of the Founding; relations between elites and the common man had taken on a new cast. Extolling the insight of his hero, William Gladstone, into the dynamics of democratic leadership, Wilson proposed that the nineteenth century had "established the principle that public opinion *must* be truckled to (if you *will* use a disagreeable word) in the conduct of government. A man, surely, would not fish for votes . . . among the minority."[15] What some saw as a vice, Wilson understood to be a precondition for governing in a democratic polity, which the United States increasingly had been since the Jacksonian revolution.[16]

While the leader's purposes might now have to be those he "interpreted" instead of proposing himself, the power wielded through successfully interpreting public opinion would be nonetheless compelling. Indeed, if anything, the power of the Wilsonian leader threatened to become overbearing, and Wilson himself seemed to suggest as much in rhetorical flights like the following: "It is the *power* which dictates, dominates: the materials yield. Men are as clay in the hands of the consummate leader."[17]

Wilson was certainly aware of the potential abuses of popular leadership. In "Leaders of Men," he defined the statesman in part by contrasting him with the demagogue: "You will find the one trimming to the inclinations of the moment, the other obedient only to the permanent purposes of the public mind" (*PWW*, 6:661). Wilson's implication, of course, was that a demagogue would be unable to sustain his leadership by pandering to temporary whims or passions, whereas the statesman, building on higher political ground, i.e., the "permanent purposes of the public mind," would be able to prosper. One might reasonably join the Founders and the modern defenders of their regime in questioning this assumption. Might not a clever demagogue be able to fool enough of the people to win office and thereafter degrade the constitutional order?

Wilson's research in the processes of political development in general, and American political development in particular, led him to think otherwise. He summarized the judgments he had gleaned from this research in other sections of "Leaders" and in doing so qualified his bold pronouncements about the power of leaders to mold public opinion as if it were clay. Even leadership of the most compelling kind had to operate within the significant constraints imposed by the natural inertia of public opinion: "That general sense of the community may wait to be aroused, and the statesman must arouse it; may be inchoate and vague, and the statesman must formulate and make it explicit. But he cannot and should not do more" (*PWW*, 6:660–61). Were the statesman to try to do more, to enact policies or reforms for which public opinion was not prepared, he would surely fail. As an organism, society could only develop in limited steps of adaptation. "What a lesson it is in the organic wholeness of Society, this study of leadership," Wilson remarked. "How subtle and delicate is the growth of the organism, and how difficult initiative in it! Where is rashness? It is excluded. And raw invention? It is discredited" (*PWW*, 6:670).

In an essay entitled "The Nature of Democracy in the United States," which Wilson also wrote in 1889, he noted that there were additional constraints on popular leadership in the U.S. polity. He cited the case of Andrew Jackson, whom he regarded as a demagogue. For all of Jackson's "childish arrogance," the constitutional tradition in the United States had kept him in check. "He was suffered only to strain the Constitution, not to break it,"

Wilson observed. After being duly elected, Jackson had to operate within "the letter of the law" and cope with "hostile criticism; and . . . he passed into private life as harmlessly as did James Monroe." Wilson also noted that amid the expansiveness and diversity of Madison's republic, it would be very hard for a demagogue to enthrall a sufficient portion of the nation to do much damage: "Thoughts which in one quarter kindle enthusiasm may in another meet coolness or arouse antagonism. Events which are fuel to the *passions* of one section may be but as a passing wind to the minds of another section." [18]

Of course these safeguards are not infallible, as demonstrated by the demagoguery that has emanated from state capitols in the South and the U.S. Senate in this century. The likes of Huey Long and Joe McCarthy, however, would not have surprised Wilson. As Stephen Skowronek and Terri Bimes have shown, Wilson regarded appeals of the sort made by Jackson, Andrew Johnson, and the politicians just then beginning to exploit the sectional issue as a real threat to the stability of the political system.[19] Indeed, in 1889, Wilson believed the danger of demagoguery in the United States was on the rise, in part because of the increasing speed with which political news could circulate among the masses, and in part because of the new waves of non-English immigrants, whom Wilson believed were more receptive to if not already advocates of radical political doctrines.[20]

It was in light of this danger that Wilson renewed his call for more responsible government: "This vast and miscellaneous democracy of ours must be led; its giant faculties must be schooled and directed" (*PWW*, 6:235). He saw his program as one that would reduce if not eliminate the danger of demagoguery. If such leaders "come temporarily to power among us," Wilson argued, "it is because we cut our leadership up into so many little parts and do not subject any one man to the purifuing [*sic*] influences of centered responsibility."[21] When power was centralized, those holding it had the ability and thus the obligation to back up their promises and accusations, circumstances that tended to temper and discipline their leadership.

Responsible government would constrain popular leaders not only by putting leaders on the spot but also, and more importantly, by tending over time to produce statesmen in the highest echelons of government who would not stoop to demagoguery. Some observers, even those sympathetic to Wilson, have suggested that he harbored an idealistic or romantic view of leadership, one that did not provide institutional solutions to the problems of what statesmen should do and how statesmen could be selected.[22] This criticism overlooks Wilson's enduring conviction that his program solved both problems. Establishing "power and strict accountability for its use,"

Wilson believed, would attract better men into politics, provide a rigorous and extended testing ground in which only the ablest statesmen could win power, and compel those responsible for ruling to adopt policies they could defend in the face of focused opposition. That Wilson's solutions were adequate is debatable; that he diagnosed the problem and offered an institutional prescription is not.

With regard to the adequacy of Wilson's program, the following issue does need to be addressed. Could an interpretive statesman serve as a historical switchman, sending American political development in the direction of responsible government? Wilson's discussion of the catalytic role of interpretive leadership, when viewed in the context of his frustration with the peculiar persistence of the separation of executive and legislative powers, indicates that he believed leaders could play a critical role in subjecting the arrangement to an informal but nonetheless fundamental evolution. The potential effects of interpretive leadership in his view went beyond fostering policy innovation and included constitutional adaptation.

But was public opinion in the late nineteenth century really amenable to responsible government? Wilson insisted that it was. The nation's mounting problems demanded responsible government for their resolution, and its political tradition, at least as interpreted by Wilson, portended this innovation. Yet if Lawrence Lowell and Sir Henry Maine were right, and the separation of powers was neither an obsolete nor an anomalous arrangement but rather vital and integral to the American political tradition, then even the most compelling statesman would have great difficulty reshaping the public opinion supporting it.

Wilson had another problem: in a sense, the Constitution had a self-defense mechanism against the Wilsonian leader. The constitutional division between the president and Congress, the bicameral legislature, the plethora of congressional committees, the pragmatic and secretive party organizations, all these features of American government and politics meant not only that there was no suitable platform for interpretive leadership in the U.S. polity, but also that any interpretive efforts to create one would be exposed to political scorn from some of the other disparate power centers.

Over the course of the 1890s, however, Wilson came to believe that despite these obstacles a platform suitable for interpretive leadership was emerging in the United States, in keeping with the progressive laws of political development, and that visionary men might use this platform to bring about more responsible government. He was increasingly convinced that such leaders might thrive not in Congress, as he had once thought, but in the presidency.

III

In late 1889, just after he drafted "Leaders of Men" and just before he embarked on more than a decade's worth of research and writing in American history, Wilson confided to his journal that:

> The phrase that Bagehot uses to describe the successful constitutional statesman I might appropriate to describe myself: "a man with common opinions but uncommon ability." I *receive* the opinions of my day, I do not *conceive* them. But I receive them into a vivid mind, with a quick imaginative realization, and a power to see as a whole the long genesis of the opinions received. I have little impatience with existing conditions; I comprehend too perfectly how they came to exist, how *natural* they are. I have great confidence in progress; I feel the movement that is in affairs and am conscious of a persistent push behind the present order.[23]

No longer an impatient physician prescribing drastic remedies, Wilson was now confident enough in his "uncommon" political insight and "the persistent push behind the present order" that he was willing to serve as a Hegelian handmaiden to reform. He would clear the way for more responsible government by describing how it was already intimated in American history. As Wilson posed the question to his journal, "Why may not the present age write, through me, its political *autobiography?*"[24] It was this grand aspiration that lay behind Wilson's discovery of the need for and possibility of presidential leadership in the United States.

It was not obvious that the presidency deserved such a rethinking in the early 1890s. Indeed, many observers were more impressed by the forceful presence of Thomas Brackett Reed, Speaker of the House, and the "Reed rules" he imposed on that body, which significantly boosted his power to control it. One was Albert Bushnell Hart, a professor of history at Harvard. In 1891, Hart expounded on the implications of the recent developments on Capitol Hill in an *Atlantic* article entitled "The Speaker as Premier." Hart implicitly chided Wilson and the rest of the "small and very earnest band of men" who had advocated parliamentary reforms of the American government. The reformers, Hart argued, had failed to see that with the augmented power of the Speaker, "there has actually grown up within our system of government an officer who possesses and exercises the most important powers entrusted to the head of the administration of England."[25]

Wilson did not find Hart's argument persuasive. "The essential feature of the [English] Premier's Leadership," he wrote to Hart, "is that he is, while he leads the House, himself constantly in the midst of administrative business." This latter business gave the leader the perspective that was crucial for crafting sound legislation, and it made the leader responsible in the sense of being accountable for the execution and effects of the laws. Because Reed was an "officer who belongs wholly to the legislature," he lacked both the perspective and the responsibility that Wilson deemed essential. Wilson put the criticism more sharply in a letter to James Bryce, who was then working on a revised edition of *The American Commonwealth* and had asked if any of the changes in Congress had significantly altered the analysis presented in *Congressional Government* (the Englishman had relied on Wilson's book when writing his first edition). The mistake of Hart and those who saw the Speaker as an emergent prime minister, Wilson argued, was that "they think what we need is concentration of power, and consequent concentration of responsibility, in the Houses merely; when what we need is the marriage of legislation and practical statesmanship—a responsible direction of those who make the laws by those who must carry them out and approve or damn themselves in the process."[26] A visit that Wilson would have with Speaker Reed later in the decade vindicated this judgment. Reed had read *Congressional Government* and told Wilson that he was quite impressed with its analysis of "government by helter skelter." When Wilson asked the Speaker where Congress was heading, Reed said he did not know; he simply did what seemed to be "most convenient at the moment."[27]

In 1893, Wilson's doubts about leadership that did not span and integrate the legislative and executive powers also led him to criticize what he regarded as Grover Cleveland's efforts to govern unilaterally from the executive branch. The worrisome sign to Wilson was Cleveland's decision at the outset of his second term to break with tradition and select personal associates instead of recognized party leaders for most of his cabinet posts. Cleveland's actions, Wilson argued, raised a fundamental question: "Are we to have a purely administrative cabinet, and individual choice of policy by the President, or are we to have responsible party government?"[28]

Although Wilson admired Cleveland's character and supported his policies, he nonetheless warned that the general precedent set by the second term cabinet "commits the country . . . in a hazardous degree, to the understanding and capacity of a single man." That the president was often elevated "hastily, by the unpremeditated compromises or the sudden impulses of huge popular conventions," made the country's reliance on his judgment even more problematic. Wilson also noted that given the limitations on the president's time, the cabinet secretaries "must decide many questions which bear directly on the general policy of the Administration." The risks of relying on an untested leader were thus compounded by the inevitable need to rely on the judgment of his personal—and unelected—associates. And men who were relatively new to governing in Washington would lack the experience to generate the "highest efficiency" in administration, efficiency that could only result from a "close cooperation and intimate mutual understanding" between the executive and the legislative branches."[29]

Instead, Wilson argued, the burdens of the executive should be shouldered by a group of men whose judgment and abilities had been proven in previous party battles—"by the conservative processes of the survival of the fittest in Congress"—and who thereby enjoyed established ties with fellow partisans in the legislature. Such men could symbolically bridge the separation of powers and bear witness that a whole party, not simply one man, was accountable for the administration's policies. In a new twist to his program, Wilson suggested that the cabinet would be more explicitly turned into such a "responsible party council" if public opinion, operating through the Senate's powers of confirmation, forced the president "to call to the chief places in the departments representative party men who have accredited themselves for such functions by a long and honorable public service." Wilson thus continued his call for the cabinet to serve as "a natural connecting link" between the executive and the legislature, though his descriptions of the mechanisms through which the link might be established were becoming more informal and ambiguous.[30]

Such were Wilson's conclusions at the outset of Cleveland's second term. By its end, however, Wilson gave a decidedly different interpretation of both the man and the office. Writing in the *Atlantic,* Wilson was speaking most of all for himself when he observed that Cleveland's "singular independence and force of purpose have made the real character of the government of the United States more evident than it ever was before. . . . He has refreshed our notion of an American chief magistrate."[31]

What was most impressive to Wilson was the way in which Cleveland had called into question the claim of *Congressional Government* that the president was simply a creature of—and could not begin to re-create—the pragmatic, parochial features of the American party system. To understand the revelation that Cleveland's example brought home to Wilson, we need to review the young political scientist's evolving impressions of contemporary politics in the 1880s and 1890s.

For all of Wilson's scholarly interest in the reform of American politics and government, after the Hayes-Tilden campaign of 1876 he grew increasingly aloof from practical politics. Wilson had a problem in that he was committed to the agenda of liberal reformers such as E. L. Godkin and Carl Schurz: civil service reform, free trade, and sound currency. However, Wilson also was a Democrat; his party was heavily populated with spoilsmen, and as he observed the month before the 1880 election, it appeared to be "allying itself, in its pursuit of power, with every damnable heresy—with Green-backers as with protectionists."[32] In 1881 he reported to a friend that he was not growing tired of politics per se, only "of the unsavory particulars of party intrigues and *personal* politics." In contrast, Wilson observed that he was increasingly interested in "political *principles,* in genuine political opinions honestly held, in political tendencies, and in the broader phases of party movements." [33]

Wilson was looking for a party to rally around a principled agenda that addressed the policy challenges of the 1880s, not the war of the 1860s. For a brief while in 1884, he thought that Grover Cleveland might be the man to bring this change about; here at last was a strong character and a Democrat with whom Wilson agreed on the issues. But Cleveland's early refusal to take an active legislative initiative, and his apparent inability to impose his principles on his party, suggested to Wilson that something more was needed. In an 1886 article in the *Boston Times* entitled "Wanted—A Party," he bemoaned the muddled lines of division between the parties and their predilection for slogging "played out" issues. He also looked forward to a day when "a new party will be formed—and another party opposed to it. All that is wanting is a new, genuine, and really meant purpose held by a few strong men of principle and boldness. That is a big 'all' and it is still conspicuously wanting." It would want a while longer. In 1889, shortly after the start of what he termed the "reactionary administration" of Republican Party regular Benjamin Harrison, Wilson reported feeling angry and despondent; his interest in affairs in Washington had "suffered a decided collapse." [34]

Then Grover Cleveland's second term in the White House piqued that interest. As Wilson viewed things from the end of that term, he identified the key turning point back in 1887: midway through Cleveland's first term, when "sick of seeing a great party drift and dally," the president threw down the gauntlet for tariff reform in his annual message to Congress. Cleveland's continued pressing of this issue during the next election year and then again in his second term, along with his spearheading the repeal of the Silver Purchase Act and his significant expansion of civil service reform—all of which he did notwithstanding the grousing of the pragmatic politicians in his party—thoroughly impressed Wilson. Here, at last, was a leader who "called himself a party man" but was nevertheless committed ultimately to what he saw as the party's long-standing principles—not the short-term success of the organization. Wilson insisted that Cleveland was no less a partisan for his priorities; rather, the president had "deemed his party better served by manliness and integrity than by chicanery."[35] That Cleveland's leadership ultimately divided and led to political disaster for the Democratic Party was beside the point. The Bryanite Democrats, running on the wrong side of the silver issue as Cleveland had defined it, had been thoroughly repudiated in 1896, or so it seemed to Wilson. Cleveland had "forced the fight" on silver and thus engaged in an act of creative destruction. He cleared the way for the rise of a new, more principled party.[36]

The "singular independence and force of purpose" that Wilson detected in Cleveland's enduring refusal to play politics as usual on the tariff and his resolute stand on silver suggested to Wilson that a president could in fact set the legislative agenda, if not control it outright, in Washington. "Power had somehow gone the length of the avenue," Wilson quipped, "and settled in one man." Maine and Lowell, for all of their championing of the nineteenth-century presidency, did not detect this capacity in the office, perhaps because in Cleveland's case the power had not come simply from the Constitution. Wilson commented of Cleveland that on the initial tariff question "the country watched him, waiting for him to speak, the only representative of the nation as a whole in the government." The circumstances compelled Cleveland to move beyond the limited, negative conception of the executive's legislative role with which he had come to the office. As he did so, he held the nation's attention. He knew this and warmed to the task: "The habit of independent initiative in respect of questions of legislative policy was growing upon him, as he felt his personal power grow."[37]

Wilson was not the only one praising Cleveland at the close of his second term. Liberal reformers Godkin and Schurz also wrote testimonials, admiring Cleveland as a moralistic repudiator, for the enemies he made. Cleveland had done what they had always wanted a president to do: say no to the party politicians in Congress, frequently and forcefully. As Godkin's *Nation* put it the day he left office, "Where other statesmen have left behind them a monument of wise laws passed, he has left a monument of foolish and base laws prevented." For his part, Schurz reserved his highest accolades for the "civic heroism" demonstrated by Cleveland in vetoing a handful of appropriation and pension bills he regarded as faulty just before leaving office.[38]

Wilson was looking for a more constructive form of leadership then were Godkin and Schurz. Cleveland's steadfastness and his willingness to use his veto pen appealed to Wilson, to be sure. But it was what was intimated in Cleveland's presidency—the possibility of a proactive, principled executive, one who could remake his party and take the legislative initiative—that Wilson most appreciated. The "direct, fearless, and somewhat unsophisticated" Cleveland had moved haltingly toward this possibility, Wilson noted, "as if in spite of himself," and he had never sought to lead Democrats in Congress with persuasion as well as mastery. His example gave Wilson a sense of what a sophisticated, willing, and persuasive president could do.[39]

The departures of Cleveland's presidency, and their ramifications for government and party politics, were especially striking to Wilson because of the broader historical context in which they occurred. Developments in the 1890s persuaded Wilson more and more that there was a pressing need for authoritative national leadership in the U.S. polity that only the president could provide. Prominent among these developments was the symbolic closing of the frontier. Frederick Jackson Turner influenced Wilson's thinking about the import of this event. Wilson had befriended Turner when they had lived in the same boardinghouse near Johns Hopkins in Baltimore. The two provincials, Wilson from the South and Turner from the West, spent many evenings discussing American history and the role of the sections in its development. The influence went in both directions; Wilson encouraged and guided Turner as the latter was working out his frontier thesis. Turner would recall later that Wilson's "emphasis upon Bagehot's idea of 'breaking the cake of custom' left a deep impression on me when I came to consider what part the West had played."[40]

Like Bagehot and Turner, Wilson understood the West not so much as a section but as a "stage of development," one that had quickened American life, given it a more democratic spirit, and widened the practical meaning of freedom in the nation. The close of the frontier raised new challenges for the polity. The American character would have to be preserved and developed further without the unique perspective borne of the frontier, and socioeconomic pressures would increase as the migrating nation turned back on itself. "The free lands are gone," Wilson warned. Americans would have to "make their life sufficient without this easy escape."[41]

At the same time that the nation was losing the safety valve of the frontier, it was being buffeted by the escalating pressures of industrialization and urbanization, a growing number of immigrants from Southern and Eastern Europe, mounting labor strife, and a surge in sectional and populist unrest. Wilson was keenly aware of the historical flux resulting from these trends. In 1897 he observed that the modernizing nation stood "unfinished, unharmonized." The situation called for "leadership of a much higher order to teach us the triumphs of cooperation, the self-possession and calm choices of maturity."[42]

Wilson recognized that the policies needed to integrate and manage the transformed society and economy were of a different sort than the distributive patterns that had predominated for most of the nineteenth century. Regulating the railroads, giant industries, and trusts; revising the tariff in the wake of industrial growth; and reforming the currency, among other tasks, all raised hard questions, pitting section against section, interest against interest. These new issues could not be settled through "a mere compounding of differences, a mere unguided interplay of rival individual forces," and they could not be avoided for much longer. In these circumstances, authoritative national leadership was essential. Yet, Wilson asked in an 1897 address entitled "Leaderless Government," who was in a position to provide such direction and judgment? "Who is to reconcile our interests and extract what is national and liberal out of what is sectional and selfish?"[43]

The answer that Wilson was reaching for was the president. In preparing the way for this conclusion—no small revision of his program—he noted the legacy of strong presidential leadership offered by the likes of Washington, Jefferson, Jackson, and Lincoln. More important, Wilson went beyond the historical precedents for presidential leadership (recently brought up to date by Cleveland) to note the potential authority and power that inhered in the presidential office as a representative institution. Only the president held a national office and represented the people as a whole. In contrast, the political vision of members of Congress, representing as they did particular constituencies, states, and sections, tended to be more limited and parochial. Wilson implied that as a result the president was in a better position to discern the public interest at home and the national interest abroad.[44]

Wilson understood that the president's ability to serve as an authoritative national leader was limited by the taint from his selection through the internecine processes of the nominating conventions as well as by the lack of any formal connections between the president and his cabinet, on the one hand, and their party's legislators in Congress, on the other. Wilson remained purposefully ambiguous about how these problems might be rectified and responsible government instituted.[45] Nevertheless, in "Leaderless Government," Wilson took a significant step: he had suggested that the platform for national leadership that he had long been calling for should be situated not in the Capitol but in the White House.

Wilson's belief that the nation had to rely on the encompassing leadership of the president to resolve the new problems it confronted in the 1890s grew even more pronounced at the end of the decade, when the Spanish American War established the United States as a world and colonial power. Many reformers worried that the American conquest marked a dangerous imperial departure in the nation's foreign policy and would distract attention from domestic reform. Yet as Wilson told himself in a personal memorandum written as the war came to a close, "The thing is done; cannot be undone, and our future must spring out of it." Moreover, after he reconsidered his program in light of the sudden change in "the scenes, the stage itself upon which we act," the future he projected was actually one of more responsible government.[46]

In his early writings, Wilson had hardly touched upon foreign affairs. Civil service reform, the soundness of the currency, and tariff revision were the issues that had animated him in the 1880s and 1890s. Insofar as he did address foreign affairs in this period, it was largely to note how congressional power, in particular the "treaty-marring" power of the Senate, tended to trammel on the president's ostensible powers in this domain. Wilson was quick to contrast this pattern with the deference that he believed Parliament accorded the Ministry as it exercised the Crown's prerogative in the making of British foreign policy.[47]

All this changed after the war with Spain. In the preface to the fifteenth edition of *Congressional Government,* which Wilson drafted in 1900, he proposed that "when foreign affairs play a prominent part in the politics and policy of a nation, its Executive must of necessity be its guide: must utter every initial judgement, take every first step of action, supply the information upon which it is to act, suggest and in large measure control its conduct" (xi–xii).

Wilson did not explicate his convictions concerning the "necessity" of executive dominance in foreign affairs, but as this passage indicates, he shared the judgments of Alexander Hamilton. The institutional efficiency of the "energetic executive," arising from the office's capacity for "decision, activity, secrecy, and despatch," made it both right and necessary that the president take the lead in matters of war and diplomacy. This initiative, in turn, effectively enabled the president to control the nation's policy.[48]

The functional logic of executive dominance in international affairs, Wilson argued, was evident in American history. When foreign affairs and war dominated the agenda, strong presidents emerged and dominated the polity. Conversely, he held that apart from the accelerating organizational capacity of Congress, the leading cause of the subordinate presidency for much of the nineteenth century was the preeminence of domestic affairs, in which Congress had more of a role to play because of its superior capacity to represent local interests and concerns.[49]

The war with Spain and the seizure of the Philippines, Wilson argued, had broken this pattern once and for all. The nation was now "in the very presence of forces which must make the politics of the twentieth century radically unlike the politics of the nineteenth."[50] The demands of imperial administration would strengthen the position of the executive branch vis-à-vis more parochial interests in the parties and the legislature. Furthermore, as the focus of party politics shifted from patronage and reconciling sectional disputes to encompass the broader scope of international affairs, the statesman bearing responsibility for these affairs would be better positioned to lead his party. The greater institutional resources and political prominence of the chief executive in turn would make it easier for him to frame the debates over domestic as well as foreign policies. Hence Wilson's pregnant suggestion as he closed out his preface to the new edition of *Congressional Government* that the recent war might "put this whole volume hopelessly out of date."[51]

The prophecy marked a significant shift in Wilson's program. In 1885, in the first edition of his book, he had been a heretical critic of the Founders' Constitution, in particular of its "radical defect," the separation of powers, which he had argued precluded responsible leadership. Now he was suggesting that such leadership could flourish in the Founders' regime. To be sure, he did not see this possibility as resulting from the Founders' constitutional provision for an independent and energetic executive power with special responsibilities for diplomacy and command. To Wilson's mind it was the necessities of foreign affairs that gave rise to the new promise of presidential leadership. But inasmuch as he was implicitly agreeing that the Constitution allowed for an ample response to the necessities, he accepted the Founders' creation. This acceptance would have no small effect on his program for responsible government.

A less dramatic event in 1898—the publication of Henry Jones Ford's *The Rise and Growth of American Politics*—bolstered Wilson's willingness to let go of long-held views on the basic dynamics of American politics. Ford, a newspaper reporter, argued that the president's national constituency and his unequaled influence on public opinion established the inhabitant of the White House as the dominant force in the polity and an unrivaled catalyst for progressive change. Wilson, of course, was beginning to believe the same thing. What distinguished Ford's account was that he believed the presidency had emerged long before to play such a role. Indeed, Ford contended that since the Jacksonian revolution and the advent of mass parties had transformed the office into a democratic, representative institution, "the agency of the presidential office has been such a master force in shaping public policy that to give a detailed account of it would be equivalent to writing the political history of the United States."[52]

Ford's book clearly had an impact on Wilson. He praised it as "lucid and convincing," recommended it on reading lists to his students as a useful counterpoise to *Congressional Government,* and successfully worked to bring Ford to teach at Princeton. The most suggestive evidence of Ford's influence on Wilson, however, comes from reading the sections of *Rise and Growth* that exult the power of the presidency to shape public opinion, party politics, and policy and the sections of Wilson's *Constitutional Government,* published ten years later, that discuss the office in remarkably similar terms. Wilson had been in the process of discovering the potential of the presidency before Ford wrote his book, and Ford's analysis served to clarify and confirm Wilson's developing thoughts on presidential power.[53]

If Henry Jones Ford's *Rise and Growth* served as the intellectual confirmation for Wilson's new understanding of the presidency, Theodore Roosevelt's vocal stewardship of the public interest served as the political confirmation. The growing tensions between the two ambitious men left Wilson hesitant to praise Roosevelt by name in his scholarly writings during the 1900s, but Wilson was not so reticent in his lectures to students and speeches to reform clubs.[54]

Several facets of Roosevelt's leadership made a profound impression on Wilson. He was struck by Roosevelt's willingness to roll up his sleeves and enter the fray of party politics. Wilson held him up as an example to reformers, who were increasingly prone to antipartisan sentiments: "The danger of our age is not partisanship, but that our thoughtful men will belong to no party. Don't form yourself into a third party. Don't isolate yourself. Go into the arena and take your active part."[55] Wilson also appreciated the active policy initiative that Roosevelt assumed in the White House. "Whatever else we may think or say of Theodore Roosevelt," Wilson told his students in 1909, "we must admit that he is an aggressive leader. He led Congress—he was not driven by Congress."[56] Finally, Wilson was impressed, albeit with some unease, by the audacity of Roosevelt's willingness, in the latter's words, "to appeal over the heads of the Senate and the House Leaders to the people, who were the master of both of us" when the president and Congress were at loggerheads over a policy.[57] Although he thought that the president's appeals were often too brash and strident, Wilson observed that at no time was Roosevelt a stronger and more popular leader than when "he spoke of any inside matter he pleased, as if it were the people's privilege to know what was going on within their government."[58]

All these developments at the turn of the twentieth century seemed consistent with Wilson's expectations regarding the progressive path of political development and the role of dynamic leaders in fostering progress. An unprecedented set of challenges at home and abroad and the bold responses to them by presidents such as Cleveland and Roosevelt were bracing the nation and opening up new possibilities of leadership.[59] Whether and how these developments would put Wilson's analysis in *Congressional Government* "hopelessly out of date" by engendering responsible government remained to be seen.

Constitutional Government
and Presidential Power

In 1906, President Nicholas Murray Butler of Columbia University asked Wilson to resurvey the territory covered in *Congressional Government,* by then more than two decades old, and present an updated analysis in a series of lectures at the university. Wilson relished the chance to do so. He had been named president of Princeton in 1902, and he had found, to his chagrin, that the administrative responsibilities of his new position crowded out time for creative thought and inquiry. In early 1907, he took a holiday in Bermuda to map out his revised analysis. He gave the lectures later that spring and published them the following year as *Constitutional Government in the United States.*[1] This book merits special scrutiny. It does in part because it integrated the studies in political development, leadership, and American history that Wilson had undertaken in the previous two decades with his earlier reform writings. He also regarded the book as his contribution to the debates over political reform then raging in the midst of the Progressive Era, stating in the preface his hope that what followed would be "serviceable in the clarification of our views as to policy and practice." Most important, it was in this book that Wilson elaborated the understandings of the American political system and presidential leadership that he took with him into the White House and that guided his conduct there.

I

In *Constitutional Government,* Wilson set out to undermine what he termed, following Henry Jones Ford, the whig theory of politics. The whig theory sought to comprehend and order the political universe much as Newton did the physical universe, in terms of fixed and enduring balances, mechanisms, and counterpoises. This theory, Wilson believed, was embodied in and perpetuated by the checks and balances and various other constraints on power in the Founders' Constitution. In place of the whig theory, Wilson sought to elaborate an alternative understanding of politics, one that relied on Darwinian metaphors and portrayed politics as an organic process of adaptation and development.[2]

Part of Wilson's criticism of the Founders' Newtonian design was based on his enduring belief (not fully accurate, as indicated earlier) that they were interested only in checking and separating power in order to prevent its abuse. Yet Wilson's problems with the Founders ultimately came from a more fundamental and accurate reading of their purposes. Wilson fully understood that the Founders had intended their Constitution to endure for the ages. The Founders had studied the history of the ancient republics and federations and pondered the universal tendencies of human behavior in order to develop a science of politics and a corresponding Constitution that would withstand the corroding influence of history. As Publius had insisted, "Constitutions of civil government are not to be framed upon a calculation of existing exigencies, but upon a combination of these with the probable exigencies of ages, according to the natural and tried course of human affairs."[3]

Wilson focused his dispute with the Founders and defenders of their Constitution on this point. He believed that the Founders' attempt to establish a permanent constitutional order was ultimately mistaken because that order had naturally and inevitably evolved over time. Government, Wilson argued, "is accountable to Darwin, not to Newton. It is modified by its environment, necessitated by its tasks, shaped to its functions by the sheer pressure of life."[4] Wilson was not arguing against the idea of constitutionalism. He only wanted to expand it to encompass what he held to be the fact as well as the promise of the living constitution.

The best proof of the Darwinian nature of politics, Wilson left no doubt, lay in the emergence of the president as the leader of both his party and national opinion, notwithstanding the intentions of the Founders to circumscribe these forms of presidential leadership with the separation of powers. "The tendency has been unmistakably disclosed," Wilson argued, "and springs out of the very nature of government itself. . . . our government is a living, organic thing, and must, like every other government, work out the close synthesis of active parts which can exist only when the leadership is lodged in some one man or group of men. You cannot compound a successful government out of antagonisms" (*Constitutional Government,* p. 60; subsequent parenthetical citations in this chapter are to this book).

The president's leadership of his party and national opinion now stood as the key to Wilson's program, for they meant that "if [the President] rightly interpret the national thought and boldly insist upon it, he is irresistible" (68). The White House was the platform for interpretive leadership that could not only provide much needed initiative and guidance on matters of policy in the short term but also expand the opportunities for the exercise of compelling direction in the long term.

Wilson's book was itself an act of interpretive statesmanship, albeit in the realm of thought, intended to discern, explain, and thus foster new possibilities for such leadership in the presidency. As an interpretive statesman in his own right, Wilson had to present a program for responsible government that people could readily grasp and accept. He could not, then, call for lodging compelling leadership in a "group of men," as he had in his early essays on cabinet government; it had to be lodged in "one man." His parliamentary plan, and the constitutional amendments it entailed, was too radical. People could more easily contemplate a dominating presence in the presidency, not least because Theodore Roosevelt currently filled the office.

Wilson's celebration of presidential power can be seen, then, as the latest in a long series of practical accommodations that began two decades earlier with *Congressional Government*. In the earlier book, he had held back from calling for the amendments he believed were essential in order to get his work published and promote his general views. He had indeed gained notice over the years, to the point where the lectures that would serve as the basis for *Constitutional Government* were reported in the New York papers. However, for all of the insight that Wilson's years of study brought to the book, the theoretical compromises upon which it rested left significant tensions and ambiguities in his analysis.

II

In championing the president's capacity to lead his party and national opinion simultaneously, Wilson challenged the assumptions of the party tradition in U.S. politics. Beginning with Martin Van Buren, American statesmen believing in the legitimacy of party action have sought to ensure that presidents remain intimately connected, through political obligations, principles, loyalties, and the means of their nomination, to a well-developed party organization. Demagoguery, factionalism, and the debasement of executive power, the argument runs, are all more likely to occur if presidents are not restrained by the institutional moderation and collective discipline of a party. Wilson's call for the president, acting on his own, to lead public opinion and thereby to wield an irresistible power ran counter to the central principles underlying the party system invoked and legitimated by Van Buren. Hence James Ceaser's charge that Wilson's talk of party government was in fact an academic's "deception," one designed to mask Wilson's intention to "destroy" the traditional parties and replace them with pseudoparties that would in fact be creatures of, and dedicated to serving, their leaders. "Parties must either constrain individual leadership," Ceaser contends, "or be undermined by it."[5]

Why did Wilson propose that the president's national leadership could and should be reconciled with his party leadership? Whatever the origins of Wilson's thinking in this regard, he was not constructing his program so that the traditional parties might be destroyed. Indeed, in *Constitutional Government*, Wilson demonstrated that he had developed, once more with the help of Henry Jones Ford, a healthy appreciation for the rough-hewn virtues of the American party system. Wilson recognized that the traditional party organizations had performed a number of indispensable integrating functions for the whig constitution over the course of the nation's development: recruiting and nominating candidates for the excessive number of elective offices at the local, state, and national level; coordinating the activities of the officeholders once in power; and, more generally, through their ideological pragmatism, muffling the sectional, class, and ethnocultural conflicts that might otherwise have riven the nation apart. And, what is more, Wilson understood that the dispensation of patronage and waffling on matters of principle that he had earlier condemned were in fact what enabled the traditional parties to perform these essential functions.[6]

In response to the criticisms of the antipartisan reformers, who at that point in the Progressive Era were at the height of their zeal and influence, Wilson quipped in *Constitutional Government*, "It is an odd operation of the Whig system that it should make such party organizations at once necessary and disreputable, and I should say that in view of the legal arrangements which we have deliberately made, the disrepute in which professional politicians are held is in spirit highly unconstitutional" (214). Moreover, at this time Wilson remained an outspoken opponent of the leading reforms advocated by the opponents of the traditional parties: the initiative, referendum, recall, nonpartisan ballots, and direct primary.[7]

Wilson's appreciation of the traditional parties, and his admonitions of those who wanted to reform them, did not go unnoticed. In its review of *Constitutional Government*, the *Nation*—the reform journal that had first whetted young Woodrow Wilson's desire for principled partisanship and parliamentary reform in the 1870s—observed that "as for the boss and the machine, no cleaner bill of health for their essential activities has lately come under our eye. It is certainly a matter of regret that, with such keen insight and so much literary skill, the distinguished author should have held his plough with so light a hand."[8]

While opposed to what he considered to be shortsighted reforms, Wilson did believe that some changes in the party system were necessary. He argued that the nation had developed and was integrated to the point where instead of moderating the debate over political issues in order to preserve consensus, the parties needed to hasten progress by articulating more coherent and timely political visions. Furthermore, the governmental integration that the parties were then providing, while essential, was less than complete: the constitutional obstacles set in their path, along with the crude methods they had to adopt in response, made party control inconsistent at best. So long as the traditional parties were integrating the executive and legislative branches and presenting slates of candidates for office in their standard fashion, the systematic legislation and professional administration that the nation needed was not likely to be forthcoming. Speaking of the traditional party system, Wilson warned that "this thing that has served us so well might now master us if we left it irresponsible. We must see to it that it is made responsible."[9]

Implicit in Wilson's concern with making the parties more responsible was the need to preempt the reformers who were capitalizing on the abuses of the party organizations in their efforts to eradicate party politics once and for all. In 1879, when he had first defended the necessity and desirability of party government against the proposed reforms of Albert Stickney, Stickney's was a voice in the wilderness. However, in the intervening twenty-five years, the antipartisan reform movement had gained many more adherents, and a wave of reforms designed to strike at the roots of traditional party politics was then sweeping the country.[10] Wilson, then, had not wavered in his commitment to party government, nor was he seeking to destroy the traditional parties. Instead, he was trying to transform the party system in order to salvage a defensible form of partisanship at a time when the antipartisanship running deep in American political culture was particularly virulent.

Wilson believed that the president's position as the sole representative of the people as a whole and as the administrative head of the federal government made it possible for him, and him alone, to provide the sort of public, principled leadership that the parties needed if they were to survive the challenges of the antipartisan reformers. Wilson proposed, for example, that presidents' control of the federal bureaucracy positioned them to wean their party organizations off baser forms of political sustenance. He admitted that "the President can, if he chooses, become national boss by the use of his enormous patronage, doling out his local gifts of place to local party managers in return for support and cooperation in the guidance and control of his party" (215). Wilson argued, however, that presidents should avoid such a perversion of the administrative ethic to suit their own political purposes.

More important, he contended that they would increasingly do so on their own, cleaning up party politics from the top down. The presidency's "conspicuous position" meant that public attention would focus on how the chief executive led the administration. In the bright light of this scrutiny, then growing in intensity, presidents would be much more likely to act scrupulously and responsibly (71, 214–16).

In addition to cleaning up organizational politics, Wilson argued that the president could use his status as national leader to extend the focus of his party in government to broader conceptions of the public and national interest. To do this, the president had to rally support behind a more encompassing vision of what the party's principles were and what policies they entailed. At the same time, the president had to work behind the scenes and take an active hand in the formulation and passage of the party's program, the step that Grover Cleveland had not taken. Wilson thus called for the president to combine the roles of statesman and politician that, he contended, were peculiarly differentiated in the United States (212–13). Through this combination, the president could lead his party in government much as Wilson's hero Gladstone had led the Liberal Party, as a visionary prime minister: "In him are centered both opinion and party. He may stand, if he will, a little outside party and insist as if it were upon the general opinion. . . . The President may also, if he will, stand within the party counsels and use the advantage of his power and personal force to control its actual programs" (69).

Wilson assumed that the organization men and elected officials, with their overriding interest in votes, would follow their party's standard-bearer even when he led them into unfamiliar (if ultimately more defensible) territory, for mutinies within or desertion from the ranks of the party would not bode well for the next election. Thus Wilson could assert of the president's standing "outside" his party, "If he lead the nation, his party can hardly resist him" (69).

In addition to the president's potentially bracing effect on the party system in the organizations and government, Wilson held that the president could best raise the issues that should appropriately animate and divide the electorate. The exercise of principled leadership in Washington and the party balance in the electorate were intimately connected. The president's sensitivity to and leadership of public opinion gave him a dominant voice on Capitol Hill. By directing government and politics in Washington with such a public voice, the president would also be "giving the country at once the information and the statements of policy which will enable it to form its judgments alike of parties and of men" (68). These quickened popular judgments, and the shifts in partisan commitments that many of them might portend, would resolve the stagnation and issue-straddling that Wilson believed had characterized the party balance in the electorate since the end of the Civil War.

In stressing the necessity of principled leadership for the redemption of partisanship, Wilson was thus holding to the claim that he had first made in "Cabinet Government" in 1879: "Eight words contain the sum of the present degradation of our political parties: *No leaders, no principles; no principles, no parties.*"[11]

James Ceaser sees this claim as proof of Wilson's general intention to subordinate partisanship to leadership, to foster conditions in which leaders could create parties and use them for their own purposes.[12] Yet as noted above, Wilson saw the emergence of such principled leadership as essential if the legitimacy of party action was to be preserved. Moreover, he held that principles, not leaders, were the dominant force in politics; leaders and their parties alike were constrained by their public commitments. To be sure, Wilson believed that interpretive leaders were needed to discern, articulate, and uphold the principles upon which legitimate partisanship—and an electoral majority—depended. However, there were significant constraints on the interpretive freedom of leaders. They could not just proclaim any set of principles and expect to rally a compelling majority that they could then use for their own political ambitions. The leaders had to be responding to sentiments and aspirations already intimated in public opinion; they had to "rightly interpret" the national mood if they wanted to garner sufficient support for their cause and sustain that support over time. Furthermore, once presidential leaders had rallied a party around a particular set of principles, the leaders and party alike would be constrained by those principles: any change in positions would have to be defensible in terms of the original principles, i.e., as extensions of rather than departures from them. Wilson recognized a phenomenon that other observers of parties, from Edmund Burke to Anthony Downs, have likewise grasped: once leaders and parties have gone on the public record with statements about where they stand and why, they change positions at their peril.[13]

It is more important to ask whether Wilson, in discussing the relationship between principled leadership and party politics, overestimated the impact of the former on the latter. Ultimately, his scenario for the creation of a legitimate and effective party system hinged on something of a theoretical deus ex machina, on his prediction that the nation was approaching a crossroads in its political development in which the parties would suddenly and uncharacteristically be amenable to leadership that would polish their virtues while ridding them of their vices. "The time is at hand," Wilson claimed, "when we can with safety examine the network of party in its detail and change its structure without imperilling its strength. . . . We are ready to study new uses for our parties and to adapt them to new standards and principles."[14] Would partisans—in Congress, the organization, and the electorate—really change their beliefs and activities so radically in response to visionary presidential leadership? For their sustenance, could the parties be weaned from patronage and the exploitation of sectional or ethnocultural antagonisms onto principled commitments and debates over truly national issues, as Wilson understood them? If so, would the parties still have the capacity to integrate the system?

These questions are particularly vexing because Wilson's own analysis of the traditional party system emphasized the considerable political inertia embodied in it. Wilson recognized the mutually reinforcing nature of behavior at all levels of the traditional party system: politicians in Washington ducking difficult issues, machine politicos struggling to control the "petty choices," and voters responding to age-old fears and loyalties. What is more, he saw that the benefits accruing from the party system, the modest integration of government and the nation, were inextricably bound up with the costs of small-time corruption and the suppression of political debate (207–10, 220–21).

Then there was the logic of responsible government that Wilson had elaborated in the first formulations of his program: to wit, that the sort of principled, programmatic partisanship he envisioned depended on the formal fusion of executive and legislative power in cabinet government. Only then, he had once argued, would the institutional incentives compel the parties to transcend their debilitating obsession with gaining access to the spoils of office and instead propose and act upon a programmatic mandate. Though Wilson had since dropped his call for constitutional amendments that would have formally integrated the executive and legislature, after realizing that it was not feasible politically, he could not escape from his own logic so easily.

Indeed, J. Allen Smith, the muckraking political scientist, reaffirmed this logic in the same year that Wilson was giving his lectures at Columbia. Like Wilson, Smith held convictions about the necessity and desirability of party government that were most unusual among progressive reformers. And, also like Wilson—indeed, basing his argument in part on Wilson's analysis of the Founders' Constitution—Smith noted how this document had thwarted the development of political parties that could serve as principled instruments of majority rule in the United States. Smith therefore insisted that so long as the separation of powers between the executive and legislature and the associated system of checks and balances remained intact, the parties would remain parochial and pragmatic institutions, i.e., unsuitable instruments of majority rule. Only when the party backed by the majority held all power and authority in its hands would democracy be established.[15]

Grant McConnell, writing some years later of Smith's theoretical conclusion, observed that "perhaps alone among the Progressives, J. Allen Smith understood the movement best. He had drawn—ruthlessly—its fullest implications." [16] Wilson had also drawn these implications; in fact, he had drawn them first. But he had opted to step back from them, in keeping with the statesman's imperative to keep his program within the realm of the possible. Whether it could still work in that realm, its core logic having been jettisoned, remained to be seen.

Wilson's proposal that the president lead both his party and the nation challenged not only the defenders of the idea of a party system but also the nonpartisan tradition in American politics. In calling for the president to capitalize on his unique authority as national leader to provide positive direction for the polity, Wilson invoked the vision of Bolingbroke's "Patriot King" that was subscribed to by the first six presidents and reflected in their leadership. However, these presidents were convinced that an important condition of such authoritative leadership was an abstention from open partisanship, at least while in office. The "presidents above party," in Ralph Ketcham's apt phrase, believed that the legitimacy to stand as the leader of the nation as a whole originated in the president's essential independence from any part, or party, of that whole. Once the president became an active player in party politics, the authoritative luster of the presidential office would be tarnished by the ensuing corruption, factionalism, and general resentment. The power stemming from that authority would be diminished as well.[17]

The notion of a nonpartisan president was gaining more adherents in the Progressive Era. Reformers increasingly proposed that the chief executive abstain from party politics altogether, governing by means of his augmented administration, attracting whatever political support was needed by leading public opinion.[18] At first glance, the idea of presiding above parties would appear to have been consistent with Wilson's evolving vision, given his new convictions about the power and authority then accruing to the presidency on account of the office's national constituency, prominence in the media, control of foreign affairs, and leadership of the administrative branch. Why did Wilson not sign on to this traditional ideal that was once more ascendant?

Wilson remained committed to the idea of party government in part because he believed it was inevitable, necessary, and desirable. Despite the pretensions of the "presidents above party," their administrations, beginning with Washington's, were nonetheless marked by some of the most contentious party battles in American history, thereby supporting Wilson's long-held belief that partisanship was an inevitable by-product of constitutional government.[19] Moreover, if the president was going to lead the nation, he required the votes of party supporters—both on election day and thereafter on Capitol Hill. In light of the political independence of and institutional jealousy between the two branches, "the President himself is cooperatively bound to the houses only by the machinery and discipline of party."[20] Beyond noting the functional necessity of parties, Wilson held them up as "an indispensable means of subordinating varieties of individual opinion to the pursuit of common principles and large objects of policy."[21] He also proposed that party leadership did not preclude the more encompassing role of national leadership for the president. For "the nation as a whole has chosen him," Wilson argued, "and is conscious that it has no other political spokesman. His is the only national voice in affairs."[22]

Of course, not every voter would have "chosen him." Could a partisan president be recognized as the nation's spokesman by followers of rival parties or by the growing number who saw partisanship in general as an obstacle to good government? This result was by no means clear, especially in light of the rancor, parochialism, and less than pristine methods that had long marked the U.S. party system. Wilson acknowledged that were the president to lead his party as a traditional politico—cutting deals with legislators over policies and appointments, building a political machine, or intervening in senatorial election contests, for example—any claim to be serving as a national leader would clearly ring false.[23]

What led Wilson to believe that presidents would avoid such naked politicking? For one thing, he proposed that the presidential nomination process, partisan though it was, made presidential abstinence from these forms of leadership more likely. In a significant revision of his earlier position, Wilson now detected broader and more coherent purposes in the functioning of the conventions. However unseemly their methods, the party chieftains who maneuvered to control the nomination were inclined to make their selection with an eye toward the symbols and principles that the candidate would represent and that, if the managers chose well, would not only rally the party faithful but also win the favor of the nation at large. "Sometimes the country believes in a party," Wilson wrote, "but more often it believes in a man, and conventions have shown the instinct to perceive which it is that the country needs."[24]

The candidate who was elected, Wilson suggested, would be apt to have a national vision and a record of integrity—a man who would be inclined and willing to "stand outside" of his party in order to make appointments, formulate policies, and raise issues in a manner consistent with the public and national interests. Presidents who adopted this more encompassing approach would preserve and enhance their authority as national leaders. Moreover, they also would set improvements in motion at all three levels of the party system—in government, the organization, and the electorate—that would make the dual exercise of party and national leadership even more conceivable. The Wilsonian president's ability to stand as a national leader, then, depended ultimately on the establishment of a new form of partisanship, a form that he believed the president was in the best position to bring about.

However, even accepting Wilson's more heroic assumptions, namely, that presidents would observe the dictates of the higher form of partisanship he was advocating and thereby could effect the transformation in the party system he had prophesied, their ability to stand as leaders of the nation would still be subject to question. For if partisanship was to become less parochial in his program, it was also to become more ideological. As the party visions became more national and coherent, they would still be visions that members of the opposing party would suspect and even fear, especially given the greater power at the disposal of the governing party in Wilson's program and the larger stakes in the party battle—the planning and execution of the new regulatory, social, and foreign policies. Thus even if the party system changed as Wilson desired, it would by no means be easier for the party leader to speak authoritatively as the national leader.

In Wilson's earliest formulations of his program for responsible government, he had called upon the president to perform a symbolic, kinglike role, serving as a unifying chief of state while leaving party leadership, and the pulling and hauling of politics, to the cabinet that he would select from Congress. In *Constitutional Government,* Wilson still cast the president as the chief of state, except now, of course, the president's national leadership role was not merely symbolic; rather, he also had to rally public opinion behind particular causes. And the president now stood as *the* leader of his party. These changes in Wilson's program meant that it had become more necessary and more difficult for the president to rise above less than encompassing political concerns and lead the nation as a whole.

III

Wilson's treatment of the president's party and national leadership was closely connected with his analysis of the president's legislative, diplomatic, and administrative leadership, the traditional roles of what Wilson termed the "legal executive." The functional demands for leadership in the traditional roles had served to bring the president to the forefront of his party and the nation, and ultimately it was in exercising these traditional roles that the Wilsonian president used the power and authority he had managed to accrue as party and national leader. At times, Wilson's reconception of the traditional roles in light of the president's emerging preeminence suggested that executive-legislative relations could be elevated to the plane of responsible government by interpretive leadership in the White House. However, Wilson's own reasoning indicated that the formal Constitution could not be so easily overcome.

One of Wilson's most striking emphases in *Constitutional Government* was his call for the president to provide positive leadership in matters of legislation, serving in effect as a prime minister. Wilson criticized what he described as the whig theory of presidential-congressional relations, under which presidents remained aloof from the legislative process, simply signing measures developed and passed by Congress, intervening only to veto unacceptable legislation.[25] Wilson argued that this conception of interbranch relations was increasingly obsolete, because Congress—for all of its continuing pretensions to be *the* government—simply could not direct itself toward any coherent, systematic ends. What was more, insofar as Congress, the House in particular, had sought to become "an instrument of business, to perform its function of legislation without assistance or suggestion . . . it has in effect silenced itself" (109). The body that was to be the organ of public opinion and was nominally the closest to it had sacrificed that position and the accompanying power by opting for efficient rather than deliberative lawmaking.

Wilson argued that in the midst of this leadership vacuum, which was growing more troublesome in its effects as the nation struggled with its new historical circumstances, a Darwinian adaptation was taking place. "Some of our Presidents have felt the need," he observed, "which unquestionably exists in our system, for some spokesman of the nation as a whole, in matters of legislation no less than in other matters, and have tried to supply Congress with the leadership of suggestion, backed by argument and by iteration and by every legitimate appeal to public opinion."[26] Wilson acknowledged that this kind of presidential leadership had yet to become the norm. Holding to the whig theory, some presidents "thought that Pennsylvania Avenue should have been even longer than it is; that there should be no intimate communication of any kind between the Capitol and the White House" (70). However, in Wilson's estimation, the reticence of the whiggish presidents could not be sustained, as it ran counter to the functional logic that properly gave the right to lead the legislature to the executive, logic that Wilson felt was particularly hard to dispute "in times of stress and change" (73).

Moreover, Wilson maintained that the whig view of the presidency rested on a cramped reading of the Constitution itself. The Founders may have been whig theorists, he argued, but their Constitution did not proscribe presidential leadership in legislation. Indeed, Article 2 of the Constitution specifically called for the president to recommend "such measures as he shall deem necessary and expedient." Wilson proposed that this clause, even when strictly interpreted, opened the way for the positive guidance of Congress by the president (72–73).

How was the Wilsonian president to lead the legislative agenda? What were the mechanisms through which he could control Congress? Implicit in Wilson's discussion of the president's ability to reshape the party system was the notion that if the principles and programs the president articulated were based on sound interpretations of public opinion, he would be less apt to face undisciplined majorities, persistent dissenters, or divided government on Capitol Hill. Nevertheless, Wilson's analysis of executive-legislative relations indicates that principled partisanship was not enough to establish responsible government in the United States.

A major problem for presidents attempting to play the prime ministerial role advocated by Wilson was that they lacked the ability to dissolve the legislature, to entice seated members with positions of power in the executive, and to influence in any significant way the nominations of their party's legislative candidates at the next election. Wilson stripped further power from the president by suggesting that a range of inelegant methods that presidents had often relied upon in dealing with Congress was unacceptable. These illicit methods included the blatant politicking discussed in the previous section and constitutional brinkmanship vis-à-vis an unyielding Congress. Not only should presidents not engage in these illegitimate activities, he argued, they could not, for these methods were sure, "in a country of free public opinion, to bring their own punishment, to destroy both the fame and power of the man who dares to practice them" (71).

In this regard, of course, Wilson's arguments were based more on his hopes than on the historical record. His hopes, though, are nonetheless revealing. On the one hand, he wanted his new model presidency to lead Congress in a fashion that enhanced, instead of degraded, the integrity of the legislative and administrative processes. On the other hand, by proposing that the president should and indeed had to lead Congress with clean hands, so to speak, within the forms of the Constitution, Wilson was attempting to show that his theory of presidential leadership had "no touch of radicalism or iconoclasm in it" (71). And with both lines of argument, Wilson was polishing the appeal of his theory of the presidency for those who might otherwise have been set aback by the idea of the head of state actively leading public opinion.

For it was through public opinion leadership that Wilson was attempting to develop an element of positive executive sanction over the legislature. The president's superior access to public opinion gave him a means "compelling Congress." Wilson celebrated the power that the active leadership of public opinion brought to the office, suggesting that through it the crucial focal point of responsibility that he admired in the British polity might be approximated in the United States (70–71). In light of some of Wilson's rhetorical flights in this regard, it is understandable that his neo-Federalist critics, most notably Jeffrey Tulis, have concluded that Wilson's was fundamentally a rhetorical presidency, that it drew and used its power through popular appeals. However, this view overestimates the role and the power of public opinion leadership in his conception of the office.

To begin with, Wilson was not suggesting that public opinion leadership was the sole or even the primary mode of leading Congress. In the same paragraph of *Constitutional Government* in which Wilson talked of the president "compelling" Congress, he emphasized the importance of "intimate communication" between Congress and the president, interactive discussions that overly zealous interpreters of the separation of powers had forsworn. Indeed, he argued that while this separation prevented the president from being able to "dominate [Congress] by authority," it nonetheless left him "at liberty to lead the houses of Congress by persuasion."[27]

The need for the president to rely more on persuasion than appeals over the heads of the legislators to the people at large was reinforced by the significant legislative role that Congress retained in Wilson's program. His account of the president's serving as a principled national spokesman coincided with a recognition that Congress tended "naturally" to predominate in "domestic questions" in which it was understandable for representatives and senators, with their personal grasp on the needs and interests of their constituents, "to make the initial choice, legislative leaders the chief decisions of policy" (58). In ordinary circumstances, "when matters of legislation are under discussion the country is apt to think of the Speaker as the chief figure in Washington rather than the President" (107–8). While the president could best lay out principles and clarify and mobilize public opinion, Congress and its leadership retained control of the basic function and the details of lawmaking. Neither partner on this legislative team could go it alone; each had to respect the role of the other.

Wilson's own analysis indicates that he saw real limits on the president's ability to rely on public opinion and hence on the element of responsibility that such leadership could bring to the American regime. His rhetorical retreat regarding the power of public opinion leadership followed the precedent of his 1889 essay, "Leaders of Men," in which he acknowledged the limits imposed on interpretive leaders by the natural conservatism of public opinion. In *Constitutional Government,* Wilson observed that in addition a president seeking to lead opinion faced institutional—indeed, constitutional—constraints.

Even in ideal circumstances, public opinion leadership was an indirect form of control. Wilson was proposing that, for example, when the House's committee structure kept what the president considered to be a necessary and widely supported measure from passing, the president could appeal to the people in order to give his side of the issues at stake. Thereafter, "if public opinion respond to his appeal the House may grow thoughtful of the next congressional elections and yield." Yet, if public opinion did not respond or if the House remained insensitive to it, then that was it; the president could not subordinate the House.[28]

More important, Wilson understood that appealing to public opinion was simply not a viable method when the president was trying to overcome opposition in the Senate. Members of the House, the ostensibly popular branch, who all stood for election every two years, might well think twice before going against the spokesman of the people unless they were sure that public opinion was on their side. But Wilson recognized that the Senate, with its staggered, six-year terms, "is not so immediately sensitive to opinion and is apt to grow, if anything, more stiff if pressure of that kind is brought to bear upon it." The only way to win over an unyielding Senate, he admitted, was for the president to seek out its counsel, communicate judiciously, and soften his demands (139–41). This imperative, though, considerably reduced the utility of public opinion leadership by the president, for on all matters of legislation the president had to carry the Senate as well as the House. And, of course, the president was completely dependent on the Senate when it came to the approval of his nominations for office and the ratification of treaties he had negotiated.

Wilson did call for presidents to focus the political debate in order to foster a consensus behind their agendas and in those circumstances where it was feasible and appropriate to appeal to the country for support. But his analysis also made clear that the president's leadership of public opinion had to complement—it could not replace—more "intimate communication" with Congress. Were presidents to capitalize on "time and circumstance and wise management," on the one hand, and their "most direct access to opinion," on the other, they had "the best chance of leadership and mastery" in the legislative process. But in the end, Wilson recognized that it was only that, a chance (110). Thus while the invigorated presidency that Wilson envisioned would help fill the leadership void resulting from more traditional conceptions of the office, it did not provide the compelling mechanisms that were needed to establish responsible government.

Wilson thought the president did not need to be as accommodating with Congress when it came to foreign policy, in part because he saw no role for the legislature in a realm in which necessity dictated the executive go it alone. And to his mind, the president could go it alone. Wilson's discussion of "one of the greatest of the President's powers . . . his control, which is very absolute, of the foreign relations of the nation," was quite brief. He simply proposed that the president held the initiative in foreign affairs "without any restriction whatever," and that this initiative effectively gave the president the ability to determine the course of U.S. foreign policy. Wilson paid little heed to the considerable powers that the Constitution gave to Congress in this domain, such as the power to regulate foreign commerce, to create and support an army and a navy, and to declare war. The one congressional prerogative that he did mention, the right of the Senate to ratify treaties, he quickly dismissed as being essentially irrelevant in the face of the president's commanding position. The president, Wilson wrote, "need disclose no step of negotiation until it is complete, and when in any critical matter it is completed the government is virtually committed. Whatever its disinclination, the Senate may feel itself committed also." The president was not only to be the dominant leader of the United States in the new century, but he would also be, "henceforth, one of the great powers of the world" and thus could use his global preeminence to trump congressional objections (77–79).

Implicit in Wilson's notion that with the nation having "risen to the first rank in power and resources," the president "must stand always at the front of our affairs" was the assumption that the nation—Congress, the parties, the media, the citizenry—would willingly stand behind the president. Thenceforth, Wilson was suggesting, politics would stop at the waters' edge, beyond which the president had to be the authoritative voice of the nation (78–79).

He was thus predicting that the Constitution's distribution of foreign policy prerogatives would no longer be, in the eventually famous phrase of his Princeton colleague, Edward Corwin, "an invitation to struggle."[29]

As presented in *Constitutional Government*, Wilson's analysis contains the basic theoretical assumptions of what Aaron Wildavsky has since termed "the two presidencies" model. Wilson acknowledged that the domestic president—his prime minister—would have to work in tandem with a Congress retaining significant control of the legislative agenda. But the higher stakes of politics between nations ruled out the debate and delay, the long marches toward compromise and consensus, that characterized domestic policy-making. As the spokesman of the nation in world affairs, the president could expect, and rightfully so, to enjoy wide freedom of action and deference from other actors and institutions in the polity.[30]

But Wilson's argument that the president could set his own course in foreign policy did not sit well alongside his subsequent observations of how the Senate, well insulated from presidential dominance, had often taken issue with the president's diplomacy and sought to dictate alternative courses of action. And, Wilson admitted, "when, as sometimes happens, the Senate is of one political party and the President of the other, its dictation may be based, not upon the merits of the question involved, but upon party antagonisms and calculations of advantage" (139). For the president to control diplomacy as Wilson hoped and predicted that he would in the twentieth century, senators and partisans not previously inclined to follow presidential leadership would have to recognize and submit to the growing functional imperative of their doing so. That they would submit was the crucial—and most questionable—assumption of Wilson's thinking about the presidential control of foreign affairs.

While arguing in *Constitutional Government* that the president's legislative and diplomatic roles were changing in profound ways, Wilson held that the job of chief executive was in an even greater state of flux. The president had less time to spend on administrative details, which were piling up as the federal government slowly expanded, because of the new demands that were levied upon him as the leader of his party and the nation. "The one set of duties it has proved practically impossible for him to perform; the other it has proved impossible for him to escape" (66–67). Responding to these imperatives, recent presidents (Wilson singled out Cleveland and Roosevelt) had increasingly delegated the administrative tasks to their cabinet officers, while taking on more of the public relations and political leadership themselves.

This functional adaptation, Wilson argued, was changing the nature of the cabinet. Less and less would it be the redoubt of party barons whom presidents took into the administration in order to better manage their party coalition or preempt their leading rivals within it. As presidents shouldered the burden of their growing political responsibility, they would choose their department secretaries primarily on the grounds of administrative expertise and personal, not partisan, connections (75–76).

By advocating the continuation of these developments, Wilson was making an important change in his own theory of the presidency and its place in responsible government, rearranging the institutional demarcation between politics and administration. In his earlier proposals, he urged that the president—essentially, the top administrative officer—be required to choose his department heads from among leaders of the majority party in Congress; they, in turn, would be the responsible political officers, directing and having to keep the confidence of the legislative bodies in which they sat. Wilson now reversed the roles: the president would serve as the political leader, the man who had to take the initiative and deal with Congress, while his cabinet secretaries would serve as administrative officers.

There were problems with Wilson's reformulation. In his old scenario, the members of the cabinet—simultaneously directors of the administration, party leaders, and congressional leaders—were in a position to prevent individual representatives and senators from involving themselves in the details and staffing of the administration. The Wilsonian president, constitutionally aloof from Congress, could not impose as many institutional and political sanctions to counter congressional interventions. Moreover, Wilson's new formulation contained no mechanisms for collective responsibility. It not only left the president without the formal means to control the legislature but also did not require that the executive leader maintain its confidence. There was ultimately no focal point of responsibility—that Holy Grail of Wilsonian politics, the source of effective government and principled politics—in the presidential system that he now celebrated. Indeed, responsibility was further occluded by the president selecting as his department heads not party leaders but private men of affairs with whom he alone had ties. The president would not have the counsel of men with established political experience and ties to the legislature, nor would he necessarily have the experience and ties himself. When Wilson had first noticed this trend during the second Cleveland administration, he had viewed it with alarm; in *Constitutional Government,* he was willing to acquiesce in and even hail it.

As Wilson concluded his discussion of the ascendant presidency, he sought to come to terms with how someone holding the office might juggle the multifaceted responsibilities that he now assigned to it. Wilson admitted that the presidency whose power he celebrated was also "the most heavily burdened office in the world" (79). In addition to the traditional presidential roles of chief of state and chief diplomat, he suggested that the president also had to serve as the leader of his party and national opinion, the prime minister of the legislature, and even as an international force in his own right. Whereas in Wilson's early program he had not assigned this last role, saw the president serving only as chief of state, and assigned the rest of the responsibilities to the prime minister of a collectively responsible cabinet, he now gave all the duties to one man, the president. Wilson recognized the potential contradictions between the roles. He also knew that the more presidents did—the more they led—the more expectations concerning their performance and leadership would increase. In light of these difficulties, perhaps only half in jest, Wilson predicted that "men of ordinary physique and discretion cannot be Presidents and live, if the strain be not somehow relieved. We shall be obliged always to be picking our chief magistrates from among wise and prudent athletes,—a small class" (79–80).

Wilson thus essentially acknowledged that his program and the presidency that lay at the center of it were problematic. In a shrug of his theoretical shoulders, he observed that the president's tremendous burdens, and the potential contradictions between and among them, could only be relieved by a constitutional amendment of the sort that he had once openly advocated, which would set up a collectively responsible executive cabinet. But this prospect "was a thing too difficult to attempt except upon some greater necessity than the relief of an overburdened office." Moreover, Wilson noted that such an amendment was unlikely to come about, not just because of the difficulty of the process but also because "it is to be doubted whether the deliberate opinion of the country would consent to make of the President a less powerful officer than he is" (80).

Wilson thus revealed the extent to which he was softening his analytical rigor regarding the preconditions, means, and ends of the reforms he desired in order to accommodate the political world as it was, to bring about the developments that might be possible within its existing confines. Attempting to put the best face on the situation, he proposed that presidents could best keep on top of their mounting burdens, "without shirking any real responsibility," by following the example of their recent predecessors, ceding mere administrative concerns to their cabinet secretaries, "regarding themselves as less and less executive officers and more and more the directors of affairs and leaders of the nation,—men of counsel and the sort of action that makes for enlightenment" (80–81). This enlightenment, Wilson might well have continued, could perhaps clear the way in the minds of citizens for more extensive changes at some point in the future.

Looking back over Wilson's program as it was presented in *Constitutional Government* and comparing it with the version that he proposed in the early 1880s, it stands as more expedient and yet, at the same time, more problematic. In a move that he understood as an act of interpretive statesmanship, he had given up on the constitutional amendments that would have established parliamentary mechanisms linking the executive and legislative branches. Wilson's subsequent elaboration of his progressive theory of political development and the catalytic role played by interpretive leadership in this process suggested that responsible government might arrive through more indirect methods. The emergence of a reinvigorated presidency in the 1890s and 1900s appeared to confirm Wilson's speculations in this regard. He now believed that amid the unprecedented and unmet functional demands that were buffeting the government of the United States—the result of sweeping social, economic, and international changes—invigorated leadership on the part of the president could bring about the adaptation in the Constitution and the party system that was required to move executive-legislative relations to a new plane. Indeed, Wilson believed that this solution to the problem of governance was already intimated in American political development.

However, Wilson's convictions concerning the Darwinian nature of political development and the power of interpretive presidential leadership were tempered by an awareness of the resilience of the Constitution and party politics as they had traditionally functioned. Wilson the reformer, who was driven by the hope and imperative of instituting responsible government, kept up his troubling dialogue with Wilson the realistic student of political life, who was keenly aware of the political inertia embodied in the American regime and the difficulties even the president would have in reversing that inertia. The analysis now turns to Wilson's more explicitly political career, in which these two personas continued, as it were, to speak their truths to each other and to his statesmanship.

❦ FOUR

Progressivism and Politics in New Jersey and the Nation

In an essay written in 1907, Wilson compared the fermenting political situation to that in the years just prior to the Civil War. "Parties have not yet squarely aligned themselves along what must of course be the line of cleavage," he mused. Accelerating social and economic changes necessitated a fundamental adjustment in politics and policies, but "party programmes are not yet explicit for the voter's choice."[1] The reason for the continued "dissolution of parties" and "confusion of issues," Wilson suggested in 1908, was a "notable absence of leadership," not so much of the party organizations "but of the leadership of the constructive thought and purpose of the country."[2] This was exactly the form of leadership that Wilson himself had always wanted to provide and for which he believed he had a special gift. And it was the form of leadership upon which his program for responsible government depended. In the years preceding Wilson's debut in electoral politics, his program quickened and focused his ambitions. At the same time, the imperatives of this debut began to alter the program.

I

The first murmurings of political support for Woodrow Wilson came in 1902, the same year he became president of Princeton. They reached a steady pitch within a few years, unaffected by his weak protests. Wilson's growing prominence on the national scene as an academic and political reformer, his dynamic presence at the podium, and—most important—his enduring and public commitment to the Bourbon principles of free trade, sound money, and efficient administration all made him an appealing figure to goldbug Democrats. Foremost among Wilson's conservative backers was Colonel George Harvey, editor of *Harper's Weekly*, who began endorsing Wilson for the presidency in 1906. Wilson maintained that his political ambitions were limited and unlikely. Nevertheless, he made sure to emphasize the conservative aspects of his political views to please his new patrons. And, using the parliamentary terms of his program, Wilson admitted to a supporter in March 1906 that he was willing to have his name put forward to help with "organizing an Opposition with which conservative men could without apprehension ally themselves."[3]

After Bryan's defeat in 1908, Wilson voiced a new resolution about what needed to be done "to organize a successful party of opposition" and the role he might play in doing it. Only a rejuvenated Democratic Party could offer a serious challenge to the Republicans, and this rejuvenation could not take place unless "men as unlike Mr. Bryan as principle is unlike expediency will devote themselves to gaining influence and control as if to a daily business, as Mr. Bryan has done." Wilson now anticipated taking the initiative himself, if it was necessary, in the fight for "a genuine rationalization and rehabilitation of the Democratic party on lines of principle and statesmanship."[4]

But if Wilson was going to lead the Democratic Party to power, he could not afford to be "unlike Mr. Bryan," at least not in terms of the policies Bryan espoused. Amid the progressivism of the time, the Bourbons and financiers whose favor Wilson was attempting to curry represented a diminishing segment of public opinion. Wilson needed to rethink his unstinting opposition to the Bryanite agenda. To do so was not conceptually troubling for him. As Wilson had told the Cleveland Chamber of Commerce in November 1907, in phrases strikingly similar to those he had used in "Leaders of Men" eighteen years earlier, "a man engaged in party contests, must be an opportunist. Let us give up saying that word as if it contained a slur. If you want to win in party action. . . . you have got to fish for the majority, and the only majority you can get is the majority that is ready."[5]

Following his own advice, in late 1908 Wilson started to warn businessmen that they held an ethical obligation to be fair and just in their dealings with "the common man." At this point in American history, Wilson argued, to be a conservative meant to be in favor of reform so as to prevent more dramatic and destructive changes. In his arguments against the protective tariff, Wilson now proposed that it had produced the trusts and was insinuated in the unseemly alliance between the Republican Party and big business. Given that Wilson's conservatism had always been organic rather than doctrinal in character, it was not hard for him to make these arguments.[6] Through these exhortations and emphases, Wilson subtly shifted his political agenda and, in the process, his attractiveness as a political candidate.

By 1910, Wilson's efforts to reestablish himself as a more progressive Democrat, one who was not beholden to party conservatives and financial interests, began to pay off. Colonel Harvey and ex-Senator James Smith, the Democratic boss of Newark (and, for all practical purposes, of New Jersey) had come to believe that Wilson was the man whom the party should run for governor. The Democrats had been in the political wilderness in New Jersey since the 1890s, when the party had been corrupted by racetrack interests and voted out of power. In the meantime, the standpat Republicans who controlled the state government had alienated the insurgent reformers in their party, known as the New Idea men, as well as the growing number of progressives generally.[7] Were the Democrats to wrest control of the gubernatorial chair, the successful candidate would have to be in a position to attract progressive support both from within and—especially—outside of his party. Wilson seemed to be just that sort of candidate. Indeed, if things worked out well for Wilson in New Jersey, Harvey and Smith anticipated that they might have a national political prodigy on their hands. As Wilson's patrons and he himself recognized, the same characteristics that made him attractive as a Democratic candidate for governor in New Jersey augured well for a presidential bid.[8]

Of course, Wilson's background made him something of an unknown. Before his sponsors gave him their active support, they made discreet inquiries about how he would treat the machine politicos. Wilson let it be known to Smith and Harvey that, in his words, "I should deem myself inexcusable for antagonizing [the machine], so long as I was left absolutely free in the matter of measures and men."[9] Wilson evidently assumed that he had been understood and could govern as he wished if elected; Smith and Harvey likewise assumed that the professor from Princeton would not be a threat to their political plans. Neither Wilson nor his patrons, it turned out, were correct in their assumptions.

As the Newark machine went about securing Wilson's nomination, it appeared to many progressives in and outside the Democratic Party that Boss Smith was using the Princeton professor as a Trojan horse with which to take Trenton. Wilson began to counter this suspicion when he made a point of declaring in an acceptance speech—which, against precedent, he chose to give himself at the convention—that he had no political debts outstanding. Furthermore, he declared, "the future is not for parties 'playing politics,' but for measures conceived in the largest spirit, pushed by parties whose leaders are statesmen, not demagogues, who love not their offices, but their duty and opportunity for service. We are witnessing a renaissance of public spirit, a re-awakening of sober public opinion. . . . Shall we not forget ourselves in making [the Democratic Party] the instrument of righteousness for the State and for the nation?"[10] As consistent as Wilson's pronouncements were with his own thinking over the years, they seemed remarkable indeed to both the machine politicians and reformers then battling in New Jersey.

A notable departure in Wilson's thinking did occur a few weeks later, however. It came about when George Record, the leader of the GOP New Idea men, on whose support the election would hinge, took up Wilson's standing offer to debate anyone on the issues of the campaign. In a public letter, Record asked Wilson to state unequivocally and for the public record his positions on a number of progressive concerns, including the regulation of public utilities, the direct election of senators, and workmen's compensation. The key questions that Record posed, however, concerned party reform, in particular the direct primary, the top concern for most New Idea men and New Jersey progressives.[11] Record and the New Idea men had good reason to be suspicious of Wilson's commitment to progressivism and party reform. After all, Wilson had previously espoused conservative policies and lectured progressives on the unsuitability of the primary as a means for serious party reform. Presently he was the handpicked candidate of Boss Smith. Record's letter presented Wilson with some stark choices. Wilson knew that if he did not answer it, his integrity, his progressivism, and his political independence would be subject to even greater speculation. At risk were the votes outside of the Democratic Party, where he needed all the support he could get. As a result, he felt compelled to ignore the advice of Smith and Harvey and issue a reply to Record.[12]

In his response, Wilson left no doubt that he would support the agenda of the New Idea Republicans. He endorsed the primary without reservation and promised to press for the abolition of boss rule. "I should deem myself forever disgraced," Wilson stated to Record, "should I even in the slightest degree cooperate in any such system or any such transactions as you describe in your characterization of the 'boss' system. I regard myself as pledged to the regeneration of the Democratic Party which I have forecast above."[13]

The force in Wilson's denunciation of machine politics was no accident. Once Wilson decided to reach out to the New Idea men and other reform-minded voters, he could not afford even the appearance of equivocation in his stance vis-à-vis traditional party politics, lest these voters continue to harbor doubts about his independence. Wilson was discovering that progressivism had a logic of its own, one that ruled out the nuanced treatment that the traditional parties had received in *Constitutional Government*.

"That letter will elect Wilson governor," George Record was reported to have said upon reading it. And, indeed, Wilson won on election day by a majority of 49,056 (out of the 433,560 votes that were cast). It was not just Wilson who ran well. In an unforeseen development, the Democrats also gained control of the assembly. Wilson's goal of appealing to Republican insurgents and independents had paid off, for him and his party. As Wallace Scudder, editor of the *Newark Evening News* put it, "Mr. Wilson owed his nomination to the Democrats. He owes his election to the independents."[14]

The latter debt, in light of its more recent incurrence and greater significance, was the one that Wilson chose to discharge in the controversy that erupted shortly after his victory, when Jim Smith told Wilson he wanted to go back to the Senate. During the campaign, Smith had led Wilson to believe that he would not seek the seat. Were Smith now elected senator, it would falsify Wilson's oft-repeated professions about his independence from his patron, not to mention his criticism of boss rule. The situation was even more ticklish because there had been a nonbinding Democratic primary for the Senate seat, in which the voters were allowed to declare their preference to guide the legislators who would later vote on the matter. Smith had not entered the nonbinding primary, in which voter participation was low. The primary was won instead by James Martine, a hapless Bryanite who had conducted several failed campaigns for various offices in New Jersey. Although Martine may have been a buffoon, his election, the defeat of boss rule, and the validation of the primary principle quickly became intertwined ideals after the election. Wilson's political future, progressive associates warned him, both in New Jersey and as a presidential candidate hinged on whether these ideals were realized.[15]

In a letter to Harvey, Wilson revealed his quandary as well as the aspirations it might thwart. He wished he could back Smith, "but his election would be intolerable to the very people who elected me and gave us a majority in the legislature. . . . the 'progressives' of both parties." The integrity of the primary principle did not concern Wilson, only the impression its violation would make. "It is a national as well as a State question," he argued. At stake for the Democratic Party was nothing less than "the chance to draw all the liberal elements of the country to it, through new leaders, the chance that Mr. Roosevelt missed in his folly, and to constitute the ruling party of the country for the next generation."[16] Wilson exaggerated. The Democratic Party was not destined to fall apart if New Jersey sent one more boss to the Senate. But if Wilson was going to instigate an enduring realignment in the party system, and if he was going to lead the transformed Democratic Party as it conducted more responsible government, both of which he was ambitious to accomplish, then for him to give in to Smith would mean disaster.

Wilson had hoped that Harvey would be able to persuade Smith to drop out of the race. But Smith was resolute in the face of Wilson's opposition to his candidacy, and a personal visit from the governor-elect on December 7 did nothing to resolve the issue. Stymied, Wilson resorted to a series of in-creasingly combative press releases and speeches denouncing Smith. Wilson combined this public coercion with extensive lobbying of the legislators who would be voting in the election. On January 24, 1911, Martine was elected senator. The college professor had given the boss from Essex County a lesson in hard-nosed politics.[17]

At first glance, Wilson's fight against Smith might seem to indicate that he was indeed dedicated to the rhetorical leadership of public opinion, the destruction of the traditional party organizations, and the establishment of direct democracy. But such an impression is misleading. The fight against Smith was, in a sense, not Wilson's, who was no defender of the direct primary until he received clear signals that his political future depended on his becoming one. Even then, Wilson worked behind the scenes in order to persuade Smith to drop out of the race; it was only when Smith refused, and dire political consequences seemed imminent, that Wilson resorted to a public showdown.

Wilson's confrontation with Smith needs to be understood as an effort not only to preserve Wilson's own fortunes but also the future of the Democratic Party. "Young men are flocking into the Democratic Party now," Wilson reminded an audience in Trenton on January 5, 1911, in the middle of one of his stem-winders against Smith. "These men will not have anything to do with the Democratic Party if it is to be dominated by the influences which in some quarters have dominated it in past years."[18] Indeed, it was not just the Democratic Party but the very idea of a party system that Wilson believed was at issue in his fight against Smith. He was attempting to salvage some legitimacy for the system as it then operated, instead of rejecting it out of hand as so many were prepared to do. "I believe in organization," Wilson asserted, "I desire to cooperate with the Democrats of every affiliation in carrying the party forward." But if Smith went to the Senate, it would only provide further confirmation of the accusations of the antiparty reformers in the state and nation, leading more and more people to "distrust both primaries and parties."[19]

That Wilson prevailed over Smith meant that for the time being, at least in New Jersey, the Democratic Party and party politics in general were spared the difficulties that might otherwise have befallen them. Wilson also reaped the political benefits that he himself stood to gain. Democrats and progressives from around the country wrote to salute his stand. The most important message came from William Jennings Bryan. "The fact that you were against us in 1896," Bryan wrote, "raised a question in my mind in regard to your views on public questions but your attitude in the Senatorial cause has tended to reassure me."[20] That Bryan was now prepared to commend him, notwithstanding their past disagreements, was a most pleasing development, for as Wilson emphatically put it, "of course no Democrat can win whom Mr. Bryan does *not* approve."[21]

But Wilson still had a way to go to win Bryan's full approval—specifically, on the initiative, referendum, and recall. While party conservatives feared these measures, the Bryanite wing of the Democratic Party had come to regard support for them as "the acid test of a man's democracy these days," as Charles Bryan put it.[22] This acid test presented a problem for Wilson. He had always argued against direct legislation by the voters as the epitome of a wrongheaded, inorganic approach to government, one that asked the voters to perform tasks of which they were manifestly incapable. However, shortly after being elected governor, Wilson had a visit with William S. U'ren, the leading proponent of the "Oregon system" of direct democracy, who urged Wilson to adopt this system in its entirety, not just the anticorruption and direct primary laws that already were planned but also provisions for direct legislation and the recall. Many of Wilson's own progressive associates in the New Jersey Democratic Party shared U'ren's views, and they also expounded to the governor the political benefits of a change in his positions. In the face of these arguments, theoretical and practical, Wilson's opposition to the initiative, referendum, and recall began to dissipate. It would soon drop altogether.[23]

In May 1911, Wilson headed out to Bryan country and the West Coast on a speaking tour in which he intended both to explore and nurture his presidential prospects. At the first stop on this tour, in Kansas City, Wilson announced his firm support for the initiative, referendum, and recall. He defended his dramatic change of heart by denying that the measures were radical: "Their intention is to restore, not to destroy, representative government." [24] When party conservatives raised their objections, Wilson would emphasize that he did not see the initiative, referendum, and recall as universal solutions; whether they would be useful depended on conditions in each state and locality. Wilson also consistently disavowed the recall of judges and judicial decisions, a reform that Theodore Roosevelt had taken to championing. Traditionalists abhorred the judicial recall, and Wilson agreed that it threatened the basic idea of constitutionalism.[25] And, as he had in the confrontation with Smith over primary reform, Wilson stated that his advocacy of direct democracy was by no means a repudiation of organized partisanship, which would always be necessary for effective political action, but only of legislators and executives controlled and corrupted by backroom politicos.[26] With his change of positions on the Oregon system,

Wilson sought to preserve the legitimacy of party action by giving voters the electoral tools they were demanding to punish the degradations of machine politics.

But this, of course, was not the whole of Wilson's endeavor. His full-scale endorsement of direct democracy, while couched in conservative terms of restoration rather than transformation, was a crucial and attractive shift in the view of Bryanites and other progressive Democrats. Throughout the remainder of the year, Wilson continued to seek the favor of these elements in the party. Toward this end, he began criticizing the money trust and distancing himself from Colonel Harvey.[27]

In January 1912, however, all of Wilson's efforts to win the support of Bryan and his followers threatened to come undone. Back in 1907, when Wilson was still an avowed goldbug Democrat, he had expressed a fateful wish to a correspondent: "Would that we could do something, at once dignified and effective, to knock Mr. Bryan once for all into a cocked hat." Five years later, this wish suddenly reappeared in the newspapers, at the very moment that the Democratic National Committee was convening in Washington for its Jackson Day meeting. Wilson knew that he had some explaining to do if he wanted to keep his presidential hopes alive. The man who, in 1908, had refused even to break bread with Bryan at a Jefferson Day banquet was now prepared to eat Jackson Day crow in front of the Commoner and the entire party.[28]

In the middle of his speech, Wilson made his apology by way of a salute: "While we have differed with Mr. Bryan upon this occasion and upon that in regard to the specific things to be done, he has gone serenely on pointing out to a more and more convinced people what it was that was the matter. He has . . . not based his career upon calculation, but has based it upon principle."[29] Wilson's testimony was remarkable, not least because it was precisely in these terms that he had previously praised Grover Cleveland and condemned William Jennings Bryan. It is hard to imagine a more profound statement of the extent to which Wilson had overhauled his Bourbon inclinations to accommodate political reality. Indeed, by the logic of his salute to Bryan, he himself was as contemptible as the Nebraskan was commendable.

In fact, Wilson held a more subtle conception of political leadership than this. To be sure, he had always praised the leader who held fast to a particular agenda, on principle, and who in the process gradually turned from a dissenter to a harbinger to a spokesman of the majority. This quality was the basis for his admiration of John Bright. But Wilson reserved more admiration for another kind of statesmanship, in which convictions and policies evolved over the years in response to the prevailing sentiments of public opinion, the logic of compelling ideas, and the experience of and responsibility for governing—the search for truth that Wilson's hero of long-standing, William Gladstone, had undertaken.

Thus despite the inconsistences that had surfaced in Wilson's positions vis-à-vis big business, political machines, and direct democracy during his initial forays into politics, and notwithstanding the political ambitions that helped bring about these inconsistencies, his actions and statements in these years had integrity at a fundamental level. In responding to public demands for reform, pursuing the logic of progressivism as it was mapped out by the likes of Record, U'Ren, and Bryan, and learning from his experience in his struggles with Boss Smith, Wilson emerged as the sort of interpretive statesman he had always esteemed, a leader who, among other things, could initiate a regeneration in the party system and the polity at large.

II

As much as his endorsement of William Jennings Bryan and the Bryanite political agenda, Wilson's legislative accomplishments during his first year as governor established him as a viable and attractive Democratic candidate for the presidency in 1912. In Trenton, Wilson sought to provide the encompassing leadership of his party, the legislature, and public opinion that he had been calling upon chief executives to exercise. His governorship served, then, as a preliminary test of his program.[30]

In October 1910, during the gubernatorial campaign, Wilson offered a preview of his brand of leadership in response to a speech by his Republican opponent, Vivian Leigh. Leigh had proposed that he would be a "constitutional governor," i.e., one who would not seek to lead the legislature actively and personally but instead only through written messages and, if necessary, vetoes. If those were the standards of a constitutional executive, Wilson proudly declared, then he would be an "unconstitutional governor" and actively lead the legislature, explaining with his own voice to its members—and to the people at large—why the measures he would propose were sound and necessary. Dismissing the whiggish scruples of his opponent, Wilson argued that his vision of engaged, public, and comprehensive executive leadership actually served the spirit of New Jersey's constitution, for it "relieves the Legislature of certain kinds of pressure which they will find it very welcome to be relieved of."[31]

Wilson wasted little time in putting his theory into practice. On January 16, 1911, the day before his inauguration, Wilson met with several Democratic legislators, party advisers, and George Record to map out the legislation he would advocate. They agreed to focus on four major proposals from the Democratic platform: a direct primary law and corrupt practices act and bills providing for workmen's compensation and a strengthening of the public utilities commission.[32] Having decided upon the agenda, in his inaugural address Wilson began the publicity campaign that he had promised on its behalf. He kept up the publicity with a barrage of press releases, public addresses, and interviews with journalists.[33] Wilson also brought his "talking" campaign to the legislature itself, taking the unprecedented step of meeting in closed sessions with the Democratic members of the assembly to explain the proposals he had put before them.[34] Wilson's visits generated considerable opposition from some members of his audience, who regarded it as a clear violation of the separation of powers. But as Wilson pointed out to them on one occasion, the New Jersey constitution mandated that "the Governor shall communicate by message to the legislature at the opening of each session, and at such other times as he may deem necessary, the condition of the State, and recommend such measures as he may deem appropriate."[35]

It was not only through public pronouncements and his ample reading of his gubernatorial prerogatives that Wilson sought to lead the legislature. He used more consensual means as well. Much to the consternation of progressive associates such as James Kerney and George Record, Wilson invited a leader of the Smith forces in the legislature to attend the January meeting at which his administration's agenda was mapped out. Once the agenda was announced, Wilson became an effective lobbyist for it, meeting frequently with members of the legislature to plead his case. He subsequently compromised with wavering legislators on numerous provisions. Various parts of the primary bill, for instance, were altered to alleviate the concerns of traditional politicians, again over the complaints of progressives. Finally, although he was not an informal man, Wilson acknowledged the need to facilitate the cooperation of legislators by swapping stories and engaging in their carryings-on. In April, near the end of the legislative session, Wilson found himself cakewalking around a dance floor with a senator. "Such are the processes of high politics," a bemused Wilson wrote to a confidant. "This is what it costs to be a leader."[36]

The synthesis of assertive and consensual executive leadership that Wilson had called for in his academic works had proved to be remarkably productive in its first practical application, facilitating the passage of the four major bills that Wilson and his aides had set as priorities in January. Reformers in the state and nation hailed Wilson's legislative success as a tremendous achievement, a result of his encompassing leadership and initiative.[37] Just after the adjournment, he sought to put things in perspective for a friend: "As a matter of fact, it is just a bit of natural history. I came to the office in the fullness of time, when opinion was ripe on all these matters, when both parties were committed to these reforms, and by merely standing fast, and by never losing sight of the business for an hour, but keeping up all sorts of (legitimate) pressure *all the time,* kept the mighty forces from being diverted or blocked at any point."[38] Wilson took pride not just in his legislative achievements but also in the methods that had produced them. No doubt he saw his success in this regard as just as much "a bit of natural history" as were the legislative achievements themselves.

Yet as Wilson was soon to realize, if he had not already, the methods and effects of his gubernatorial leadership were not completely consistent with his program. The Darwinian evolution of politics upon which this program was premised lagged somewhat, at least in New Jersey. It is interesting to note that even when writing to a close friend, as he was in the passage above, Wilson felt the need to note parenthetically that he was, of course, exercising only "(legitimate)" pressure on the legislature. What might constitute illegitimate pressure? In *Constitutional Government* and in his prophetic, preelection declaration that he would be an "unconstitutional governor," Wilson identified two particularly egregious forms of pressure that executives had been known to resort to: using patronage to purchase votes in the legislature and setting up a political machine of their own to fight their political opponents.[39] Wilson had in part developed his conception of interpretive leadership, in which the leader drew strength from his public elaboration and defense of a principled program, so that executives might free themselves, and the public interest, from the debilitating influence of "mere partisanship."

Thus on March 20, 1911, when New Jersey Democratic Party Chairman James Nugent, Jim Smith's son-in-law and henchman, accused Wilson of using the very same illicit methods of partisanship that the governor had repeatedly condemned, an enraged Wilson chucked the politico out of his office, thereby adding to his growing reputation as the scourge of the bosses. However, what the press took for righteous indignation might well have been anger generated by a guilty conscience.[40]

Recall that Wilson failed to resolve a fundamental ambivalence if not a contradiction in his program regarding party politics. On the one hand, he proposed that executives could and should refuse to stoop to the rough-hewn methods by which party leaders had traditionally secured votes in the legislature and the electorate. On the other hand, he had come to appreciate the integrating functions of the traditional party organizations and the extent to which a party's performance of these essential functions hinged on their making the "petty choices" of politics, especially at the state and local level.

Notwithstanding Wilson's mounting criticism of the boss system, criticism in large part driven by the progressive tide he was attempting to ride in New Jersey and the nation, he retained his realistic understanding of what made for effective party action after he embarked on his political career. His realism in this regard led him to ask Joseph Tumulty, an ex-assemblyman and a regular in the Hudson County machine run by Robert Davis, to be his secretary. Like several other reform-minded Davis men, Tumulty had first come into the Wilson camp when it appeared that candidate Wilson was turning away from his patron, James Smith, whose Essex County machine was the chief intraparty rival of their own. During the rest of 1910, Wilson appreciated and benefited from Tumulty's practical advice and support, especially in the early days of the showdown with Smith. In early January, when Wilson was realizing more and more the extent to which he would have to beat Smith at his own game, he offered Tumulty the job "in order that I may have a guide at my elbow in matters of which I know almost nothing." [41]

In addition to practical advice on how to proceed in the fight to deny Smith the Senate seat he coveted, Wilson relied on Tumulty to recommend men for virtually all of the appointments he made as governor. Not wanting to handle this duty himself but recognizing that it had to be done, and done well, Wilson assigned it to his new assistant. Tumulty's heartier scruples and broader experience made him, as Wilson no doubt knew, a better man for the job. Tumulty had received his political education in a system where bosses kept tight control over the sustaining spoils. He was caught off guard even as he was delighted by this "most remarkable assignment." [42] In consultation with his friend James Kerney, a Trenton newspaperman who, like Tumulty, coupled an appreciation for Wilson's vision with a realistic understanding of what was needed to make it work, the young aide filled in the roster of appointments. Kerney later recalled that "Tumulty and I made a sincere effort to pick men who would be a credit to Wilson and who furthermore had rendered party service and would not be offensive to the organization." Acting upon Tumulty's advice and upon their implicit mutual objective of reconciling progressivism and politics, Wilson completely cut out the Smith machine in making his appointments; nevertheless, the state Democratic chairman could later boast that Wilson had filled 80 percent of the jobs at his disposal with party regulars. More important, Wilson kept most of his appointments in hand until after his legislation had made it through the statehouse, keeping the carrot out in front of the legislators expected to hold the party line. [43]

Tumulty and Wilson, though the governor was not prepared to admit it, were not only interested in securing votes in the legislature but also in the

New Jersey electorate before the legislative elections in 1911—and in any elections that Wilson might be standing in the following year. Tumulty prepared his patronage lists with an eye to fostering a Wilson machine throughout the state that could defeat the Smith faction. The crown jewel of his strategy was to capture as much of the Hudson County machine, then in flux after the death of Bob Davis, as was possible, thereby establishing for Wilson a major urban base (Jersey City) to balance that controlled by Smith (Newark).[44]

This plan, however, entailed Wilson's warming up to some Jersey City politicos with more than just patronage. Thus in the primary season of 1911, for example, during which Wilson took what he pointed out with a boast was the unprecedented step of stumping the state to condemn the intraparty opponents of his policies, most of whom were Smith's men, he shocked his progressive supporters when he did not come out against two Hudson County assemblymen who had been among the most recalcitrant in opposing his legislative agenda. Having the sole virtue of not being in Smith's pocket, the two bosses from Jersey City received Wilson's stamp of approval.[45]

Wilson's tacit collaboration with machine elements in New Jersey politics, opportunistic and hypocritical though it may have seemed to James Nugent and New Idea men alike, was in fact rooted in a nagging contradiction in his program. Other problems surfaced with the returns and aftermath of the 1911 elections. According to Wilson's program, these elections should have produced Democratic majorities. He and his party had run on a progressive platform and carried it out systematically, precisely the circumstances that he had always believed would produce a groundswell of electoral support. "You voted for the forecast. Are you going to confirm the reality?" Wilson asked voters in Morristown on October 16. Later that day, in Madison, Wilson bluntly told his audience: "If you don't vote to return a Democratic Legislature on November 7 you lied when you voted for me last fall."[46]

Arthur Link documents that Wilson's leadership and the Democratic record of 1911 do appear to have spurred on the Democratic vote. Whereas Republican candidates for the legislature, taken as a whole, had run up statewide majorities of 61,586 votes in 1908 and 41,502 votes in 1909, in 1911 they were outpolled by their Democratic rivals by 3,100 votes. Nevertheless, in 1911 the voters of New Jersey sent Republican majorities to both houses in Trenton. The GOP won thirty-seven of the sixty assembly races and five of the eight Senate races. What produced the defeat? The Wilson ticket had been knifed by Smith's machine. Had the Democrats carried Essex County, they would have had majorities in both houses, but the silence of Smith's papers during the campaign and his machine's deliberate refusal to get out the Democratic vote in Essex County, which fell from 40,516 voters in 1910 to 23,360 in 1911, kept this from happening.[47]

Wilson was caught off guard by the returns and enraged by Smith's pyrrhic vengeance. His conception of party leadership had suddenly been confounded: notwithstanding his successful execution of his mandate, he—the prime minister—now faced the prospect of having to deal with a legislature controlled by the opposition. The day after the election, Wilson stated tersely, "I look forward with great interest to the next session as affording an opportunity to the Republican leaders to fulfill the very explicit pledges of their platform." He was clearly putting the onus for constructive legislation on the GOP.[48]

In the next few months, Wilson became precisely the sort of "constitutional governor" that he had earlier derided. Apart from a proposal for administrative reorganization, Wilson took no initiative in matters of policy, in stark contrast to the previous session. He also reacted against Republican measures by issuing some fifty-seven vetoes (as compared with thirteen the year before), many of which were drafted in acerbic form.[49] Having effectively buried the separation of powers in the New Jersey constitution in 1911, Wilson exhumed the arrangement and used it to fight a rear-guard action against the Republican majorities in 1912.

Wilson's record as governor of New Jersey provides an early glimpse of the central insights and contradictions in his program for responsible government. The comprehensive leadership he had provided in 1911, combining as it did public and private, forceful and consensual means, was by all accounts masterful and a major factor in the remarkable legislative achievements of that year. At the same time, however, Wilson's program did not map an easy route through the maze of traditional party politics; its key assumption about the translation of legislative success into electoral reaffirmation was overridden at the polls; and it offered no effective formula for—indeed, it appeared to exacerbate—the circumstances of divided government.

III

Wilson's apparent abdication of gubernatorial leadership in 1912 no doubt stemmed partly from his increasing preoccupation with the presidential campaign. At the same time that his program was being sorely tested in Trenton, it was also being put to the test at the national level. Wilson's advocacy of his candidacy and his party's platform in the months leading up to the presidential election rested in large part on a defense of his program against the standpattism of Taft and the Republicans, on the one hand, and the radical departures envisioned by Theodore Roosevelt and the Progressive Party, on the other. On questions of political economy, for example, Wilson denounced the Taft administration's willingness to rely on the Sherman Act to cope with the problem of monopoly and its support for high protective tariffs. But Wilson insisted that the remedies to these problems in the Progressive platform were likewise unacceptable.

Theodore Roosevelt and sympathetic intellectuals such as Herbert Croly and Walter Lippmann disdained what they regarded as the heavy-handed and all too often parochial attempts by Congress and the political parties to solve increasingly complex social and economic problems by means of formal laws. They thought it far better to turn over these vexsome tasks to independent commissions, in which expert administrators, well insulated from political pressures, would be in the ideal position to discern and act upon the public interest. The Progressive Party platform reflected this argument in planks that called for the establishment of independent commissions to regulate business and oversee the setting of tariff rates.[50]

To be sure, Wilson believed in experts and the need to grant them sufficient discretion. However, he had long insisted that to be legitimate, agencies had to be directly controlled by political leaders and parties that were in turn directly accountable to the electorate. Independent boards and commissions not only violated the ideals of political responsibility and the rule of law but also increased the likelihood that private interests would capture such agencies and use them for their own purposes. In 1912, Wilson insisted that more partisanship, not less, was the solution for problems like the tariff and the trusts—that is, responsible partisanship of the sort that produced coherent and systematic legislation.[51]

But was such partisanship possible? At a more fundamental level, Wilson had to defend the idea of responsible partisanship against the alternative notions embodied in the campaigns of his rivals. William Howard Taft's campaign was both an unabashed display and defense of traditional party politics against the antipartisan insurgency led by Theodore Roosevelt. The Republican presidential machine cracked the patronage whip with great efficiency as it lined up convention delegates for the incumbent. Taft's forces also squelched calls for primary reform, which stood to benefit the more popular Roosevelt, ignoring the outraged protests of the Bull Moose and his supporters. Determined to stand against such "radicalism and demagogy," Taft vowed that "even if I go down to defeat it is my duty to secure the nomination if I can, under the rules that the Republican Party Convention has established, in spite of all the threats to bolt or to establish a third party."[52] The resolve of Taft along with that of Elihu Root and Henry Cabot Lodge, who joined the incumbent in his stand against Roosevelt, was ultimately prompted by Roosevelt's championing of direct democracy, especially the judicial recall, which horrified constitutional conservatives.[53]

Undaunted by the determined opposition of his former associates, Roosevelt continued his demands for more direct democracy, even on constitutional questions, and pressed his assault on "the spoils politicians and patronage mongers," in his graphic phrasing, by lashing his candidacy directly to the cause of primary reform. In June, on the eve of the Republican National Convention from which he would soon bolt, he declared, "I have absolutely no affiliation with any party."[54] The progressives who followed Roosevelt out of the convention had likewise given up on party politics. In its first platform plank the Progressive Party condemned "The Old Parties" as obsolete and corrupt and deemed itself "a new instrument of government through which to give effect to [the people's] will in laws and institutions." It went on to endorse a sweeping program of direct democracy, including the judicial recall at the state level, intending to drain the power from "the state of courts and parties" that Taft and his supporters were defending. As Sidney Milkis and Daniel Tichenor have observed, the Progressive Party was a paradox, "a party to end party politics."[55]

It was between these two extremes, the uncritical acceptance or principled rejection of party politics, that Wilson was trying to navigate in 1912. His criticism of the stultifying effect that the traditional parties had on political debate, legislation, and administration—criticism that he had sharpened after his entrance into electoral politics in 1910—continued as he campaigned for the White House. So did his recently adopted advocacy of the direct primary and the initiative, referendum, and recall (though he continued to oppose Roosevelt's judicial recall as inconsistent with the rule of law). That a progressive politician in Wilson's day would criticize backroom politics while advocating direct democracy is not surprising. What is striking is Wilson's insistent efforts to defend responsible party government.

Wilson emphasized two main themes in this defense. First, he sought to redefine party politics. "A boss isn't a leader of a party," Wilson insisted in a recurring campaign argument. "Parties don't meet in back rooms; parties don't have private understandings; parties don't make arrangements which never get into the newspapers."[56] In lieu of this common conception of party politics, he offered an alternative view in which principles and public policy, not patronage and political power, were what animated and united the partisans. Thus it was that Wilson told an audience in New Jersey, while wrapping up his presidential campaign, "I look upon the party as an instrument, not as an end. I do not limit my view by the Democratic Party, but I look through the Democratic Party to the destinies of the United States."[57] If ever the two diverged, he continued, he would stick with the larger destinies. He knew that if parties could be seen in this light, as instruments oriented to the public and national interests, then party government could take on a new legitimacy.

At the same time that Wilson was attempting to redefine partisanship, he continued to stress the importance of political organization. Indeed, whenever he endorsed direct democracy as a reform agenda, he almost always urged that it be considered not as a substitute but only as a correction for an organization gone awry. Wilson expounded on these imperatives in the first plank of a draft platform that he proposed for the national Democratic Party in 1912: "Political organization is absolutely indispensable to the successful action of parties, and should . . . be fostered so long as it constitutes the means of carrying out the principles of a party and of serving the public interest. It becomes hurtful or illegitimate only when it is perverted and degenerates into a mere 'machine' for the advancement of personal fortunes (either economic or politic)."[58]

Both reformers and party regulars doubted, albeit for different reasons, whether the creation and maintenance of such an organization, at once principled and effective, was possible. Certainly the history of party politics in the United States gave ample evidence for their doubts. Wilson acknowledged the difficulty of the juggling act he was proposing but also argued that the legitimacy and efficiency of the party organization were not opposed but in fact intertwined. On September 12, 1912, when Wilson addressed the leaders of the New York State Democratic Party, in which machine and reform elements were at loggerheads, he elaborated as follows: "The strength of a party, the fighting strength of a party, lies in its organization, but the strength of an organization lies in the purpose which it has in view. Without the right purpose, organization can't succeed in the long run. With the best of purposes, you can't succeed without organization. And that is the whole quandary of politics."[59]

It was indeed a quandary. In formulating his program and attempting to put it into practice in New Jersey, Wilson had yet to reconcile the demands of party legitimacy and efficiency. His opponents in 1912 had forsaken the attempt altogether, Taft digging in with his organization to defend the old ways, Roosevelt and his followers bolting with their principles and faith in direct democracy. But Wilson himself remained convinced, or at least was not ready to give up his lifelong hope, that a leader of vision who abstained from the baser methods of party management but nevertheless stayed within the party fold would be able to solve the quandary of party politics in the United States.

The three different views on party politics held by Taft, Roosevelt, and Wilson in 1912 ran parallel to differences in the candidates' views on presidential leadership. Taft, for his part, came close to embodying the whig presidency that Wilson had criticized. After leaving the White House, Taft would argue that "the President can exercise no power which cannot be fairly and reasonably traced to some specific grant of power or justly implied and included within such express grant as proper and necessary to its exercise."[60] Taft did not always hold to such a narrow and lawyerly view of presidential power, as demonstrated by his unstinting campaign against Roosevelt in 1912. That being said, Taft's famous definition of the constraints on the executive reflected a conception of the office that was much more limited than those held by his rivals in the 1912 election.

Wilson and Roosevelt believed that the president could and should take much more initiative in leading Congress and public opinion.[61] But there were clear differences in their approaches. In Wilson's estimation, public opinion leadership primarily involved the recognition and explanation of emerging political developments. Insofar as the leader's speech was inspirational, it should be because of the powerful truths and principles that were being explained. Roosevelt, in contrast, subscribed to a heroic conception of leadership that inspired more of an emotionally charged, even spiritual response. Although Wilson regarded Roosevelt as something of a demagogue, other progressive thinkers warmed to his outbursts. Herbert Croly admired him as "Thor wielding with power and effect a sledge-hammer in the cause of national righteousness." Walter Lippmann remarked that Roosevelt "haunts political thinking. And indeed, why shouldn't he . . . government under him was a throbbing human purpose. . . . I believe we need offer no apologies for making Mr. Roosevelt stand as the working model for a possible American statesman at the beginning of the twentieth century." Roosevelt's thunderous rallying cry to his fellow progressives in 1912—"We stand at Armageddon and we battle for the Lord"—is a perfect example of the heroic, radical rhetoric that set his leadership apart from the more professorial, interpretive approach of Wilson.[62]

Wilson also held that the executive leader was connected with his party in ways that Roosevelt ultimately found unacceptable. The two leaders' behavior leading up to the 1912 election is revealing on this point. Wilson had, over time, moved toward the progressive majority in his party. Roosevelt, in contrast, sought to impose his more progressive views on a party, and when it was clear that he and his policies were going to lose, he appeared in person to denounce the proceedings and led his supporters away. During the Democratic Convention, Wilson disavowed any personal appearances and ordered his delegates to be released when he concluded that he could not win the nomination. Unwilling to give up so easily, Wilson's floor managers did not carry out his instructions, and subsequently, through the vagaries of the two-thirds rule and some old-fashioned back room dealing, the Wilson men prevailed. The outcome notwithstanding, the contrast between Wilson's and Roosevelt's behavior reflects different convictions concerning the relationship between leaders and their parties.[63]

Looking at the 1912 election, then, it is apparent that the program embodied in Roosevelt's candidacy and theorized by Croly and Lippmann was the source of the unsettling ideas for which James Ceaser, Jeffrey Tulis, and others have criticized Wilson.[64] While Wilson shared many of the concerns of Roosevelt and his followers, he proposed to conserve and refine many aspects of the old order. It is in the Bull Moose's candidacy that one finds a highly distilled call for the subordination of the Constitution and traditional party politics to plebiscitarian leadership and direct democracy. It is particularly revealing that the self-conscious defenders of the Founders' regime felt compelled to defeat Roosevelt's program. That doing this required Taft, Root, and Lodge to turn on a friend and former leader, to sacrifice knowingly the political fortunes of the Republican Party in 1912, and to allow the Democrats to take control of the government reveals the intensity of their convictions about the radicalism of Bull Moose progressivism. Conversely, it reflects the less objectionable nature of Wilson's program to the friends of the Constitution and the traditional party system.

The contrasts among the candidates in 1912 also point to the continuity in Wilson's thinking over the years, the altered institutional dynamics of his program notwithstanding. In the 1880s, Wilson had defended the idea of party government against Albert Stickney's call for a nonpartisan administration of the "best men" at the same time that he had opposed Sir Henry Maine's and A. Lawrence Lowell's endorsements of the constitutional and political status quo. In 1912, Wilson was occupying the same ground for the same reasons. He still did not believe that party government could or should be rejected in favor of an omnipotent executive and an expanded bureaucracy. Yet Wilson also remained convinced that the constitutional balance of power between the executive and legislature, as well as the means and ends of party politics, needed to be adjusted if the nation was to cope with its new predicaments.

IV

Another perennial aspect of Wilson's program figured prominently, and was of more immediate relevance, in his 1912 presidential campaign: the need for a realignment that would sweep away the last remnants of Gilded Age politics, define a more principled and relevant debate between the parties, and establish the Democrats as a reform-minded majority in the process. As David Sarasohn has demonstrated, the wide agreement within the Democratic Party on a progressive agenda and the electoral surge that it had recently been enjoying in some key states and Congress made the prospects for a realignment look very good indeed in 1912.[65] Wilson's desire to help foster and then to benefit from this realignment had informed his entrance into electoral politics in 1910 and shaped his political leadership in New Jersey. He understood that his fortunes in national politics as well as the fate of his program for responsible government would ultimately depend on such a sweeping change in the party system.

In the spring of 1911, as Wilson tacitly opened his presidential campaign with a cross-country speaking tour, he drew attention to the ferment in the American polity. "Party lines are resting lightly on the people these days," he contended in Indianapolis on April 13. "I do not believe there will be any new parties, but I believe there will be a redistribution of the voters between the parties."[66] Wilson was optimistic in this regard because of what he interpreted as fundamental changes occurring in voting behavior. In Kansas City on May 6, Wilson proposed that "the voters now are becoming what might be called detachable voters. They don't have to be pried off with a crowbar. They follow their convictions. There was a time, you remember, when a man couldn't have been torn from his party for anything. But the times have changed. . . . The old arguments of the parties do not ring [true] any more. The people want new proposals and the party that offers them will win."[67] In noting the erosion of the fervent partisan identification that had characterized party politics in the "party period" of the nineteenth century, and in drawing attention to the difficulties that the two major parties were having in accommodating the issues that had come to the fore in the Progressive Era, Wilson was pointing out developments that have since been confirmed by political scientists and historians. But at the same time he was also attempting to "interpret" a realignment that would bring him and the Democratic Party to power.

To spur along the realignment, Wilson urged that citizens put aside family traditions and sectional and ethnocultural loyalties when they entered the voting booth. Voting decisions—or nondecisions, in Wilson's estimation—

arising from these factors had contributed to the political and governmental stagnation that had constrained the nation's development for too long. "We have made a mess of voting sentimentally," he argued at the height of the 1912 campaign. "We have made a mess of being disinclined to vote tickets which our fathers wouldn't vote." Instead, Wilson proposed that voters decide on the basis of what he believed were national, contemporary issues.[68]

Were voters to decide on the issues, on which party's programs were the best suited for the nation's problems, then Wilson had no doubt that the Democrats not only would win the election but also acquire, through a realigning shift, the support of a majority in the electorate. The Republicans, Wilson argued, had been thoroughly corrupted by their years in power and their de facto alliance with large industrial and financial concerns. The insurgent protests and the schism within the Republican ranks were apt reflections of the corruption of the GOP. But the insurgents were fooling themselves by attempting to form a third party, an effort that could not result in any constructive change. Only the Democratic Party—the Opposition Party—was in a position to produce such change. Having been out of power for so long, it was free of the corrupting effects of holding power, and its economic program sought to countervail rather than collude with powerful economic interests. Therefore, Wilson reasoned, the Democrats were both the deserving and the only suitable recipients of the progressive voter's loyalty.[69]

It would be easy to dismiss Wilson's discussion of realignment, and his general defense of responsible partisanship, as the campaign rhetoric of a politician seeking to line up votes, which Wilson certainly was. But there was more to his speeches. They expressed ideas that had always been at the core of his program for responsible government. Wilson understood his own victory and the Democratic capture of both houses of Congress in the 1912 elections as a profound historical confirmation of his ideas. "There has been a change in Government," Wilson announced at the start of his inaugural address on March 4, 1913, in distinctively parliamentary phrasing. His party, the emerging majority party, had a mandate to govern: "No one can mistake the purpose for which the nation now seeks to use the Democratic Party. It seeks to use it to interpret a change in its own plans and point of view."[70]

Looking back at 1912, political scientists and historians have generally disagreed with Wilson's confident judgment and have been inclined instead to see the Democratic victory in 1912 as a historical accident produced by the divided GOP ticket. Were Roosevelt's 4.1 million votes and Taft's 3.5 million votes pooled together, this line of analysis runs, the Republicans easily would have overcome Wilson's 6.3 million votes. The electoral troubles that Wilson eventually encountered were to be expected: he was only presiding over a deviating "Democratic interlude," as Walter Dean Burnham has put it, that shook up but did not realign the Republican-dominated electoral "system of 1896."[71]

Looked at from another angle, however, the election of 1912 takes on a different light. The three-way race in 1912 was not an accident but rather the result of deep fissures that had been brewing in the Republican Party for some time. Taft, Roosevelt, and their respective supporters were in fundamental disagreement over the appropriate forms of party politics and constitutionalism in the United States. The two campaigns also had divergent understandings of how and to what extent the government should intervene in the industrial economy. It is far from clear, therefore, that Taft's and Roosevelt's votes simply can be combined after the fact. The evidence indicates that a significant percentage of Republican and progressive voters just could not have brought themselves to vote for the rival faction. Had either Taft or Roosevelt run alone, Wilson still may well have won.[72]

That Wilson and the Democrats may not have been predestined for decimation by a return to Republican normalcy in 1920 is given further credence by a reconsideration of the process of partisan realignment itself. Recently, political scientists and historians have suggested that while the process of realignment begins with shifts in the electorate, it concludes and is ultimately distinguished by the achievements of the officeholders invested with power by those shifts. In this conception of realignment, leaders and parties in government, as much as voters in the electorate, serve as the "mainsprings" of American politics. Presidents and their congressional parties secure realignments by undertaking reforms and making policies that consolidate and sustain a majority base in the electorate. Such a top-down understanding of realignment suggests that the electoral fate of Wilson and the Democrats was not yet determined in 1912–1913; instead, this fate would hinge on the leadership and policies that would follow.[73]

When considered from this angle, the prospects for a Democratic realignment looked promising as Wilson was taking office in 1913. There was widespread support in public opinion and in Congress for action on the three items at the top of Wilson's agenda: tariff revision, banking and currency reform, and antitrust legislation. In the elections of 1912, the Democrats considerably increased the House majority they had won in 1910, holding 291 out of 435 seats; in the Senate, they gained 10 seats and a new majority of 6. These majorities were eager and organized to work with the president, and 114 of the House Democrats were freshmen elected with Wilson on the New Freedom ticket. Since the overthrow of Speaker Cannon in 1910, the delegation had organized and disciplined itself through the party caucus under the leadership of Majority Leader and Ways and Means chairman Oscar Underwood of Alabama, who was heading up the tariff revision. In the Senate, the slimmer majority was partially offset by the influx of several progressive Democrats, the likely support of the administration's economic reforms by Republican insurgents, and the selection of John Worth Kern, a progressive from Indiana and Bryan's running mate in 1908, as floor leader.[74]

The election of 1912, then, opened a window of opportunity for Wilson and the Democrats that boded well for legislative achievement and a re-alignment of the party system. To secure these policy and political goals, Wilson had to begin to put his program for responsible government into practice. He knew that if he was going to exercise systematic leadership of the domestic agenda at this critical juncture in American history, he needed to bridge the constitutional divide between Congress and the president with authoritative leadership and to turn the Democratic Party into a party that was animated more by principles and policies and less by patronage and parochial concerns. The resulting reputation for masterful leadership and the creation of a more progressive Democratic Party, in turn, would certainly enhance if not guarantee the political fortunes of Wilson and his party, not to mention a fuller establishment of his program for responsible government.

✵ FIVE

Wilson's Program and
the New Freedom

In February 1913, one month before taking the oath of office, Wilson wrote a revealing letter (which he intended for public consumption) to Democratic Representative A. Mitchell Palmer of Pennsylvania. In what came to be known as the Palmer letter after its release, Wilson argued that the presidency was "passing through a transitional stage." To have so many expectations for leadership increasingly centered on the president was "quite abnormal and must lead eventually to something very different." The president was expected to be not only the chief executive but also the "leader of his party," a "prime minister as much concerned with the guidance of legislation as with the just and orderly execution of the law." And the president stood as "the spokesman of the nation in everything, even the most momentous and most delicate dealings of the government with foreign nations." Up to this point in his letter to Palmer, Wilson had essentially summarized the findings of *Constitutional Government*. For a tantalizing moment, though, he went further than he had in his book, suggesting that reform was needed to relieve the "quite abnormal" burdens and tensions of the presidency, reform that would provide for more responsible government. Eventually the president "must be made answerable to opinion in a somewhat more informal and intimate fashion—answerable, it may be, to the Houses whom he seeks to lead, either personally or through a cabinet, as well as to the people for whom they speak." Yet Wilson still left open the question of how and when this change would occur: "That is a matter to be worked out—as it inevitably will be, in some natural American way which we cannot yet even predict." [1]

If Wilson could not predict the way and time in which responsible government might be established, he was nevertheless seeking to "interpret" such a change in the Palmer letter. His interpretation embodied both the ambiguity and the optimism of his revised program. The ambiguity stemmed from a tension that he had long tried but ultimately failed to resolve between his conviction that the nation would "inevitably" resort to responsible government as the solution for its mounting problems of governance, on the one hand, and his awareness that the Constitution, party system, and political culture of the United States all worked against this solution, on the other. For all of his theoretical difficulties in this regard, Wilson remained remarkably confident about the prospects of his program for responsible government. Over the years he had developed considerable faith in the progress of history, in the functional adaptation that occurred when mature polities like the United States were confronted with new challenges. Wilson also believed that wise and compelling leaders, by interpreting the course of progress for their followers, could serve as the handmaidens for political development. Given that he himself would be exercising interpretive leadership in the White House, Wilson had even more reason to be confident of the eventual realization of his program.

I

Wilson's confidence in this regard was clearly reflected in his remarkable acts of interpretive leadership upon taking office. He called the 63d Congress into a special early session in order to revise the tariff downward, the perennial goal of Wilson and the Democratic Party. He decided to take the extraordinary step of convening the session by going to Capitol Hill and speaking to the legislators in person. No president had done this since John Adams; Thomas Jefferson had stopped what he regarded as the royalist practice of his Federalist predecessors. When writing *The State* in the late 1880s, Wilson had argued that Jefferson's decision had effectively dashed the first intimations of responsible government in the United States; with his decision to reverse Jefferson's reversal, Wilson intended to put American political development back on course.[2]

Several members of Wilson's cabinet were unsettled by his intention and conveyed their lack of enthusiasm to him. When word of Wilson's visit reached Congress, there was a more pronounced protest as legislators with whiggish scruples, most notably John Sharp Williams, Democratic senator from Mississippi and Jefferson's biographer, inveighed against the very idea of such an address from the throne. Wilson, in his comments to the press before going to the Capitol, sought to alleviate congressional fears by explaining that he had nothing more radical in mind than open communication. Yet some discomfort was still apparent on the afternoon of April 8, 1913, when Wilson walked into the joint session, the representatives and senators before him on the floor, the galleries packed with diplomats, journalists, and onlookers. To reassure the restive members of his audience, Wilson began by observing that he was glad for the opportunity to prove he was "not a mere department of the Government hailing Congress from some isolated island of jealous power" but rather "a human being trying to co-operate with other human beings in a common service."[3]

Wilson was not yet done breaking with precedent. The next day he returned to the Capitol to confer with the Democratic senators of the Finance Committee on the tariff revision. He was the first chief executive to use the President's Room in the Capitol since Lincoln had during the Civil War. Wilson's opting to participate in his legislative party's deliberations, like his address on tariff reform the night before, was a matter of some controversy. Nevertheless, he assured the reporters gathered outside the Capitol that his return visit was by no means a "national crisis" but only another effort to reach out to Congress in a cooperative spirit.[4]

Wilson undertook his initiatives deliberately, as a symbolic unification of the executive and legislative branches whose separation had long troubled him. "That is perhaps the reason why I have done some very unconventional things in this very conventional town," he told the Gridiron Club on April 12, as the hubbub over his initiatives was starting to recede. "This business of the division of powers, carried to the point of punctilio to which it has been carried, amounts to a permanent misunderstanding, to a permanent incapacity to get together."[5] With his deeds and his words, then, Wilson was exercising interpretive leadership. In an age when people were more and more inclined to look to the executive for constructive direction, Wilson's departures from tradition, however unusual, could be seen as natural and potentially helpful developments, the success of which would ultimately hinge on the president's discretion. "Never can there have been a case where the tone will so clearly make the song," as the *Nation* put it. Wilson's initial tone, combining as it did assertive and accommodating elements, held considerable promise.[6]

In addition to the speech on tariff revision, Wilson appeared on Capitol Hill to call for currency and banking reform and for antitrust legislation. He kept his addresses relatively short and stuck to what he saw as the problems that needed to be solved and the key principles at stake with each reform. Wilson delivered these concise and resonating messages every few months, as the time grew ripe for each new piece of legislation. They were thus focused upon and widely disseminated in their entirety by the newspapers. It was not only Congress, then, but also the nation at large that Wilson was addressing.[7]

That Wilson's appearances on Capitol Hill drew the spotlight of public opinion was in keeping with his intention of introducing many of the forms and, he hoped, the benefits of parliamentary government in the United States. His admiration of the Westminster regime originated in large part because the executive's presence in the legislature sharpened debate and captured the public's attention. With his appearances, Wilson was attempting to signify that responsibility for governing had indeed been invested in the executive and his legislative party. In his address on currency and banking reform, he aptly summarized the motivation behind each of his appearances: "I have come to you, as the head of the Government and the responsible leader of the party in power, to urge action now, while there is time to serve the country deliberately and as we should, in a clear air of common counsel." [8]

While on one level Wilson's traveling to the Capitol bespoke a desire for open communication, "a clear air of common counsel," there was also a coercive element in his addresses. He used his appearances to influence the timing of the legislative agenda and to outline the general form that the bills needed to take, putting the parties as well as the institution of Congress on the spot in the process. Wilson's proclamations about party responsibility gave the Republicans notice that the Democrats were governing. At the same time, his unflinching descriptions of the duties of the governing party made it difficult for congressional Democrats to stand in the way of the reforms he was advocating.

Wilson combined his formal addresses to Congress with a more informal and interactive mode of presidential-congressional relations. His visit to the President's Room the day after his tariff address was not merely symbolic. At the Capitol, the White House, and over the direct phone line that Wilson had installed between the two buildings, the president was continually conferring with legislators, working with the Democratic committee chairs and floor leaders as they drafted and shepherded the New Freedom bills, marshaling a consensus among the various factions of his party, and buttonholing undecided Democrats before key votes. And the communication along Pennsylvania Avenue went in both directions. Wilson was not imposing legislation upon but rather drawing it out of Congress. With each of the New Freedom measures, he was refining and advocating bills that originated in Congress, not the administration. To be sure, Wilson put his stamp on the legislation. It was at his insistence, for example, that the "Democratic" commodity of sugar was not exempted from the tariff reduction. But Wilson also accommodated the legislators, such as when he bowed to the demands of Bryanite Democrats that the federal government, not private bankers, control the central board of the new banking system and underwrite the currency it issued.[9]

Thus Wilson was not being disingenuous (though he was downplaying the importance of his own unprecedented, systematic legislative leadership) when, in November 1913, he responded to a reporter's question about *his* trust program by declaring

> You know, my trust program is largely fiction. . . . Of course, I have certain ideas which I am earnestly [intent] on seeing carried out, and about which I have already conferred in an informal way with Senator Newlands and the chairman of the House committee. And I think from those conferences that we really are, at any rate, thinking along very much the same lines, that it is very feasible to do what I have usually done in these matters. I haven't had a tariff program. I haven't had a currency program. I have conferred with these men who handle these things, and asked the questions, and then have gotten back what they sent me—the best of our common counsel. That is just what I am trying to do in this case.[10]

Wilson's portrait of himself as merely the interlocutor and coordinator of Congress, not its dominating master, was certainly consistent with the discretion of his public rhetoric. Consider, for example, his most publicized statement in this period, his dramatic denunciation of the intense lobbying that was bogging down the revision of the tariff. He issued his warning on May 26, 1913, as the bill came before the Senate, where tariff reform had traditionally been sabotaged and where certain legislators, including some Democrats, were apparently prepared to collaborate with the interests once again. Though Wilson knew who they were, he did not single out the collaborators. Instead, he focused public attention on the lobbyists—"so numerous, so industrious . . . so insidious"—and positioned himself as the defender of Congress: "I know that . . . I am speaking for the members of the two houses, who would rejoice as much as I would, to be released from this unbearable situation." The attention generated by Wilson's statement made it impossible for senators to conduct tariff politics as usual—indeed, they eventually passed deeper cuts than the House did—yet his phrasing was such that they could not easily take public offense to it.[11]

Wilson had even more occasion to criticize members of Congress directly and publicly in October 1913, when he faced what would be the sharpest challenge to his leadership of domestic legislation during the New Freedom. Three Democratic renegades on the Senate Banking Committee, James O'Gorman from New York, Gilbert Hitchcock from Nebraska, and

James Reed from Missouri, were refusing to sign on to the Federal Reserve bill. Their refusal endangered the product of Wilson's painstaking labors during the summer to get the Bourbon and Bryanite factions of his party to agree on a compromise reform plan.[12]

Wilson urged the Democrats in the Senate to force the dissidents back into the party fold. Newspaper reports suggested that Wilson was even prepared to read O'Gorman, Hitchcock, and Reed out of the party and to speak out against them in their states if they did not acquiesce. Wilson was indeed furious with the three senators, but he was well aware of the need—and took care—to keep his temper and respect senatorial sensitivities in order to win approval of the bill. With the issue still hanging fire, Wilson told reporters that he had no intention of appealing to the constituencies of the dissidents. He also wrote to the *Washington Post,* which had reported his alleged threat of party ostracism, as follows: "I am quoted in your issue of this morning as saying that anyone who does not support me is no Democrat but a rebel. Of course, I never said any such thing. It is contrary to both my thought and character, and I must ask that you give a very prominent place in your issue of tomorrow to this denial."[13] Wilson then continued to hold his temper and abstain from public criticism of his opponents. After more negotiations with the dissidents, the Federal Reserve bill was dislodged from the committee and before the end of 1913 was passed by Congress.

These examples are not meant to suggest that Wilson's leadership in the New Freedom period was not forceful or that it did not rest in large part on his leadership of public opinion. Wilson's protests and denials notwithstanding, with his formal addresses before Congress and with public statements such as his denunciation of the tariff lobby, he sought to drive the legislative agenda and compel wavering legislators to support the New Freedom bills. Reports of his conversations with individual members of Congress indicate that he was apt, politely but resolutely, to speak of the duty to follow public opinion in private settings as well.[14] Nevertheless, Wilson carefully avoided public criticism of congressional Democrats opposed to his policies, worded his statements so that public opinion, not he himself, stood as the "boss," and pursued his policy goals by working with and through the Democrats on Capitol Hill. Indeed, it was as much their agenda as his.

But this was, of course, not all that Wilson was trying to do. By the end of September 1914, as Congress prepared to pass the Clayton Antitrust Act, the last of the major New Freedom reforms, Wilson had good reason for confidence in the success of his program for responsible government. Indeed, it was at this juncture in his presidency that he had the conversation with

Colonel House, noted at the outset of this book, in which the president suggested that constitutional amendments were unnecessary because he could transform the political system through the power of his personal leadership.

Several editorial observers were reaching similar conclusions. They had been struck by how Wilson's systematic leadership of Congress was unlike anything they had witnessed and pointed to new possibilities in American politics. Even the *New Republic,* the fledgling progressive journal of opinion at which Herbert Croly and Walter Lippmann served as editors, acknowledged that Wilson's legislative leadership transcended that of its own patron saint, Theodore Roosevelt. The editors observed that Roosevelt had "made no consistent attempt to work through and by means of Congress," relying primarily instead on "arousing public opinion." Wilson also had led public opinion, but more adeptly, in ways that did not keep him from reaching out to and working with legislators. As a result, he had been more productive. While the editors worried that Wilson's approach might lead him to make too many compromises with the Democratic majorities, they concluded that "in establishing regular forms of co-operation and a better general understanding between the President and Congress, Mr. Wilson is accomplishing an immediately beneficent constitutional reform."[15]

The judgments of Wilson's contemporaries have since been confirmed by students of the historical development of the presidency. In this regard, Wilfred Binkley's claim that during the 63d Congress "Woodrow Wilson's formula for responsible government was working as planned" seems hard to refute.[16] However, when it came to remaking party politics—a task that, as Wilson knew, was an inextricable part of his program for integrating the separation of powers—his formula was proving to be more problematic.

II

Wilson's program rested on the assumption that the president could rely on the support of disciplined party majorities in Congress. Insofar as this discipline needed bolstering, the president could accomplish it by publicly committing the party to the legislation that corresponded with its principles, on the one hand, and by working actively behind the scenes to build a consensus in support of the measures, on the other. This was what Wilson was trying to do in the New Freedom years. Yet his adroit reconciliation of such divergent roles was not enough. He also had to rely on the imposition of a party line in closed legislative caucuses and the enticements of the spoils system.

At the end of the 63d Congress, a congress in which the legislative caucus flourished as it never had before, or since, in American history, a Democratic legislator wrote to President Wilson to complain about the frequency and force with which the party whip had been applied. Unmoved by the objections, Wilson told the dissident that while freewheeling debates were appropriate in the caucus, the party had to present a united front on the legislative floor. "I do not see how party government is possible," he argued, "if individuals are to exercise the privilege of defeating a decisive majority of their own party associates in framing and carrying out the policy of the party." To buttress this judgment, Wilson added that it had been borne out in both his "years of study" and his "recent years of experience."[17]

Wilson's letter was misleading. His political experience may have convinced him of the imperative of caucus discipline, but as noted earlier, he had not been so convinced in his "years of study." The young Woodrow Wilson had looked forward to the day when instead of a cigar-smoking politico the force of public opinion would serve as the real "boss" of the legislative delegations and impose a purified form of party discipline.

Wilson began his presidency with these hopes intact, but they were not shared by the Democratic leaders on Capitol Hill, particularly in the House. In 1910, following the revolt against Speaker Cannon, the House Democrats had won a majority of seats, and they had invested controlling power in the caucus. In 1913, with a Democrat entering the White House, the leaders who would shepherd the reform legislation through the 63d Congress, most notably House Majority Leader Oscar Underwood, were determined to retain the caucus to secure the safe passage of the Democratic agenda, beginning with the tariff revision that would quite fittingly bear Underwood's name.[18]

Wilson understood that the Democratic leaders were so inclined, yet as he noted to reporters, he had always been a critic of the caucus mechanism. The president suggested to the congressional leaders that the party could at least hold its caucuses in public, which would eliminate the specter of "hide and seek" politics that he was wont to denigrate. However, Underwood and the Democratic leadership, knowing that an open caucus was really no caucus at all, ignored his advice.[19]

It was not long before Wilson saw for himself that a vote tainted by the smoke of the caucus counted just as much as one that floated on the pure air of public opinion—and that the former were more readily marshaled. Given that he needed votes more than he did theoretical consistency, at least in the short term, he dropped his objections to the closed caucus soon enough. Indeed, even before the struggle for tariff revision was over, Wilson had become an ardent defender of the caucus and supported his legislative lieutenants in their efforts to set a party line. Thereafter, his doubts about caucus rule resurfaced on occasion, but there was no mistaking his political reliance on the institution.[20]

Wilson's reliance paid dividends. The caucus played a critical role in the Democratic Party's achievements of 1913–1914. In the House, Underwood drove a veritable steamroller that repeatedly ran over the intraparty opposition to the tariff, banking and currency, and trust legislation. In the Senate, the tradition of legislative individualism, the body's more informal organization, and the consensual approach of the Democratic leader, John Worth Kern, meant that the imposition of caucus discipline was less frequent and compelling. Even so, the "conferences" (as Kern preferred to call them) among Democratic senators figured prominently in the passage of the Underwood Tariff and especially the Federal Reserve Act.[21]

Ironically, while expediency led Wilson to drop his opposition to the legislative caucus, thereby facilitating the party triumphs in the New Freedom years, the course of events demonstrated that there was nevertheless considerable wisdom in his original views. As Wilson could have predicted, the controlling influence of the Democratic caucuses set off vehement protests: from progressives and Republican insurgents who had been hoping to collaborate with the administration but were effectively shut out from deliberations over the reform agenda; from Republican regulars whose opposition was pointless before the Democratic steamroller; and, most tellingly, from renegade Democrats who braced against the new expectations of regularity. Criticisms leveled earlier against the tyranny of Speakers Reed and Cannon were now directed, from both sides of the aisle, at the hidden machinations of "King Caucus."[22]

The criticism resonated with the age-old suspicions of legislative cabals and party wire-pullers that figure prominently in the American political tradition and that were furiously circulating in the Progressive Era. The enforcement of party discipline on the floor of the legislature by a body that met secretly outside of it, while evidently necessary for responsible government in the United States, promised to be a difficult practice to legitimate. The more efficient the enforcement, the harder the interpretive task became, and Wilson's previous opposition to the practice only made his problems in this regard more formidable.[23]

If the need for caucus rule pointed to unrealistic assumptions in Wilson's program concerning the willingness of legislators to vote with their party on their own accord, then the persistent criticism of the practice suggests that in another important respect he was right (in expecting it). Whether Wilson could successfully "interpret" the caucus system, though, would soon be turned into a moot question, as profound divisions among the congressional Democrats concerning national security policy, brought to the surface and inflamed by World War I, ruled out even the modicum of agreement needed to put the caucus system into effect.[24]

The coercive legislative caucus was, for a time, an effective but insufficient means of lining up votes for the Democratic agenda on Capitol Hill. Wilson also had to bend his program in another, more collusive fashion: dispensing federal patronage to congressional Democrats in exchange for their support. Much like the caucus, the administration's use of the spoils system, while evidently necessary for legislative success in the short term, was exceedingly difficult for Wilson to legitimate in the political atmosphere of the Progressive Era.

As with the caucus, Wilson entered the White House with the best of intentions. He vowed that he would appoint "progressives, and only progressives" to administrative positions, and that he would not consult with the old guard Democrats on Capitol Hill when filling offices. In keeping with his program, he intended to wean his party off of the spoils of office simply by refusing to traffic in them.[25]

Subsequent events, however, showed that Wilson went back on his vows. His political deputies, most notably Joseph Tumulty, who he brought down from Trenton to serve as his personal secretary, and Albert Burleson, his postmaster general, funneled the administration's patronage through the politicians belonging to the dominant Democratic machine or faction in any given area, i.e., the men best able to deliver votes. This practice led the administration into some decidedly unprogressive relations with bosses from the South and the northeastern cities—even with Tammany Hall and the hated Essex County Machine in New Jersey—where insurgents had made some inroads but had not yet toppled the regulars.[26]

There were more jobs to pass out, too. Wilson acceded further to the congressional Democrats' thirst for patronage by agreeing to Burleson's opening up for political appointments some 36,000 postmasterships (they had been classified into the civil service list by Taft before he left office). Wilson also signed off on bills that excluded from civil service classification many of the administrative positions in the agencies created by the New Freedom bills, such as the Internal Revenue Service, the Federal Reserve Board, and the Federal Trade Commission.[27]

What led Wilson to stray so far from his professed intention of separating politics from administration? The standard account is that Burleson persuaded Wilson to change course at the start of the administration. Burleson, a Texas politico with long experience in the House, was alarmed by Wilson's declarations regarding patronage. He warned the president that if the administration were to abstain from the conventional distribution of jobs to party loyalists, its legislative agenda would falter. "It doesn't amount to a damn who is postmaster at Paducah, Kentucky," Burleson argued, "but these little offices mean a great deal to the Senators and Representatives in Congress." Though Wilson was obviously discomforted by the dilemma, it was not long, Burleson later recalled, before the president turned him loose to conduct politics as usual.[28]

Wilson probably did have conversations with Burleson in the early days of his administration that followed the pattern recounted by the latter. Nevertheless, the hard truth that Burleson purportedly explained to Wilson—how the "petty choices" of the spoils system engendered receptive majorities in the legislature—was a truth that Wilson had already acknowledged in his program. The problem was, of course, that Wilson had never reconciled his acceptance of this reality with his vision of a responsible party whose unity came from principles instead of patronage, a party whose leader could therefore preside over a nonpartisan administration all the while enjoying the disciplined support of his compatriots in the legislature.

This programmatic contradiction between the imperatives of party politics and sound administration, moreover, was manifested in Wilson's leadership well before his talks with Burleson. Governor Wilson had effectively consented to the construction of a Wilson machine in New Jersey by delegating his appointing power to Joseph Tumulty. Complain as he did that Tumulty could not "see beyond Hudson County, his vision is so narrow," Wilson nonetheless brought him to Washington to serve as his personal secretary.[29] Wilson knew that the former ward heeler had the political instincts and sensibility that were crucial for party management but that he himself lacked. Likewise aware of Burleson's background and political orientation, Wilson chose him to be his postmaster general and the administration's chief liaison to Congress for the same reasons that he kept on Tumulty.[30] Despite Wilson's subsequent ambivalence and dissembling over the dilemma of patronage, he himself laid the foundation for the patronage policy of his administration with the unresolved ambiguities of his program, his selection of political deputies, and his delegation of the appointment power to them.

The gap between Wilson's program and practical necessity caused problems in another regard. Wilson left up to his cabinet secretaries the staffing, basic policies, and daily administration of the departments. In turn, he devoted the majority of his time and energy to legislation,[31] thereby fulfilling the prophecy in *Constitutional Government* that presidents would resort to such a division of labor in view of their increasing political responsibilities. The freedom this division gave Wilson to concentrate on legislative affairs was a significant factor in the passage of the New Freedom bills. But he had premised this part of his program on the assumption that the cabinet would consist not of party politicians with their own agendas but rather of experienced men of affairs who would be dedicated to the president's agenda and serve as efficient administrators. Wilson could not and did not fill his cabinet exclusively with such men—political expediency dictated otherwise—and the standards of administration during his presidency suffered accordingly.

Burleson, for example, was an inveterate spoilsman who Wilson included in his cabinet in order to have an experienced broker with congressional Democrats. Yet Burleson's selection as postmaster general and his subsequent manipulation of his department's offices were perhaps to be expected, as his position was the one most likely to call for such politicized administration. A more striking departure from Wilson's program was the naming of William Jennings Bryan as secretary of state. Bryan's selection was obviously intended to reward (and pacify) a party baron and the sizable wing of the party under his direct influence. A long-standing opponent of administrative reform, Bryan quickly set to work finding places for "deserving Democrats." To help make room for them, he turned out many of the professional foreign service officers who had been promoted to unclassified positions by Wilson's Republican predecessors, believing that they harbored GOP loyalties. Then, in the best Democratic tradition and in consultation with Wilson, Bryan took care to divide the spoils at his disposal among various state and ethnic constituencies. That Wilson himself made several political appointments in the upper reaches of his administration, not least in staffing the State Department, no doubt left Bryan with a sense of license in these matters.[32]

Although Bryan and Burleson were the clearest examples of political secretaries in the cabinet, Wilson appointed others, such as Secretary of the Navy Josephus Daniels and Secretary of the Treasury William McAdoo. It was not that these men were not capable administrators; it was just that they had more on their minds. Wilson's complete deference to them in departmental affairs hastened the conflation of politics and administration during the early years of his presidency. In perhaps the most notorious example, he gave the go-ahead for several southerners in his cabinet to undertake a concerted effort to remove, segregate, and otherwise discriminate against the blacks working in their respective departments, thereby opening up more favorable opportunities for Democratic office-seekers.[33]

To be sure, this kind of management was not an across-the-board prob-

lem in the cabinet. Wilson's delegation of administrative power to his secretaries meant that in those instances where he appointed able men who
were not interested in playing politics, such as Secretary of Agriculture
David Houston, Secretary of War Lindley Garrison, and Secretary of Labor
William Wilson, the standards of professionalism lauded by progressive reformers were advanced.[34] The problem was that these administrators were
more the exception than the rule.

What were the effects of Wilson's politicized administration? The most
immediate was the support it purchased for the administration on Capitol
Hill: sated with spoils, the regulars stood by their unexpectedly benevolent
president. For his part, Wilson acknowledged and appreciated the old guard's
support, stating later that "no wheelhorse in harness ever pulled harder than
they did in the direction of the party's program of progress. I did not have
to lie awake at night knowing what they were going to do."[35]

However, Wilson's patronage policy also drew widespread criticism.
Democratic insurgents in various state and local organizations dispatched
protests to the White House when sustaining aid was given to the party
conservatives whom they had battled in Wilson's name in 1912.[36] At the
national level, reformers and progressives complained that Wilson appeared
to be doing nothing less than simply turning his administration over to the
spoilsmen. Herbert Croly spoke for this group when he complained that
"Mr. Wilson is the only President, Democrat or Republican, since the original civil service law was passed, who has not only done nothing to raise the
standards of administration but who has actually lowered them."[37] As with
the caucus, Wilson once more fell victim to one of his own predictions: in
this case, that presidents who resorted to the blatant use of spoils would, in
light of the mounting calls for professional administration, be condemned
for their sins.

The protests clearly got to Wilson, and he urged his deputies to avoid
excesses. Though accepting the need for patronage politics, at least in the
short term, Wilson also knew all too well that it tended to keep the sights
of legislators fixed on the mundane activities suited to gaining and keeping office and away from what he considered to be more appropriate aims—
using power for systematic and collective purposes. As long as the patronage
system was in place, broad-minded and principled politicians, the type of
party men needed for Wilson's program to work as intended, would be less
apt to flourish.[38] And, of course, in such circumstances what Wilson regarded
as one of the leading by-products of responsible government, the disentan-
glement of politics and administration, could not be established. But Wilson

knew that to shut off the flow of jobs would impinge on the legislative successes that were necessary for him and his party to be sustained in office by the electorate, hence his dilemma. "It is a thorny and difficult matter altogether," he admitted to a progressive critic of his patronage policy, "in which I have not satisfied myself and am grieved to learn that I have not satisfied my friends."[39]

⚛ SIX

Toward Party Reform and Realignment

Although the New Freedom period demonstrated the promise of Wilson's approach to relations between the president and Congress, it also demonstrated the limitations imposed on it by the state of the U.S. party system, in particular the Democratic Party. From 1914 to 1916, Wilson undertook several initiatives in the hope of making his party a more suitable instrument of responsible government. His attempts to overhaul his party, while not completely in vain—they helped him demonstrate his progressive bona fides, which proved crucial to his reelection in 1916—were largely unsuccessful. By the end of his first term, he was more and more convinced that at least so long as the separation of powers was in place, the president could not transform his party through personal leadership.

I

Wilson's first serious attempt to reform party politics came in 1914, after the initial year of the New Freedom, when he began pushing his plan for a national presidential primary. Although his support for the direct primary had at first been extorted by progressives in New Jersey, he had since come to be persuaded that the primary was one way of transcending what he regarded as the debilitating constraints of traditional party politics. In the Palmer letter of February 1913, Wilson argued that the popular nomination of presidential candidates not only would guard against the temptation to construct a presidential machine for reelection purposes (as Taft had notoriously done in 1912) but also would establish an unmistakable bond between the successful presidential candidate and the dominant trend in public opinion. Popular nominations would thus reduce the president's need to rely on the usual, objectionable methods of party management while carrying out the multiple duties of his office.[1]

Wilson also became an advocate of the presidential primary because he believed it would deflate support for another popular reform that would do more harm than good: a constitutional amendment establishing a single, six-year term for presidents. The activities of the GOP machine on behalf of Taft's campaign for reelection had only bolstered support for the amendment, which passed the Senate in early 1913. Wilson held that one extended term would be too long for a bad president, too short for a good one. He therefore proposed in the Palmer letter that it was better to clean up presidential politicking with the primary rather than attempt to eliminate it with one six-year term.[2]

In Wilson's first annual message to Congress, on December 2, 1913, he proposed that the Democrats follow up on their presidential primary platform plank and called for federal legislation instituting presidential primaries nationwide. The party convention, in Wilson's plan, would simply ratify the choice of the primary voters. Wilson gave his plan a notable twist, though, by including an idea he had discussed in the Palmer letter. He proposed that the party's platform be drafted by the convention delegates, in his plan an exclusive group consisting of the politicians then holding or campaigning for federal office under the party's rubric, along with its national committee. Their platform would be the equivalent of a parliamentary mandate, on which the party-in-government would stand at the November election and for which it could be held responsible thereafter. Because the party line in Wilson's program would be ratified (or not) by voters before its influence was felt, the resulting discipline would not suffer the same criticisms as that imposed by the caucus.[3]

Wilson's party reform figured prominently on his agenda in early 1914, and he met with legislators to discuss how to frame it. However, as he admitted, there were more pressing policy matters to be taken up than this political reform, most notably the trust package.[4] A few months later, the president and Congress were preoccupied with the international upheaval resulting from the outbreak of war in Europe. The course of events pushed the primary bill into the background, but so did the nature of the reform itself. There were considerable doubts on Capitol Hill concerning the propriety of the federal government dictating to the states and the parties the means by which candidates for the presidency were to be selected. Constitutional objections aside, Wilson recognized that aligning the timing and form of the states' nominating processes would be a formidable job. He also was aware that were a presidential primary bill to pass, it might only have the ironic effect of increasing the influence of money and political managers in the nomination process, the concern that had prompted Wilson's earlier opposition to the direct primary.

By the fall of 1914, in the face of these complexities, he announced that the party reform package was being put on hold. Then, in March 1915, when a Senate report indicated that Wilson's primary plans required a constitutional amendment, the administration was given a pretext to drop the matter altogether.[5] Thereafter, Wilson paid occasional lip service to the idea of presidential primaries but did nothing about them in practice. In the 1916 Democratic platform, which Wilson drafted himself, the primary plank of 1912 fell from view.[6] While the distinguishing features of the traditional party system discomforted Wilson, he concluded that the struggles that would arise from attempting to change those features with his reform proposal would be even more troublesome.

Notwithstanding this retreat, Wilson's support for the presidential primary has figured prominently in interpretations of his historical legacy. Many political scientists argue that his advocacy of popular nominations had a significant influence on the establishment of presidential primaries in the 1960s and 1970s, even going so far as to blame Wilson for the erosion of both the strength of the party organizations and the veneration of the Founders' constitutional design that have accompanied modern primary reform.[7] Such criticism seems hard to sustain given that Wilson's active support for the presidential primary came relatively late in the Progressive Era and was short in duration. Furthermore, Wilson proposed his presidential primary plan not to undermine but rather to help salvage party government and a Founding principle. His primary plan would have convened a well-defined set of party elites, candidates, and officeholders to put together the party's legislative agenda. By creating this symbolically compelling mechanism of collective responsibility, Wilson's twist on the conventional presidential primary stood ready to counter the political individualism that otherwise would flourish with popular nominations. In addition, his advocacy of the presidential primary stemmed in large part from his desire to preserve a key component of the Founders' design, namely, the reeligibility of the executive, by deflating the movement for a single, six-year term. Indeed, the argument that Wilson pressed against this constraint on the president in the Palmer letter was essentially a reaffirmation of that of Hamilton in *Federalist* 72.

II

In December 1914, after Wilson had come to realize that his primary plan was not feasible, he took another tack in his efforts to transform traditional party politics. His new approach was traditional in its own right, reminiscent of actions taken by Presidents Garfield and Cleveland in the Gilded Age. In a straightforward assault on "senatorial courtesy," a linchpin of the spoils system, Wilson made several recess appointments of U.S. marshals, revenue collectors, district attorneys, and postmasters without observing the norm of consulting the Democratic senators in whose jurisdictions the positions were being filled, namely, James Reed of Missouri, James O'Gorman of New York, and James Martine of New Jersey. Throughout the struggle for the New Freedom bills, these senators had been persistent critics of Wilson's policies and his encompassing leadership. Now that the major pieces of legislation had been passed and Wilson was not so reliant on Congress, he opted to test the system of senatorial privilege by refusing to name the henchmen of the three renegades.[8]

After the 63d Congress reconvened in December 1914 for its last session, Wilson put forward his recess appointments for regular positions. The first two of Wilson's nominees, for postmasterships in Buffalo and Kansas City, respectively, were unanimously rejected by the Senate upon the advice of Reed and O'Gorman. The New York Times reported that Wilson's defeat was "almost unprecedented in the history of the Government. Few Presidents had the control of their party that Mr. Wilson has exercised; but no one can recall so sudden and sharp a rebuff administered to a President by a House of Congress in which his party had safe control."[9]

Undaunted, Wilson decided to escalate the confrontation: he sent another slate of recess appointments to the Senate, and administration sources let it be known that if necessary Wilson was willing to wait and reappoint the nominees rejected by the Senate to new recess appointments. For its part, the Senate promised to reject all such candidates. It also set up a special committee to investigate the constitutionality of Wilson's tactics. The confrontation soon focused on one Ewing Charles Bland, a municipal judge whom Wilson had given a recess appointment for a U.S. marshal's post in western Missouri without consulting Reed. Wilson was determined to install Bland in office, and Reed was just as determined to prevent it. The president's sudden refusal to grant senatorial courtesy attracted widespread interest, and not just among reporters looking for interbranch intrigues. At long last, it appeared to reformers, the professor who had lectured on the public administration ethic in the classroom was going to stand up for it in the White House.[10]

In early January 1915, Bland's appointment came before the Senate. Once again, the Senate was unanimous in rejecting Wilson's nominee. Once again, Senator Reed, whose opposing arguments were supported by Senator

O'Gorman, carried the debate. Now Wilson faced a hard choice: to escalate his showdown with the Senate, which had thus far been more than equal to his challenge, perhaps by waiting and appointing Bland to another recess appointment, or to back down and withdraw his nominee, thereby losing face and leaving the spoils system even more solidly entrenched.[11]

The bold, uncompromising rhetoric of the Jackson Day address that Wilson delivered on January 8, 1915, two days after the defeat of Bland's nomination, in which the president warned his fellow Democrats that "the Democratic Party is still on trial. . . . the country is not going to use any party that cannot do continuous and consistent teamwork," suggested that he was prepared to go public in the face of the Democratic senators' obstructionist tactics.[12] But now Wilson also had legislative concerns of the sort that had made him hesitant to stop handing out patronage during the New Freedom period. Among other things, he had begun pushing a controversial shipping bill, and the opposition to it was strongest in the Senate. If Wilson and the Senate were at loggerheads over patronage, the former's shipping bill, not to mention the rest of his legislative priorities, would hardly be well received by the latter. Word soon filtered out of the administration that the president was willing to withdraw Bland's name and put forward another candidate for the U.S. marshal's post, one acceptable to (if not selected by) Senator Reed.[13]

Once again, political expediency limited how far Wilson was willing to go to reform the party system. And once again, Wilson relied on a constitutional pretense in order to justify his retreat from party reform. In a report that made its way into the newspapers, Attorney General Thomas Gregory instructed that Wilson's course, if maintained, would amount to a departure from constitutional tradition. Wilson wrote a letter of apology to Bland, explaining that he felt honor bound "to live up, not only to the letter, but to the spirit of the Constitution."[14]

Wilson's decision not to press ahead with party reform and his persisting difficulties in separating politics from administration were disappointing but not surprising to the editors of the *New Republic*: "It would be unreasonable to expect any such sacrifices from Mr. Wilson. He is seeking above all to govern by means of his party and to give renewed vitality to the system of party government. Congressional control over patronage is essential to the partisan system as it has been built up under American conditions. The President who seeks to destroy it must be ready to get along without organized partisan support and without any but indispensable Congressional cooperation."[15] These men looked forward to the day when presidents would forget about party leadership. Wilson was not willing to forgo his program, however, notwithstanding the conundrums of government and politics he was encountering because of it.

III

Although Wilson gave up on his primary plan and his attack on senatorial courtesy, both of which would have profoundly reformed the Democratic party-in-government and the party organization, he did not give up on party reform. He pursued it at another level, continuing his efforts, first undertaken as a gubernatorial candidate in New Jersey, to make the Democratic Party a progressive electoral majority. Remaking the party in the electorate promised to alleviate the frustrations that Wilson and his program for responsible government were meeting with at the other levels in the party system.

The imperative of an electoral shake-up became all too clear to Wilson in the wake of the congressional elections of 1914. Before these elections, he took it for granted that the voters would reward his party for passing the key planks in the 1912 platform during the 63d Congress. The voters disappointed him. While the Democrats picked up five seats in the Senate, bringing their majority in that body to sixteen, they lost sixty-one seats in the House, reducing their majority to twenty-five. The falloff in the Democratic vote in the midterm elections was predictable. Apart from the normal decline at such a juncture, the Democrats were also hurt by the economic turmoil resulting from the New Freedom reforms, whose benefits were not yet fully realized, and the drift of Progressive Party voters back to the GOP. Indeed, considering the circumstances, many Democratic analysts were inclined to interpret the returns favorably; the outcome certainly could have been worse. But Wilson was surprised and rendered distraught by the returns. He regarded the defeat suffered by congressional Democrats as a repudiation of the party's collective efforts during the 63d Congress and thus of his administration.[16]

Wilson and the Democrats were going to have to do better if they were to retain power in 1916. Clearly their electoral fortunes would hinge on whether they could pick up sustaining support from the many voters estranged from the two major parties in 1912, a group amounting to 5.3 million voters, or 35 percent of the presidential electorate in that year. Wilson revealed his grasp of the situation with his widely commented upon Jackson Day address of January 8, 1915. After noting the crucial role that the "independent" voter would play in 1916, he proposed that in light of the stand-patters' dominance in the GOP and the proven progressive record of the Democratic Party, this voter's natural home was in the latter. For his part,

Wilson was going to see to it that such a realignment occurred: "I have this ambition, my Democratic friends—I can avow it on Jackson Day: I want to make every independent voter of this country a Democrat."[17]

Wilson had taken steps toward this objective well before his Jackson Day vow, most notably by presiding over the establishment of the Federal Reserve Board and the Federal Trade Commission. In working to create these agencies, which were insulated from direct political control and given considerable latitude to intervene in the economy, Wilson had reversed his earlier avowed opposition to independent—i.e., "irresponsible"—commissions.

The reversal was prompted in large part by politics. The president realized that a public, semiautonomous Federal Reserve Board was perhaps the only way to meet the demands of the progressive wing of the Democratic Party for government control of the banking system without completely alienating Bourbons who were fearful of a Bryanite seizure.[18] With the Federal Trade Commission, Wilson was seeking to preempt the criticism that was destined to surface in the election of 1914 from progressives and businessmen if the Democrats did nothing about the trusts except to bolster the prohibitions and sanctions of the Sherman Act.[19]

Yet more than political expediency was involved. Once Wilson entered office and began hashing out these policies with his advisers and the Democratic leaders in Congress, he was persuaded that independent government agencies were the best course to follow in terms of policy. It increasingly appeared to him that the problems of the money supply and monopoly could not be adequately resolved on an ongoing basis (as they needed to be) through the normal legislative, administrative, and judicial channels. Wilson's search for a solution in both instances was helped along considerably by the fact that Louis Brandeis, his chief economic adviser, had concluded that a combination of governmental control and administrative autonomy was needed to deal with the problems of the financial sector and the trusts. After receiving Brandeis's counsel, Wilson came out strongly for the Federal Reserve Board and the Federal Trade Commission in the forms that they eventually assumed.[20]

In early 1916, Wilson initiated a move that led to yet another independent agency, a tariff commission that was to have considerable investigatory power to gather information concerning tariff rates and advise the president and Congress as to how and where they should be set. The idea of such a commission had long been an anathema to most Democrats, including Wilson; they regarded it as a Trojan horse for protectionism. However, given the havoc the war in Europe was wreaking on international commerce, the problems accompanying the inflexible and frequently haphazard character of congressionally mandated tariff schedules were becoming insufferable. The circumstances of global war overwhelmed the Democratic Party's nineteenth-century tariff truisms. Wilson's economic advisers convinced him to go with a tariff commission, and in this case, too, good policy was also good politics. Progressive Democrats such as Senator Robert Owen made it clear to Wilson that a commission would make a profound impression upon Bull Moosers still inclined to see the Democrats as a party committed to outdated Jeffersonian policies.[21]

The tariff commission, along with the Federal Reserve Board and the Federal Trade Commission, did indeed change some minds, most notably at the *New Republic*. In September 1916, its editors proposed that the belated, ironic embrace of the independent commission by Wilson and the Democrats pointed to "their readiness to discard obsolete principles and to consult realities in the preparation of their legislation." That Wilson had persuaded the Democrats to raise certain questions above party politics indicated to Walter Lippmann and Herbert Croly that more and more the president was becoming a national, progressive leader deserving the support of the voters who four years earlier had stood with Roosevelt at Armageddon.[22]

Wilson's efforts to establish a tariff commission came to fruition in 1916. This achievement was but one of several initiatives with profound implications for domestic affairs and the party balance that Wilson and the congressional Democrats agreed upon and enacted before the November elections. In January, Wilson gave his enthusiastic support to a bill erecting a system of rural credits for debt-ridden farmers, a measure that populists in the South and West had long been advocating. In July, he provided critical assistance to progressive Democrats as they successfully fought for bills that limited child labor and extended workmen's compensation to federal employees. Wilson also signed off on the plans of southern radicals for a sharply progressive income tax hike that put the onus of paying for military and naval improvements on the northeastern establishment that had been most vocal in demanding them. Finally, at the end of the summer, he pushed through the Adamson Act, which resolved a railroad strike by granting workers the eight-hour day they had sought, much to the protests of the railroads and businessmen generally. With virtually all of these measures, Wilson was only facilitating—albeit skillfully and with important results—progressive legislation developed under the initiative of congressional Democrats.[23] He was once more displaying his penchant for accommodation with his party's legislators in domestic affairs; their policies became his policies.

What made his support of these measures particularly striking was that, as in the case of independent commissions, they represented a clear reversal of his previous positions. Wilson had not supported the federal regulation of child labor because he thought it would be held unconstitutional (as indeed the Supreme Court soon deemed it in *Hammer v. Dagenhart*). And he had considered it a matter of principle to oppose "class" legislation framed at the behest of farmers, labor, aggrieved sections of the nation, and so on.[24]

What explains Wilson's dramatic move to the left? More than anyone, Wilson knew, as he reminded a conservative Democratic senator in May, that "our whole fortune in the coming election depends on whether we gain or do not gain the confidence of the independent voters."[25] Hence his striving to win over the social justice advocates, workers, and agrarian radicals whose votes were up for grabs in 1916. Yet Wilson's support for a far-reaching progressivism in 1916 was also the result of a genuine rethinking on his part, one related but not reducible to political considerations, of how to secure fully the liberty and fair competition that had been promised in the rhetoric of the New Freedom. This rethinking was certainly pressed along by his experience in government, grappling with practical issues of how best to frame and administer laws that would turn the rhetoric into reality.[26] Wilson's views would continue to be transformed in this way, in keeping with his ideal of interpretive statesmanship.

To facilitate the electoral realignment he was seeking, Wilson combined the policy shifts in 1916 with active and progressive leadership of the Democratic Party during the campaign. Here, too, the advice of Senator Robert Owen bolstered the president's progressivism. In a series of letters solicited by the White House, Senator Owen stressed the importance, both as a matter of principle and of political expedience, of including a plank on social justice similar to that which had been included in the Progressive Party platform. Wilson asked Owen to send him a sample plank and incorporated the senator's suggestions in the draft that he sent out to the St. Louis convention. In this draft Wilson endorsed, among other things, the general concepts of workmen's compensation, a minimum wage, an eight-hour day and a six-day workweek, vocational training and assistance for the unemployed, and the regulation of child labor.[27] With an eye toward winning over pacifists and progressive internationalists, Wilson also included planks on the Democratic commitment to peace and a preliminary outline of a "feasible association" that would guarantee world peace after conflict in Europe was over.[28]

Progressive platform aside, Wilson still had a problem. He led a party that was widely perceived to be dominated by unreconstructed southerners and the bosses of the big city machines and wedded to the spoils system it had created in the Jacksonian period. To accommodate the nonaligned leaders and voters who were willing to support the president but not yet the Democratic Party, Wilson and party chair Vance McCormick set up organizational halfway houses. In July, with Wilson's enthusiastic support, volunteers led by Representative William Kent of California established the Woodrow Wilson Independent League.[29] In August, after extended negotiations, Wilson and McCormick persuaded seven prominent ex–Bull Moosers to join an auxiliary wing of the Democratic Campaign Committee—the Associated Campaign Committee of Progressives—under the direction of Bainbridge Colby, the New Yorker who had given the nominating speech for Roosevelt at the Progressive convention in 1912.[30] For his part, Wilson interpreted the endorsement of these "independent men whose convictions I share" as a clear indication "that the political processes of the country are clearing for a new and more effective combination."[31]

Wilson had good reason to be encouraged about the prospects for the realignment he had long prophesied. In addition to the leaders of the Independent League, the Associated Campaign Committee, and *New Republic* editors Croly and Lippmann, the list of progressive intellectuals, journalists, and public figures who endorsed Wilson eventually included, among others, Amos Pinchot, Jane Addams, Ida Tarbell, John Dewey, Harry Garfield, Max Eastman, Lincoln Steffens, John Reed, Upton Sinclair, and Helen Keller. On November 1, eleven of the nineteen members of the platform committee of the Progressive Party in 1912 announced they were supporting Wilson, claiming that he had made good on twenty-two of their thirty-three planks.[32]

However, while Wilson was apparently winning over those whose votes hinged on progressivism and political reform, he was losing ground among certain groups of voters whose loyalties were determined more by their ethnocultural ties. Wilson's understanding of party realignment rested on the assumption that voters responded to the broader questions raised in policy debates. He continued to criticize the Americans whose views of national politics were influenced by their loyalties to a foreign nation, the so-called hyphen vote.[33]

Wilson's foreign policy, though, stirred adverse reactions among at least two important ethnic groups. His administration's hostility to the conservative Huerta regime in Mexico (which was aligned with the Catholic Church) drew the ire of many Irish-Americans. Their anger was only heightened by the apparent British tilt in Wilson's proclaimed neutrality vis-à-vis the European belligerents, in which he acquiesced in the British navy's aggressive and expanding blockade while taking a harsh stand against German submarine warfare. And, of course, Irish complaints about a de facto Anglo-American alliance were reiterated with considerable vehemence by German-Americans: on October 1, 1916, the *New York Times* reported that out of the more than one hundred German-language newspapers in the United States, Wilson was receiving the active support of only one.[34] Just as World War I had strained the Democrats' time-honored positions on issues like the tariff, so too was it jeopardizing the party's political coalition.

Wilson made a point of denouncing the ethnic groups' concerns, "corruptions of the mind and heart" he termed them in his annual message of 1915. He inserted an "Americanism" plank into the 1916 Democratic platform that singled out as "subversive" and "destructive" any group "political or otherwise, that has for its object the advancement of the interest of a foreign power." Finally, in a highly publicized exchange in September 1916, Wilson lashed out at Jeremiah O'Leary, a prominent Irish-American leader and critic of the administration's foreign policy. The president declared that he would be "mortified" to receive the votes of O'Leary and his followers, "disloyal Americans" all.[35]

The fact was, of course, that whether or not Wilson wanted the support of the hyphenated voters, he knew that he and his party needed it, especially when it came to the Irish, Catholic, and recently immigrated ethnic groups who provided the voting base for the Democratic Party in the North.[36] After the O'Leary exchange had established Wilson's "Americanist" bona fides, he substantially muffled his criticism of the hyphenates. What was more, the Democratic National Committee, the activities of which Wilson was fully informed about, surreptitiously set up special bureaus in order to make tailored appeals to ethnic voters in Yiddish, Polish, Italian, Spanish, French, Norwegian, and Russian.[37]

When the results of the vote finally were established in 1916—Wilson's managers stayed up most of election night thinking he had lost—the president had defeated Charles Evans Hughes. In the popular vote, Wilson prevailed with 9,126,300 votes (49.24 percent) to Hughes's 8,546,789 (46.11 percent). In the electoral college, Wilson defeated Hughes by a vote of 277 to 254.[38] In light of the previous discussion, several aspects of the 1916 vote merit attention.

Wilson's attempt, through his rhetoric and policy shifts, to stand as the candidate of progressivism and peace was relatively successful; indeed, it was the key to his own reelection. Demographically, women (where they could vote), farmers, and workers were the most prominent converts to his coalition. In terms of parties, historians have estimated that Wilson garnered approximately 20 percent of the 4.1 million voters who backed Roosevelt in 1912 and approximately 33 percent of the 900,000 who voted for Debs in that election. The support Wilson received from former Bull Moosers and Socialists was most apparent west of the Mississippi River, where he won all but four states and where in most cases the new members of his coalition provided him with his margin of victory. By adding the West to the solid South and the border states of Missouri, Kentucky, and Maryland, Wilson built the intersectional electoral base that Bryan had thrice essayed but never established. With the support of two northeastern states—he won Ohio and New Hampshire—this new foundation proved sturdy enough to elect a Democrat to the presidency in a two-way race.[39]

However, while many nonaligned voters responded positively to Wilson's policies and the progressive rationale underlying them, the president did not fare as well among German- and Irish-Americans. To be sure, there was no mass defection among these groups, and in some locations Wilson ran surprisingly well among them. Roosevelt's belligerent speeches and the Democratic claim that Wilson had "kept us out of the war" softened the ethnic reaction against the administration.[40] Nevertheless, as David Sarasohn and Meyer Nathan have demonstrated, the Irish-and German-American dissatisfaction with his administration's pro-British leanings cost him and his party votes. Wilson did not experience the same surge in support from these groups as he did generally in 1916. Indeed, in Irish and German wards and counties the vote for Wilson typically dropped below his previous percentages as well as below the percentages that Democrats running for other offices were receiving in 1916 and the surrounding years. While it is bold to suggest, as Sarasohn does, that the drop in support from hyphenates in 1916 prevented a realignment of the sort that took place during the 1930s, the returns from that year nevertheless indicate that to Wilson's disadvantage the ethnocultural loyalties disparaged by him continued to be a leading determinant of voting behavior in the American electorate.[41]

Another defining characteristic of the vote in 1916 was that Wilson's victory was largely personal. The worries of Wilson, House, and McCormick about the image of their party proved to be justified, as many voters pulled the lever for Wilson but not for his legislative supporters. Nationwide, while Wilson was winning 49.24 percent of the popular vote, Democratic candidates received only 46.27 percent of the total vote cast for the House of Representatives.[42] This result translated into a loss of fourteen seats and the complete erasure of the Democratic majority in the House (though with the help of a handful of minority party candidates the party would still be able to retain organizational control over the body when it convened the following year). The Democrats retained a majority of eleven seats in the Senate, but one of the three seats they lost belonged to floor leader and staunch Wilsonian John Worth Kern of Indiana.[43]

The results in the congressional elections indicated that the clarifying realignment that Wilson had been attempting to invoke in 1916, and for many years before that, had not occurred. After the election, he admitted to a member of the Associated Campaign Committee of Progressives that he was befuddled by the persistence of these traditional patterns of voting behavior. The "rigidity of party association so far as it affects a very large proportion of the voters" made the question of how to bring about a fundamental shift in the electorate "one of the most puzzling questions." Though answering it, Wilson noted, would be "by no means easy," doing so remained "the fundamental job in the next four years. I gladly open my mind to instruction on the subject."[44]

IV

That Wilson would open his mind to practical instruction in this regard was not out of the question. He was doing just this with the prospects for informal constitutional change and the place of the presidency in the political system. Wilson came into the presidency assuming that the office was emerging as the linchpin of responsibility in the U.S. polity, and that this emergence would continue by means of the evolutionary processes of political development and interpretive leadership on the part of visionary presidents like himself. The New Freedom period confirmed Wilson's reading of American political development in this regard.

However, in the next two years, as Wilson came into increasing conflict with Congress and members of his own party, he called these views into question. In private conversations, Wilson began arguing that the institutional jealousy and political independence of the executive and legislature resulting from the separation of powers required a formal remedy after all. He returned to his original plan for responsible government, in which a constitutional amendment would clear the way for a parliamentary-style executive cabinet in Congress.[45]

After a dinner at the White House in early 1915, for example, Wilson read to some friends from his chapter on the presidency in *Constitutional Government,* noting that it was the first time he had revisited his famous chapter since he wrote it in 1907. In the conversation that followed, Wilson confided that he was discouraged because the "irresistible" power that he had ascribed to the presidency in theory simply did not exist in practice. He now concluded that "the ideal form of leadership in this country" (which he promised to write a book about at some point) was one in which "the President should be a mere figure-head like the King of England. The leader of the Party should be the leader in Congress and heard in debate fully."[46]

But the establishment of parliamentary government in the United States would obviously require far-reaching political and constitutional changes. As president, Wilson was no more able than he had been as a graduate student to give a realistic account of how those changes might come about. And he recognized that until they did come about, the presidency would remain the dominant institution, to the extent that there was one, in the political system, especially when it came to foreign affairs.

In early November 1916, with the race between Hughes and Wilson still too close to call, Wilson's thinking in this regard presented an immediate problem. What if Hughes won? He would not be inaugurated until March. Yet the United States was engaged in delicate negotiations with the European belligerents to end the war, and the issue of American involvement might well surface during the talks. A president turned down at the polls, Wilson believed, could not serve as an authoritative leader in such circumstances.

Colonel House, the adviser with whom Wilson was wont to discuss the issues accompanying constitutional reform, proposed a remedy. House suggested that if Wilson lost, he should name Hughes to be his secretary of state, and then the president and vice president should both resign. Under the rules of succession, Hughes thus would become president without having to await an inauguration five months later, and the United States would continue to have a responsible leader handling affairs of state. Wilson found House's plan compelling. In order to commit himself to following through on this contingency and to insulate himself from charges, should they arise, that he was resigning in spite, two days before the election Wilson wrote a letter to his secretary of state, Robert Lansing, outlining the plan and stating his intention to pursue it if he were defeated.[47]

Wilson adopted the resignation plan for two reasons. The first stemmed from his belief that, as he wrote to Lansing, "the choice of policy in respect of our foreign relations rests with the Executive." Citing the unprecedented "critical circumstances" the United States faced, Wilson concluded that "it would be my duty to step aside so that there would be no doubt in any quarter how that policy was to be directed, towards what objects and by what means." Second, he noted that the resignation appealed to him because "all my life long I have advocated some such responsible government for the United States . . . as such action on my part would inaugurate, at least by example. Responsible government means government by those whom the people trust."[48]

Wilson did not have to set this example. He defeated Hughes, albeit narrowly. And the passage of the Twentieth Amendment in 1933, which moved the presidential inauguration date from March 4 to January 20, alleviated what Wilson had singled out in his letter to Lansing as "the extreme disadvantage of having to live for four months . . . under a party whose guidance has been rejected at the polls." His resignation scheme thus stands as a remarkable "what if" in American political history, an indication of the lengths to which he was willing to go to institute more responsible government in the United States.

But perhaps what is most interesting about Wilson's resignation scheme is the contradiction it embodied. On the one hand, he insisted that the "choice of policy" in foreign affairs was exclusively the executive's. On the other hand, he indicated that in order to exercise this choice effectively, the executive had to depend on a popular and partisan mandate for his leadership. Over the course of Wilson's presidency, in the pointed debates about American participation in the Great War and the peace that followed, his attempt to resolve this contradiction had momentous consequences.

⚝ SEVEN

Diplomacy, War, and Executive Power

During the New Freedom period of 1913–1914, there was one unmistakably sour note in Woodrow Wilson's relations with the Democratic majorities in Congress. It came in early 1914 with his decision to push for a repeal of the lower rates and exemptions that would be enjoyed by U.S. ships traveling through the Panama Canal, which was due to open later that year. Great Britain argued that the special treatment would amount to a violation of the Hay-Pauncefote Treaty. However, the Democratic platform of 1912 (and candidate Wilson, before he was swayed by the British arguments) endorsed the privileges for American shipping. Many congressional Democrats, including House Majority Leader Oscar Underwood and Speaker Champ Clark, still did. In light of Wilson's continual demands of fellow Democrats that they uphold the party line, his reversal provoked considerable outrage. Indeed, the *New York Times* called the tolls dispute "the most sharply drawn issue between the Executive and Congress that this Administration has seen." [1]

Wilson sought to explain himself to his followers by arguing that the tolls issue raised doubts abroad about the willingness of the United States to live up to its international agreements and was, as a result, undermining his diplomacy. The nature and international stakes of the dispute ruled out compromise; in this instance, congressional Democrats needed to defer to their president's leadership. "As for the platform," Wilson argued, "I feel that no promise made in a platform with regard to foreign affairs is more than half a promise." [2]

Wilson eventually succeeded in getting majorities for his repeal in the House and Senate, as he had with the major domestic reforms of the New Freedom. In this instance, however, he was neither treating Congress as the legislative partner of the president nor working with the Democratic leaders to advance traditional party policies. Rather, as Wilson acknowledged, he

118

was dictating his views to his followers and demanding that Congress accept the president's foreign policy.[3]

However inconsistent Wilson's leadership in the tolls dispute might have been with the rest of his legislative leadership during the New Freedom, it was quite consistent with his theoretical conclusions about "the two presidencies." The domestic president needed to work in tandem with his party followers in the legislature, i.e., as a prime ministerial figure. However, necessity dictated that the president could and should exercise "very absolute" control of the nation's foreign affairs. During the struggles over American preparedness and neutrality prompted by the escalating war in Europe, Wilson had to act upon his theoretical convictions in increasingly assertive and controversial ways. Congressional Democrats (not to mention Republicans) did not accept his assumptions about the president's exclusive control of American national security policy. In the face of this opposition, Wilson came to rely on an argument that he first made in a speech to Congress on the tolls repeal, in which he maintained that he was "charged in a peculiar degree, by the Constitution itself, with personal responsibility" on questions of foreign affairs.[4]

There was nothing unusual in Wilson's claim; presidents had long asserted and exercised special prerogatives in this domain. Indeed, the historical ability of presidents to do so was the major reason why he had come to believe that in an age of new and persistent international challenges the president could dominate the American polity. But the stance on issues of war and peace that Wilson assumed as an independent and energetic president made it harder for him to stand as a cooperative prime minister, working through and with his partisans in Congress, on the domestic agenda. As he assumed personal responsibility for the nation's diplomacy and later its war effort, and as he sought to defend his control in constitutional terms, he blurred the parliamentary divide between the "government" and "opposition" parties that he had established during the New Freedom. In its place appeared the more familiar constitutional struggle between the president and Congress over the control of American diplomacy and national security. By the end of World War I, the exertions of this interbranch struggle put Wilson in the unlikely position of defending, both in practice and in theory, the Founders' separation of powers and the independent executive office it secured.

I

The outbreak of war in Europe prompted a new departure in Wilson's approach to legislative leadership. Concerned about preparing the nation for war, were it to become involved in the conflict, he began submitting bills to

Congress that had been developed by his administrators. No longer was he content to speak on the general principles, then draw out the details of legislation from his party in Congress. Rather, Wilson presented these bills to Congress as vital for the nation's security—matters that he, as chief diplomat and commander in chief, could best understand and act upon and for which he was responsible. Wilson discovered, however, that members of Congress believed that they, too, were responsible for these matters and would not pass the administration bills as a matter of rote.

The first measure stemming from the war proposed the establishment of a federal shipping board. The outbreak of World War I had quickly diverted or waylaid many of the foreign ships that had been carrying fully 90 percent of the American goods bound for overseas markets. To alleviate the sudden dearth of shipping, Treasury Secretary William Gibbs McAdoo drafted a bill empowering a commission to build and purchase merchant ships, then operate them in international commerce. In his annual message in December 1914, Wilson urged Congress that "such legislation is imperatively needed and cannot wisely be postponed."[5]

However, Republican senators led by Henry Cabot Lodge and Elihu Root feared that the administration's shipping board might purchase some of the German ships left stranded in American harbors, thereby involving the United States in a diplomatic imbroglio with the British and the French.[6] Wilson grasped this danger and repeatedly stated that the administration would not undertake ship purchases that would generate international controversy. Nevertheless, despite the importuning of his friends and associates, he refused to accept an amendment, sponsored by Lodge, that would have proscribed the purchase of German ships, nor would he explicitly disavow any intention to purchase German ships. To do so would qualify both Wilson's reading of the rights of neutral nations, which it was his policy to uphold, and the president's control of American diplomacy.[7]

To overcome the Republican challenge to his policy and prerogatives and to retain the support of congressional Democrats, many of whom shared the objections of the GOP, Wilson sought to frame the bill as a domestic issue, as yet another fight against the "interests" in which disciplined partisanship was therefore not only legitimate but necessary. Yet Wilson's partisan tone, in what was essentially a demand for executive discretion in foreign affairs, only hardened the resentment of the Republican senators filibustering against the bill and the seven dissenting Democrats who gave them crucial support.[8]

The filibusterers won out. Wilson and the Democratic Party in the end could not unite what the Constitution had put asunder. That there was no

British-style responsibility in the American regime was by no means a complete disaster for Wilson. He was therefore able to stay in power in the wake of an unmistakable legislative defeat and to continue to fight for his policy. Over the next eighteen months, Wilson and McAdoo kept pushing for shipping legislation. It eventually passed in 1916, but only after a provision similar to that embodied in the Lodge Amendment, forbidding the purchase of belligerent ships, was included.[9]

The other major legislative initiatives of the administration in response to the war were bills enhancing the preparedness of the army and navy. Wilson initially denied that the war in Europe required changes in the size and organization of the U.S. armed forces (as many were contending, most notably—and stridently—Theodore Roosevelt). However, the *Lusitania* crisis in the spring of 1915 and the risks accompanying Wilson's insistence on standing up for the rights of neutral nations under international law led him to reconsider. In July, he asked the secretaries of the War and Navy Departments to consult with the military leadership and develop plans for preparedness.[10]

Later that year, when Wilson introduced his administration's preparedness legislation, he declared that "for the time being, I speak as the trustee and guardian of a nation's rights, charged with the duty of speaking for that nation in matters involving her sovereignty."[11] He certainly was not speaking for his party. Indeed, the bills went nowhere in the Democratic Congress, opposed as they were by pacifistic Bryanites and southerners, including House Majority Leader Claude Kitchin of North Carolina, who objected to the augmentation of federal military power. The Democratic disunion was aptly spoofed at a meeting of the Gridiron Club by two men in a donkey costume: the front end answered to the call of preparedness calmly and steadily, while the rear end kicked and struggled.[12]

In early 1916, to overcome the congressional opposition to preparedness, Wilson headed out to the Midwest for a weeklong publicity tour, the first of his presidency. In his opening speech, he emphasized that "we live in a world which we did not make, which we cannot alter, which we cannot think into a different condition from that which actually exists."[13] Necessity dictated that if the United States was to protect its rights and deter attacks that might lead the nation into war, then something had to be done. Wilson reiterated his claim to be the officer best situated to determine what this might be, telling his audience in Pittsburgh, for example, "I want you to go home determined that, within the whole circle of your influence, the President—not as partisan, but as representative of the national honor—shall be backed up by the whole force that is in the nation."[14]

Wilson's weeklong swing impressed many observers, most notably Herbert Croly of the *New Republic*. Croly had been increasingly critical of the compromises necessitated by Wilson's efforts to govern with the Democratic regulars in Congress. His inability to unite his party on preparedness confirmed Croly's deep suspicion that the Democratic Party was an especially unfit instrument for policies that were truly national in scope. While Wilson believed that leadership of his party and national opinion were compatible, indeed synergistic roles, Croly saw them as mutually exclusive. The president's decision to appeal to the public on the matter of preparedness, undertaken in large part to pressure members of his own party, in the manner of Theodore Roosevelt, indicated to Croly that Wilson had at last recognized the futility of party government and opted instead for national leadership. "He has ceased to be a responsible Prime Minister," Croly proposed, "and has become an independent executive whose power rests on his direct influence on popular opinion."[15]

However, this power, for all of the drama accompanying Wilson's exercise of it, had not generated congressional majorities for the administration's proposals, as he discovered upon his return to Washington. Wilson thus had little choice but to strike a bargain with congressional Democrats who wanted to preserve more of a role for the locally based National Guard than the administration's initial plans for a large federal army allowed. Through persistent negotiations with Congress, in which Wilson played off the House bills against the stronger measures passed in the Senate, which was more inclined toward a larger army and navy, he salvaged the essence of "reasonable preparedness" that had been his goal from the start.[16]

That Wilson ultimately had to make compromises in reaching this goal led some advocates of preparedness, including Croly's *New Republic,* to suggest that for all of the sound and fury of his preparedness tour, the president had ultimately backtracked to playing politics as usual with congressional Democrats, as he had earlier during the New Freedom. Yet, as the president's critics admitted, had Wilson not compromised, no preparedness legislation would have been likely to pass.[17] This certainly was the lesson of the initial fight over shipping in 1915. Moreover, Wilson had gone to considerable lengths—the greatest of his presidency—to lead public opinion on the issue, to stand as an executive above partisan concerns, to move policy in a direction opposed by the Democratic majorities in Congress, and to assert his authority over legislators in matters involving national security. If circumstances prevented Wilson's leadership on the preparedness issue from being exclusively that of Croly's uncompromising "independent executive," it was nonetheless closer to this role than to that of a "responsible prime minister."

II

In February and March of 1916, when congressional Democrats rebelled against Wilson's diplomacy, he was in a much better position to assert control of national security policy, and he did so sharply. After Germany declared that armed merchant ships in the war zone would be sunk without warning, Democrats in both the House and Senate formulated resolutions that would have warned Americans traveling through the war zone on such ships that they did so at their own risk. Supporters of the warning resolutions believed that the president, by insisting that he would hold the Germans strictly accountable for the safety of American passengers, in accordance with his interpretation of the rights of neutral nations, would take the nation into the war.[18]

The Democratic leaders in Congress, who were virtually unanimous in opposing their president's position, urged Wilson to allow them to let the warnings lie dormant on the congressional agenda, thereby avoiding an embarrassing intraparty showdown. Of course, doing so would have left open the question of which branch had the final say in the matter of U.S. neutrality and was thus unacceptable to Wilson. Through public statements and intensive administration lobbying, he moved to spike the resolutions as quickly as possible.[19] Wilson bypassed the Democratic leadership in Congress by writing directly, and publicly, to an administration supporter on the House Rules Committee, urging him to force a vote as soon as possible. Wilson acknowledged the unusual nature of his request but justified it by appealing to both necessity and the Constitution: "The matter is of so grave importance," he argued, "and lies so clearly within the field of Executive initiative."[20]

Wilson's campaign to defeat the warning resolutions soon came to fruition. Within a week, both houses debated and voted them down by wide margins. Afterward, Walter Lippmann, like Herbert Croly wont to complain about Wilson's collaboration with Democratic legislators in domestic concerns, declared, "Mr. Wilson eliminated the legislature from diplomacy . . . he abolished . . . the democratic initiative in the conduct of foreign affairs; he smashed a rebellion."[21] But this triumph was not unambiguous for Wilson. In the process of "smashing" the congressional rebellion, he also gave considerable affront to the many dissident Democrats and heightened the interbranch jealousy that he had long sought to eradicate. The *Nation* made a telling observation after Wilson's defeat of the warning resolutions: "He won, not after the fashion of a Prime Minister of England, drawing out the opinion of the House, but after the fashion of a President of the United

States demanding that Congress stand by the Government in its dealings with a foreign nation. As a precedent, the incident of the past week does not carry us towards, but rather away from, the approximation of the role of the President of the United States to that of a Prime Minister of England."[22]

Was Wilson giving up his long-held convictions regarding party government in the course of his disputes with congressional Democrats over preparedness and neutrality? In May 1916, Ray Stannard Baker posed this question to the president in a revealing interview at the White House. Baker's notes record that Wilson "reiterated again his belief in 'responsible government,' & a closer working together of party and president. . . . He thought some modification of the English system would bring about better team work in public affairs." And Wilson argued that his success during the New Freedom was due to the logic of party government, "having a definite program—approved by the people & in the party platform, which he carried out." He explained the New Freedom anomaly of his push for a repeal of the Panama Canal tolls by simply noting that it "concerned foreign affairs & was properly within the initiative of the president." In discussing his leadership of "the new program which came in with the war," Wilson cited the arguments he had presented in *Constitutional Government:* "In times of peace when domestic problems are uppermost Congress comes to the front, but when foreign affairs intrude the people look to the president. His foreign affairs policy must then be his own."[23]

The unilateral trend of Wilson's leadership on issues relating to the war was even more evident a year later in yet another serious interbranch confrontation over American neutrality. In February 1917, U.S. shipping came to a standstill in the wake of the German commencement of unrestricted submarine warfare. Wilson decided to go to Congress and seek the funds and authority to arm American merchant vessels, if he deemed it necessary, in order to restore overseas trade. He did so even though some in his inner circle, most notably Treasury Secretary William Gibbs McAdoo, argued that he did not need legislative permission to arm the ships.[24]

The prospects for permission being granted were not promising. A unanimous Senate Republican caucus had already agreed to filibuster essential appropriations measures through the end of the 64th Congress, which would force Wilson to call a special early session of the 65th Congress, bringing legislators wanting to oversee his diplomacy back to Washington. As Lodge wrote to Roosevelt on February 27, "Although I have not much faith in Congress we should be safer here with Congress than we should be with Wilson alone for nine months."[25]

In his address to Congress on February 26, an angry Wilson sought to resolve both the immediate issue of armed neutrality and the broader question of who controlled American diplomacy. Wilson emphasized that he was not asking for permission to arm the ships: "No doubt I already possess that authority without any special warrant of law, by the plain implication of my constitutional duties and powers." What he did want was a symbolic ratification of his leadership. "I wish to feel that the authority and power of Congress are behind me in whatever it may become necessary for me to do."[26] Standing confidently as president, Wilson at the same time wanted to cloak his policy with the sort of legislative confidence that a prime minister might enjoy.

On March 1, an overwhelming majority in the House of Representatives, braced by the White House's release of the Zimmermann telegram, granted Wilson authority to arm the ships. But in the early morning of March 3, eleven Senators (six Republicans and five Democrats) began a filibuster. These senators refused to grant the president the complete control over American neutrality that he sought, and they ultimately blocked every attempt to bring the matter to a vote before the 64th Congress adjourned the next day.[27]

In Wilson's screed against the "little group of willful men" who had thwarted him, he charged that in a moment of crisis they had left "the great Government of the United States helpless and contemptible."[28] However, the U.S. government was not as helpless as he had proposed. After Congress adjourned, he went ahead and armed the ships anyway, acting upon his stipulated premise that he already had the power to do so.[29] Denied the confidence of the legislature, Wilson nevertheless had the capacity, as an independent executive within the separation of powers, to proceed as he wished. His leadership during the controversy over armed neutrality anticipated the general direction his presidency would take during the U.S. involvement in World War I.

III

In the weeks after the dispute over arming merchant ships, the tensions between the United States and Germany that had flared up with the initiation of unrestricted submarine warfare and been exacerbated by the Zimmermann telegram continued to mount. As there was little that even armed merchant vessels could do to defend themselves against the U-boats, the reluctance of U.S. shippers to sail for Europe continued. And between March 16 and 18, German submarines sunk three American vessels, two without warning, killing sixteen sailors.[30] Would the United States acquiesce in the face of these attacks or was its entry into the war necessitated by them? Wilson's efforts to deny his cabinet and Congress a significant role in answering this question speaks volumes about his determination to exercise single-handed control of the nation's diplomacy, even in the most fateful days of his presidency.

That Wilson would largely freeze out his cabinet in making his decision for war was not surprising. In the Palmer letter of 1913, Wilson had spoken of the president's need to serve as the nation's spokesman in "even the momentous and most delicate dealings of the government with foreign nations." In keeping with this imperative, Wilson had essentially been his own secretary of state on issues relating to the war, writing many of the key communiques to the belligerents, including the protests to Germany over the sinking of the *Lusitania*. What Wilson could not do, he entrusted not to his secretaries of state but to Colonel House, the personal associate with whom he believed he had a rare communion of views. Wilson's domination of American diplomacy vis-à-vis the war lay behind Bryan's resignation in 1915, as well as the selection of a replacement, Robert Lansing, whom Wilson (and House) could easily subordinate.[31]

Wilson's cabinet nevertheless expected to have a say in the decision for war. In a meeting on March 20, after Wilson had been pondering on his own for ten days the question of whether to go to war, he at least paid his secretaries the courtesy of soliciting their views. They were unanimously and forcefully in favor of war. An inscrutable Wilson merely thanked his colleagues for their advice. Secretary of State Robert Lansing observed afterward that "the ten councilors of the President had spoken as one, and he—well, no one could be sure that he would echo the same opinion."[32]

During the next two weeks, cabinet members could infer the president's decision for war from his calling Congress into special session and the executive orders he issued on military matters, but Wilson was not forthcoming about what he planned to say to the legislators. Secretaries Burleson and McAdoo came to talk with Wilson about the war message, but he refused to see them. When Colonel House, whom Wilson had taken into his confidence, asked him why he had not shown the message to the cabinet, "he replied that, if he had, every man in it would have had some suggestion to make. . . . He said he preferred to keep it to himself and to take the responsibility. I feel that he does his Cabinet an injustice. He should not humiliate them to such an extent."[33]

While drafting his message, Wilson also took care to limit Congress's role in the declaration of war, which was not easy to do, of course, given that the Constitution invested the legislature with this power. Amid the rampant rumors and apparent drift in administration policy that marked the days immediately preceding Wilson's address to Congress, Secretary Lansing prepared a statement for Wilson to release that announced that the president's silence was only a product of his deference to Congress's prerogatives. While it no doubt would have helped alleviate the growing unrest and uncertainty, Lansing's statement also would have offered a constitutional interpretation that contradicted Wilson's desire to reduce the legislators' influence on American statecraft. Wilson thus instructed Lansing not to release it.[34]

Colonel House observed in his diary that in this period Wilson was wrestling with the question of whether "he should ask Congress to declare war or whether he should say that a state of war exists, and ask them for the necessary means to carry it on."[35] The former course gave an active, determinative role to the Congress and, as House warned Wilson, portended a more acrimonious debate. In contrast, asking Congress simply to acknowledge that a state of war existed left it with a passive role, in which the legislators would accept the international imperatives laid out by the executive. Wilson opted for the latter, asking Congress to "declare the recent course of the Imperial German Government to be in fact nothing less than war against the government and people of the United States, that it formally accept the status of belligerent which has thus been thrust upon it."[36]

IV

Although Wilson implicitly proposed that the decision of whether the United States would go to war was essentially the president's, he was more explicit in his assumption that once the nation was at war he should and would receive unusual deference from Congress, not only in executing the war effort but also in framing the legislative preparations for it. In Wilson's war message, after discussing the necessity of raising and supporting a larger army and navy and mobilizing the country's economic resources, he noted that he would have his administrators prepare and submit bills to Congress for these purposes. Wilson went on to "hope that it will be your pleasure to deal with them as having been framed after very careful thought by the branch of Government upon which the responsibility of conducting the war and safeguarding the nation will most directly fall."[37]

Almost immediately after the declaration of war, the administration began sending sweeping bills down Pennsylvania Avenue for ratification by Congress. These included plans for a draft that would marshal American conscripts for the war in Europe, an espionage bill containing expansive provisions for government censorship of the press and control of exports, and a bill creating a food administration empowered to regulate the production and consumption of foodstuffs.

The administration's controversial proposals incited bipartisan opposition. For the same reasons that they had opposed preparedness, southern Democrats led the opposition to conscription and joined the movement of Theodore Roosevelt and his supporters for a volunteer army.[38] Prominent Democratic leaders like Speaker Champ Clark and Senator Robert Owen sided with the Republicans protesting against government censorship of the press.[39] And Democratic populists from the South and West, notably T. P. Gore of Oklahoma and James Reed of Missouri, were the most vocal opponents of the Administration's food bill.[40] Wilson, however, was unwilling to compromise on the controversial provisions of the bills, even with members of his own party, insisting that the legislators had to defer to the executive judgments embodied in the administration's proposals. The concessions that Wilson eventually did make, such as the elimination of some of the censorship provisions, were forced upon him by the need to secure the key components of the administration bills.[41]

The intense congressional reaction to the proposals stemmed not only from their content but also from the way in which the administration demanded that the legislators—the ostensible lawmakers—simply endorse, without qualification, these unprecedented requests. During the debate over the administration's conscription bill, for example, Hubert Dent of Alabama, the Democratic chair of the House Military Affairs Committee and an avowed opponent of the bill, declared that he would resign his seat before he would accept "the argument . . . that, in time of war the executive department shall draft its legislation and send it to Congress, and Congress shall not exercise the right to cross a 't' nor dot an 'i'."[42] The same resentment boiled over in the Senate on May 16, during a debate on an emergency appropriation bill submitted and termed essential by the administration. Furious, the senators voted to go into a closed session, where for more than three hours various members, and reports observed that they came from both parties, railed against the administration's presumptuous treatment of Congress.[43]

The legislators' protests were by no means unprecedented. During the Civil War, Lincoln had encountered similar criticism from radical Republicans for his dramatic assumption of the policy initiative, which extended to his taking the then unprecedented step of sending drafts of proposed legislation to Congress.[44] That Wilson was receiving a similar response from a wartime Congress controlled by his party, while not surprising, did put the lie to his hope that the administration bills would be readily accepted on Capitol Hill.

V

While members of Congress bemoaned the administration's usurpation of their legislative role, they also sought, again like their Civil War counterparts, to extend their oversight of the administration's prosecution of the war effort. Wilson strenuously and successfully opposed the plans for special oversight, claiming that they were prompted by partisan Republican opposition to his presidency, a claim that has since been reiterated by historian Seward Livermore. However, the most serious efforts to set up a Civil War–style congressional committee on the conduct of the war were bipartisan; indeed, they were spearheaded by Democratic leaders and derived crucial support from members of Wilson's own party.[45] The bipartisan nature of the efforts, though, did not keep him from reacting to them as illegitimate encroachments on his constitutional powers or from vigorously using the energy those powers put at his disposal to thwart them.

Democratic Senator Robert Owen offered a proposal for a Joint Committee on Expenditures in the Conduct of the War as an amendment to the administration's food bill on July 21, 1917. Fifteen Democrats joined with the thirty-eight Republicans in favor of an oversight committee and provided the votes necessary for the amendment's passage.[46] In urging Wilson to accept his proposal, Owen argued that the oversight was only fitting, given the massive sums Congress was appropriating for the war effort. Owen also noted that the committee would be controlled by Democrats and that the idea was consistent with Wilson's oft-repeated belief in "common counsel"—the sort of give-and-take that Wilson and Owen had engaged in, for example, during the crafting of the Federal Reserve Act of 1913 and the social justice plank for the Democratic Party platform in 1916.[47]

In a sharply worded public letter, however, Wilson declared that the Owen proposal would "render my task of conducting the war practically impossible." War was an executive business; common counsel was out of the question. A congressional initiative merely to supervise the financial aspects of that business, even one controlled by his legislative supporters, would still "amount to nothing less than an assumption on the part of the legislative body of the executive work of the administration."[48] By issuing this declaration, twisting arms, and throwing down a veto threat, Wilson was able to get the Owen Amendment stripped and the food bill passed in the Senate.[49]

The next congressional attempt to expand oversight of the war effort came at the end of 1917. It was prompted by sensational hearings in December before the Senate's Military Affairs Committee, chaired by Democratic

Senator George Chamberlain of Oregon. Given the comparatively under-developed status of the American administrative state, the sudden mobilization for World War I was destined to be plagued by serious problems and inefficiencies. And, indeed, the committee's hearings aired several horror stories of poorly constructed, disease-ridden camps and soldiers who lacked not only guns and equipment to train with but even winter clothing. In response to what appeared to them to be a crisis of management, Chamberlain and his Democratic colleague Gilbert Hitchcock drew up plans for the creation of an executive Munitions Ministry to coordinate the war effort. Chamberlain's plan was supported by a majority of the Armed Services Committee, and its provision for a new executive body bypassed Wilson's earlier objections to congressional oversight. Still, the plan was being proposed by Congress and provided for Senate confirmation of the new munitions secretary. Wilson could not accept it. He would not be seen as conceding to Congress, even to members of his own party, the right to structure the prosecution of the war. After private efforts to dissuade the bill's proponents failed, Wilson, determined to stave off the proposal, went public with a letter declaring that the plan would undermine his ability as a commander in chief to coordinate the war effort.[50]

However, two weeks later, after the administration imposed a "coal holiday" in order to resolve a chronic shortage of fuel on the eastern seaboard, there was no stopping Chamberlain. The order appeared to Congress, the newspapers, and the public at large—not to mention many Wilsonians—as yet another example, albeit the most unsettling one, of the administration's mismanagement of mobilization. The senators on the Military Affairs Committee began formulating plans for the creation of a war cabinet. The proposal called for the president to appoint, with the advice and consent of the Senate, "three distinguished citizens of demonstrated ability" and to grant them control over all the aspects of his administration that pertained to the war.[51]

Wilson struck back quickly and vehemently. He told legislators that if there was to be a war cabinet, it would happen not simply over his veto pen but over his dead body. He also issued a vitriolic public attack on Chamberlain and his proposal, contending that it "sprang out of opposition to the administration's whole policy rather than out of any serious intention to reform its practice." The vociferous GOP support for the proposal, which Chamberlain openly welcomed, gave credence to the president's charge.[52]

Nevertheless, Chamberlain had been a staunch defender of even the most controversial war policies that the administration had pressed upon Congress, and he had voted against the Owen Amendment the previous summer.[53] Moreover, when the plan for the war cabinet was first announced, it was widely supported among Democrats in Congress, especially in the Senate.[54] Whatever else it may have been, Chamberlain's war cabinet bill was also a bipartisan attempt by legislators to exercise, albeit indirectly, the influence over the war effort that they believed was rightfully theirs but that Wilson had thus far managed to deny them.

Wilson was able to fend off Congress using his standard formula of arm-twisting, veto threats, and public confrontation. Once more he defended and exemplified the Hamiltonian idea of an energetic and independent executive. By spiking the Chamberlain plan, Wilson enhanced the overall efficiency of the war effort and protected the constitutional position of his office against legislative encroachment. For all of the shortcomings that were then bedeviling his administration's prosecution of the war, the legislators' efforts to boost their oversight and influence no doubt would have compounded the problems. At the same time, Wilson's vigorous executive leadership required him to put aside his own notions of responsible government and "common counsel." The same trend is evident in the administrative changes that Wilson made in the wake of the last of these battles with Congress.

VI

The idea of an "administrative presidency," in which the president takes firm control of the executive branch and actively seeks to shape policy by means of this control, is implicit in the Founders' executive office. The personal responsibility that presidents bear for the executive branch sooner or later bids them to preside in such an energetic and independent fashion. This tendency is true even of presidents whose initial predispositions are to delegate responsibility for administration to lower-ranking officials and pursue a "legislative strategy" of cooperation with Congress.[55] This logic played itself out in Woodrow Wilson's handling of the war effort.

Wilson's initial view of his office did not leave him inclined to take firm control of the executive branch; as noted above, his method was to serve as the political leader and leave the administrative details to his cabinet secretaries. This division of labor also entailed that the chief task of the department heads was to serve independently as administrators, not as a council of political advisers. The U.S. entrance into World War I did not change things; Wilson let his war administrators handle their departments and agencies essentially as each saw fit. He did so even though several of his advisers, including Colonel House, William McAdoo, Herbert Hoover, and Bernard Baruch, urged him to create and rely on an administrative "war machine," in House's phrase, in order to foster the requisite efficiency and coordination in the mobilization.[56]

Wilson's adherence to his theory was no doubt reinforced by his feelings for the two administrators drawing the most criticism (the men whose power the advocates of a "war machine" wanted to get their hands on): Newton Baker and Josephus Daniels, the secretaries of the War and Navy Departments, respectively. Baker, a professed pacifist and reform mayor of Cleveland, and Daniels, a teetotaling, Bryanite editor from North Carolina, were unlikely warlords. Wilson had selected them because of their personal loyalty and political service. They also shared his views on administration.[57] To replace or subordinate these men in a wartime reorganization of his administration would only validate his critics.

Wilson's administrative philosophy in the early phases of the war and the congressional ire it produced, especially in light of the appearance of faulty management, were aptly represented in an exchange between Secretary Newton Baker and Senator John Weeks, Republican of Massachusetts, on January 12, 1918. The setting was a congressional hearing on Chamberlain's plan for a Munitions Ministry. Baker argued that "if you are omniscient and have an omnipotent man to run things you have the ideal. My idea is that you have a multiplicity of wisdom, although a decrease in speed, in a number of men. Consultation makes for accuracy." To this, Senator Weeks protested: "What is being done in the War Department is opposed to the theory of the Government at this moment. The Government has asked for and obtained, at the hands of Congress, broad power of centralized control, yet you scatter it."[58] For his part, Wilson maintained, "I would be willing to have a minister of munitions if I had a superman to put in the place. But it requires a superman, and there is no superman."[59]

In the end, however, Wilson had little choice but to alter his direction of the war effort in order to ward off congressional encroachments on his administration.[60] His first step, taken in conjunction with his attack on the war cabinet bill, was to push through the Overman Act. Drafted in the administration, this measure granted the commander in chief virtually complete freedom to create, reorganize, and fund executive agencies as he deemed appropriate for the war effort. Legislators protested Wilson's demand for what seemed nothing less than the "abdication by Congress of its lawmaking power," as Democratic senator Gilbert Hitchcock put it.[61] But under the circumstances, the legislators found they had little choice but to grant Wilson the authority he sought. In a skillful bit of rhetorical judo, Wilson argued that "Senator after Senator has appealed to me most earnestly to 'cut the red tape.' I am only asking for the scissors."[62]

Wilson's second administrative initiative was to enhance the power of Bernard Baruch and the War Industries Board he chaired. In February 1917, at Wilson's urging, Newton Baker finally bowed to the arguments of Baruch and others regarding the need for a "legal, authoritative, responsible, central-ized agency for the purpose of coordinating the demands of the fighting forces." [63] In March, Wilson placed the board under Baruch's personal control and authorized him to coordinate and set priorities for the procurement, production, and conservation of war supplies needed by the federal govern-ment and the Allies. To be sure, Baruch's newly empowered board was not an omnipotent agency. The War and Navy Departments retained control of their purchasing, and while Baruch had a seat on the administration's price-fixing committee, it was chaired by Robert Brookings. Wilson, having fought off Chamberlain's Munitions Ministry, was not going to create one himself. Nevertheless, through the enhanced War Industries Board, Wilson had created the interagency clearinghouse, under the control of one hand-picked administrator, that he long had been resistant to establishing. [64]

Wilson's other major administrative initiative was the creation of an in-formal war cabinet that began meeting on March 20, 1918, in lieu of one of the biweekly meetings of the regular cabinet. The usual participants were Wilson, Baruch, and Secretaries Baker, Daniels, and McAdoo; the food, fuel, and shipping administrators; and the chairman of the War Trade Board. Thus the war cabinet brought together the men in charge of the key aspects of the war effort. In their meetings, Wilson and his top administrators attempted to hash out the broader questions of policy and conflicting administrative objectives that arose during the remainder of the war—"to keep together and obtain a common bird's eye view of the whole situation," as Newton Baker put it. [65]

By 1918, then, on top of his duties as the political and national leader that he aspired to be, Wilson also was taking up questions concerning the basic structure and day-to-day operation of the administration over which he was presiding. If serving as a chief executive in this way was not what he had in mind upon taking office, it was part of the Founders' conception, and it was toward the latter view that Wilson was moving during the war.

VII

Paradoxically, at no point was Wilson's shift in this regard more evident than when he issued his surprising and ill-fated appeal for a Democratic Congress just before the midterm elections in 1918. Edward Corwin proposed that with this appeal, "Wilson was asking the country for a vote of confidence for himself and his party. His action is therefore in line with his own peculiar conception of the President as Prime Minister."[66] Upon closer scrutiny, however, it is clear that Wilson appealed as a president, not a prime minister, for if he truly was asking for a parliamentary vote of confidence heading into the peace negotiations, then he would have resigned after the Democrats lost control of Congress.

Wilson might well have taken such a dramatic step; indeed, he was prepared to take it in 1916, when it appeared as though he might lose his bid for reelection to Charles Evans Hughes. But this option was never a part of his plan in 1918. In September, a month before Wilson gave the appeal (which was already in the works), a friend familiar with the 1916 scheme asked him if he would resign should the Democrats lose Congress. Wilson said he would not: "I cannot do it on account of the world-wide situation, in which American influence is very important and may be decisive. It happens to be a case where, even if defeated by the people, I shall try to obtain the objects for which we went to war."[67]

The Republican reactions to Wilson's appeal charged that it posed a severe threat to the separation of powers; Wilson was asking for control not only of his branch, they alleged, but also of the legislature. This criticism missed the basic thrust of his appeal. For partisans to make appeals during wartime elections was no radical innovation; indeed, the GOP had done it in 1864, 1898, and 1918 as well.[68] That Wilson would not resign if the vote of confidence failed was likewise not a radical stance but rather in keeping with the independence of the constitutional executive. The radical challenge to the separation of powers would have come had Wilson resigned in 1918, but he had no intention of doing so.[69] The change in Wilson's stance from the election of 1916 to that of 1918 reflected the ways in which the experience of leading the United States during the war had led him to harden his conception of his office; for the time being, it was grounded not on public opinion or party mandates but on the Constitution itself.

Striking evidence of the transformation in Wilson's views in this regard is found in a conversation that he had with friends and reporters on the deck of the *George Washington,* the liner that was transporting the president and his entourage to Europe for the peace negotiations in December 1918. In this conversation, Wilson saluted the separation of powers for enabling him to preside as he had during the period of American belligerency. While he had not given up his faith in the parliamentary system, he was now prepared to admit that it was not always the best form of government. Wilson's physician recorded his remarks: "The President said that [parliamentary] government has a greater responsibility to the people than our own government. He added however that he thought our present form of government was the best in time of war. This was indicated by the fluidity of the situations developing and overturning the cabinets on the other side; whereas, ours was compact all the time."[70]

The leading critic of the "Newtonian" Constitution thus had come to view it differently in the sharp light of his wartime experience. The war had forced Wilson's program and leadership to take startling new directions. The controversies in Washington arising from the conflict in Europe overwhelmed a tenuous assumption of his program, namely, that legislators and politicians would defer to the necessity of presidential leadership in matters of war and peace. In doing so, the war presented Wilson with a stark choice between his two presidencies. He could still push to control national security policy, but to do so in the face of opposition in Congress and within his own party would require him to act as an independent and energetic executive, not as the prime minister of a responsible party. The pressures of governing during a World War, when combined with Wilson's theoretical belief in the necessity of executive control in diplomacy and command and with the incentives, powers, and perspective that the Founders' executive office gives to its inhabitants, bid him to act unilaterally, boldly pursuing his own course and warding off challenges to his power. Although Wilson had assured members of Congress in his first appearance before them that he would not preside as an "isolated island of jealous power," by the end of World War I that is exactly how he stood.

鄹 EIGHT

Party and National Leadership in World War I

Between the docking of the *George Washington* in France in December 1918 and the opening of the peace conference in Paris a month later, Wilson basked in the hero's welcome given to him by massive throngs in Paris, London, and Rome. Little more than two years later, however, at the end of his presidency, he surrendered leadership of his own nation surrounded by ill feelings and controversy. What led to Wilson's dramatic fall? The answer lies in part with his failure to bring more supportive Democratic majorities to Congress in 1918. This failure, in turn, stemmed from the U.S. entrance into World War I, which constrained Wilson's ongoing efforts to build a progressive Democratic majority in the electorate. The war also raised a number of divisive issues, despite his efforts to suppress them, that wreaked havoc with his coalition. What is more, the control that Wilson sought to exercise over the American war effort and subsequent peace negotiations increased both the need for and the risks of a presidential intervention in the congressional elections of 1918.

I

In the aftermath of the 1916 elections, several prominent progressives who had supported the president analyzed the implications of the returns. In light of the crucial boost in support that Wilson received from progressives in and outside of the Democratic Party and the failure of machine politicos in the North to deliver the key states of New York, New Jersey, Indiana, and Illinois, his would-be advisers urged him to forsake the bosses and forge ahead with his efforts to build a center-left coalition. The editors of the *New Republic* summarized for the president what the new model Democratic Party had to do in order to prove its progressive bona fides and consolidate the support that had sustained Wilson in 1916: "It must be prepared to emancipate the administrative departments of the government from petty distracting political interference. . . . It must be prepared to shed the newer-worldly provincialism of American foreign policy and to promote the participation of the United States in . . . a working international organization. Finally, it must recognize the existence of a class of wage-earners which . . . suffers from more or less exploitation, and for whom special provision must be made in the reorganization of American society."[1] Civil Service reform, liberal internationalism, and social welfare legislation—this was the progressive prescription for the Democratic Party. Wilson wasted no time in following it.

Braced by postelection letters from prominent reformers who were friendly to his administration but criticized his reliance on the spoils system, Wilson vowed to Colonel House that he would put a stop to blatantly political appointments in the upper reaches of his administration. Even more dramatically, Wilson decided to issue an executive order instructing Postmaster General Burleson thenceforth to fill all first-, second-, and third-class postmasterships—some 10,000 positions—in accordance with the merit system.[2] Wilson now was prepared to assume without qualification the progressive stance against patronage that he had called for as an academic and briefly assumed in late 1914.

After the announcement of the new policy in March 1917, a protest quickly and predictably brewed on Capitol Hill. Democratic legislators implored Wilson to reconsider for the sake of the party's future. Champ Clark warned that the new classification would lead to electoral disaster, as was demonstrated, the Speaker argued, by the effects of the administration's previous efforts to classify fourth-class postmasters: "That raised more cain in politics than anything else, and it is one of the main reasons why the next House is so close. People in a Democratic district want a Democrat in office as a Postmaster."[3]

Despite the protests, the president stuck to his new position. As for chastened Postmaster General Burleson, while his implementation of Wilson's executive order was not completely free of politics, it was sufficiently neutral to draw the ire of Democratic regulars. Progressives were generally pleased. "President Wilson's order," commented George Keyes, president of the National Civil Service Reform League, "is one of the most progressive that any president ever issued. It stops the shameful spoilsmongering that has been going on with these offices for the past 80 years."[4]

Wilson also pursued his vision of a new world order through his efforts to mediate a "peace without victory" among the European belligerents and his address on the subject to the Senate in January 1917. Of course shortly thereafter, in the wake of the unrestricted submarine campaign by the Germans, Wilson gave up on mediation and led the United States into the war, actions that shook the faith of some of the die-hard pacifists who had warmed to his earlier pronouncements. However, many progressive internationalists, and Wilson himself, had come to believe that U.S. participation in the war was essential if the president and the ideas he espoused were to have any influence on the subsequent peace. As Wilson put it in the conclusion of his war message, the crusade he was prepared to lead looked forward to "a universal dominion of right by such a concert of free peoples as shall bring peace and safety to all nations and make the world itself at last free."[5]

As historian Thomas Knock has documented, however, the appeal of Wilson's crusade to progressives was quickly diminished by the reactionary aspects of the administration's handling of the war effort. The Espionage Act passed by Congress at Wilson's urging in July 1917 gave Attorney General Thomas Gregory and the Justice Department the power to prosecute those deemed to have jeopardized recruitment for or loyalty in the armed forces. The act also empowered Postmaster General Albert Burleson to withhold from the mail printed material that likewise undermined the war effort or that could generally be construed as fomenting treason or insurrection. Liberally interpreting the illiberal law, Gregory and Burleson cracked down on socialist and pacifist leaders and publications. Their zealousness profoundly disturbed new Wilsonians such as John Reed, Max Eastman, Amos Pinchot, Herbert Croly, and Walter Lippmann, who warned the president of the damage that Burleson was inflicting on both civil liberties and Wilson's coalition. He was sensitive to this criticism, but he was not a civil libertarian. And, as Wilson's push for the Espionage Act demonstrated, he believed that the war necessitated a curtailment of personal freedoms. In keeping with his general inclination to defer to cabinet members, Wilson accepted the judgments of Burleson and Gregory in almost every case.[6]

The irony is that even as the Wilson administration's curtailment of civil liberties was convincing many progressive and independent observers that the president was, at heart, a reactionary, his opinions on social policy and domestic reform continued to shift to the left. In February 1918, Wilson told Colonel House that he found the Fabian socialist program that the British Labor Party had just put forward to be a compelling reform agenda. In his diary, House recorded the subsequent conversation:

We discussed the trend of liberal opinion in the world and came to the conclusion that the wise thing to do was to lead the movement intelligently and sympathetically. . . . He spoke of the necessity of forming a new political party in order to achieve these ends. He did not believe the Democratic Party could be used as an instrument to go as far as it would be needful to go and largely because of the reactionary element in the South. . . . Again let me say that the President has started so actively on the liberal road that I find myself, instead of leading as I always did at first, rather in the rear and holding him back.[7]

House's comments show that Wilson's conversion to advanced progressivism before the 1916 elections was as much intellectual as political in its origins. It also reveals that Wilson still sought to preside over a realignment in which disparate progressive elements would be brought together in a new majority. Indeed, Wilson was now contemplating leaving behind the conservative wing of his own party in order to forge it.

Wilson did not just confide his changing convictions to Colonel House. On March 20, 1918, he sent a letter to the New Jersey Democratic Party in which he declared that the economic and social forces unleashed by the war needed to be channeled toward "greater opportunity and greater prosperity for the average mass of struggling men and women, and of greater safety and opportunity for children." Subsequently, he drafted a platform for the Indiana Democratic Party's convention in June 1918. Building on the exhortations of his New Jersey letter, Wilson looked ahead to the postwar reconstruction and called for "the sympathetic aid of the Federal Government . . . to the allocation of labor, the development of its skill, and the establishment of proper labor conditions." Moreover, in vague phrasing that he adopted in order to mute arguments that Tumulty and House found too radical, the president proposed government control over "raw materials and all universal essentials, like coal and electric power" as well as the rail and water transportation systems. The *New Republic* remarked that the new tone of Wilson's views "indicates for the first time the direction in which his mind is working and the burden of radicalism which in his opinion a responsible political leader can afford to carry."[8]

Yet Wilson's discussion of the future direction his party should take regarding social and economic policy received surprisingly little attention. The discussion was overshadowed because as Wilson himself said in the first sentence of the Indiana platform, "The immediate purpose of the Democratic party, the purpose which takes precedence over every other, is to win the war." He therefore told government officials that legislation geared toward social and economic reconstruction and not immediately connected with the war effort would have to await the conclusion of hostilities.[9] In the meantime, all that Wilson could offer the advocates and potential beneficiaries of the proposed domestic agenda were promises. Not least because of his treatment of their civil liberties, many progressives were skeptical.

II

The American involvement in the war was causing Wilson additional headaches by raising the divisive questions of prohibition, women's suffrage, and southern domination of the Democratic Party. The war thus revealed the extent to which Wilson's party was riven by cleavages along religious, cultural, and sectional lines and, conversely, the extent to which it diverged from his programmatic ideal of a party united on and animated by encompassing national issues.

Wilson had maintained the "local option" position on prohibition during his governorship and his first term in the White House. In doing so, he sought to avoid alienating either side in an intraparty debate that pitted immigrants in the urban Northeast and "wet" enclaves in Wisconsin, Kentucky, and Tennessee against the progressive, southern, and Bryanite Democrats fighting for a nationwide ban on alcohol. However, American belligerency, and the accompanying demands for the conservation of foodstuffs and the concentration of virtue, gave strength to the prohibitionists. In late 1917, Wilson told Tumulty, "I should like very much to keep out of the prohibition mixup," but this tactic proved to be impossible. Despite his covert efforts to dissuade them, persistent Anti-Saloon Leaguers and their supporters in Congress managed to attach a series of riders to wartime legislation that sharply curtailed and then finally banned the production of alcohol. Wilson paid a price coming and going: his reluctant acquiescence did not merit the approbation of the dry forces but nevertheless earned him the opprobrium of the wets.[10]

Wilson faced similar difficulties over suffrage. Western and progressive Democrats were pushing for a constitutional amendment granting women the vote, while southerners, who saw in the proposed amendment the thin end of a political wedge that would open the way for black voting rights, were opposing it. Wilson had long sought to defuse this controversial issue by maintaining that it should be settled at the state level. As with prohibition, the war made it impossible for him to stay on the fence. The suffragists had the president over a rhetorical barrel: how could he claim to be leading a crusade to make the world safe for democracy, they asked, when he refused to push for its full establishment in the United States? Wilson endorsed the amendment in January 1918 and thereafter was an increasingly forceful advocate on its behalf. However, he could not budge most of the southern Democrats in the Senate. In September 1918, fifteen out of twenty-two of them voted against the amendment, which failed by two votes. At the same time that Wilson had succeeded in antagonizing these senators, he and his party nevertheless had failed to meet the suffragists' demands and had to face the political consequences as a result.[11]

The outcome of the prohibition and suffrage controversies also threw stark light on the most divisive threat to Wilson's coalition: the widespread perception that southerners held firm control of the Democratic Party and were bent on using the party's control of government to the benefit of their own section and to the detriment of the rest of the nation. This accusation was an old one, of course, stretching back to the bloody-shirt campaigns of the Gilded Age and the alleged dominance of a slaveholding oligarchy in the years leading up to the Civil War. It reappeared during World War I in part because Wilson himself and many of his top aides and officials, e.g., House, Burleson, Gregory, McAdoo, Houston, and Daniels, were southerners. Although there was no monolithic "southern" view in Wilson's circle— Daniels was as progressive as Burleson was conservative—the diversity was lost on the administration's critics. The critics also could level accusations at Capitol Hill, where southern Democrats had capitalized on the one-party system characteristic of their region and the nascent seniority system in Congress to wield a remarkably disproportionate influence, controlling the vast majority of the major committees in both the House and Senate.[12]

The controversies of agricultural price-fixing brought the question of southern domination squarely to the fore. The Wilson administration kept the price for the 1917 and 1918 wheat crops set at $2.20 a bushel, making prices manageable for American consumers and the British government, which was purchasing vast amounts of wheat. Yet Wilson's decision roused vociferous opposition in the wheat belt, the region that had swung behind him in 1916.[13] Meanwhile, the South was enjoying what chief administration price-fixer Robert Brookings termed a "runaway market" for cotton (prices would ultimately quadruple over the course of the war). Cotton was less essential to the war effort than wheat; fixing its price would be more a symbolic act than an economic necessity. That being said, the disparity in regional fortunes, and the potential electoral consequences, clearly troubled the president. In September 1918, he indicated that cotton prices would be controlled. However, a sudden drop in the market and an immediate protest by southern Democrats led him to forgo his plans, giving more credence to the charges of southern dominance.[14]

That southerners were enjoying an economic boon in the war seemed particularly unjust to observers in other sections of the country in light of the opposition of many southern Democrats to the mobilization. The focal point of the antisouthern sentiment in this regard was House Majority Leader Claude Kitchin of Great Neck, North Carolina, who confirmed the suspicions of many about the "Americanism" of southern Democrats. Kitchin had led the campaign against preparedness and even voted against the declaration of war; thereafter, he was a frequent hindrance to Wilson's war legislation. To make things worse, Kitchin, from his chair on the Ways and Means Committee, was quite vocal if not vindictive in his pronounced intentions to throw the cost of the war on the industrialists and financiers of the North. In 1918, the cry of "Kitchinism" emerged as not only a ready-made epithet for GOP strategists but also a succinct encapsulation of the difficulty that Wilson was having in holding together the divergent elements of his coalition in wartime.[15]

III

Confronted with these difficulties in reaching out to progressives while holding together the Democratic coalition, Wilson felt compelled to make a series of personal interventions in the 1918 congressional elections. In his influential study of politics during World War I, Seward Livermore has suggested that these interventions were thoughtless and self-deceptive, ultimately born of Wilson's "strong personal antipathies."[16] However, Wilson was fully aware of the risks involved with intervening in these difficult political circumstances and wrestled with how to proceed amid them. He fully understood—but could not resolve—the tension in his program between the president's roles as party and national leader. Here, too, the war complicated his task.

In 1914, Wilson had sought to support the Democratic candidates for Congress from a discreet distance. In a public letter written before the congressional elections of that year to the chairman of the Democratic Congressional Campaign Committee, Wilson observed that as president he bore a "two-fold responsibility": on the one hand, he was the prime minister, the leader of his party supporters in Congress, while on the other hand he was the leader of the people as a whole, the executive who needed to act and speak for the nation with respect to the war in Europe. Wilson observed that the former role might well be perceived as conflicting with the latter role. Given the supreme importance of national leadership in a time of crisis, his party leadership had to be subordinated to it, and he could not actively campaign. Instead, he issued a general endorsement in which he commended the work done by the 63d Congress, expressed confidence that grateful voters would return its Democratic majorities, and left it at that.[17]

The self-restraint that Wilson had publicly adopted in 1914 seemed even more necessary in the congressional elections of 1918, for now Wilson was the commander in chief of a nation at war. At the same time, though, even more was at stake, notably, control of the war effort as well as the subsequent peacemaking and domestic reconstruction. The high stakes gave Wilson powerful incentives to intervene in the elections, both to preserve Democratic control of Congress and to ensure that his ostensible supporters responded more consistently to his direction. On several occasions during the 1918 congressional campaign, Wilson put aside his ambivalence and acted as a party leader. The mixed results his interventions met with, however, appeared to validate the wisdom in Wilson's earlier, more reticent stance. Leading both the party and the nation in such critical times was an impossible juggling act.

In March 1918, Wilson made his first political intervention in a special election for a Wisconsin Senate seat. The Democratic candidate, Joseph Davies, had asked Wilson for an endorsement. Wilson could not decide whether or not to give him one and turned to Albert Burleson for advice. Braced by the unabashedly partisan Burleson, Wilson sent a letter to Davies that made note of the Democratic candidate's support of the administration on the warning resolutions and armed neutrality. His letter implicitly criticized Irvine Lenroot, the GOP candidate, for not having backed the president on the issues that provided "an acid test in our country to disclose true loyalty and genuine Americanism."[18]

The voters of Wisconsin, many of whom were of German origin, willingly failed Wilson's "acid test" and elected Lenroot. Wilson's political intervention was widely decried, by friends and enemies of the administration alike, as an action that not only demeaned the authority of the president through unseemly party maneuvering but also met with the electoral fate it deserved.[19] Apparently chastened, shortly thereafter Wilson gave his "politics is adjourned" speech to Congress, in which he publicly subordinated his fight as a party leader to the fight he was presiding over as commander in chief.[20]

Although Wilson was willing to put his campaign against the Republicans on hold, he could not abstain completely from party leadership. The Democratic primary campaigns were under way in the summer of 1918, and Wilson, against his expressed intentions, was eventually drawn into some of them. Several considerations lay behind Wilson's hesitance to choose between and among competing factions and candidates at the state and district level. The spurned Democrats would obviously harbor a grudge, and given the prevailing attitudes toward the president in many regions, they might well be able to wear Wilson's admonishment as a badge of honor. A repudiated candidate's nomination would only highlight the administration's weakness. Wilson also sensed that his taking a stand in one primary campaign would make it impossible to avoid the exhausting and controversial task of vetting candidates in every race, even when none of those running met the "acid test." Hence Wilson's statement, repeated in various forms to those who inquired in the early months of 1918, that "I do not feel at liberty . . . to suggest who shall be candidates for Congress or who shall be preferred at the elections. I think that would be going beyond my prerogatives even as leader of the party."[21]

However, while publicly disavowing such activities, Wilson was in fact working behind the scenes in various races, rallying support for the most promising proadministration candidates; attempting to unite factions opposed to antiadministration renegades; avoiding even the appearance of validating the campaigns of his personal opponents and their political allies; encouraging congressional supporters who were contemplating retirement to mount yet another campaign; and instructing inconsistently supportive Democrats who appealed for a presidential endorsement that none would be forthcoming.[22] With all of this activity, however, Wilson continued to hold back from publicly endorsing or condemning candidates in the Democratic primaries. Only in late July and August 1918 did he change course.

Wilson did so in part because in two Senate primaries his covert efforts to thwart candidates who had been irascible in their hostility to his administration, Senators Thomas Hardwick of Georgia and James Vardaman of Mississippi, appeared increasingly likely to fail. Wilson either had to put aside his qualms about direct intervention in the primaries or face the unsavory prospect of having to endure the barbs of Hardwick and Vardaman for the rest of his presidency. Wilson discussed his ambivalence with his cabinet. Most members who spoke urged him to continue his policy of not embroiling himself in primary controversies. Albert Burleson, as was his wont, weighed in on the other side, and the partisan postmaster evidently persuaded the president to put aside his doubts. Wilson proceeded to send out public letters repudiating Hardwick and Vardaman. Whether or not his letters were the deciding factors is hard to estimate, but both men were defeated in the primaries.[23]

In what appeared to be arbitrary political overkill, Wilson also publicly condemned two House Democrats, James Slayden of Texas and George Huddleston of Alabama. These repudiations were more a result of local partisans wanting to use the president's authority as party leader for their own purposes than of Wilson's proclivities. Predictably, his repudiations generated considerable criticism, and in Huddleston's case the presidential blackball did not even hold up. Commenting on the Alabamian's primary victory, the *Nation* quipped that "somehow this does not look as if the American electorate were disposed to take directions from the White House as to how it should vote."[24]

The *Nation's* judgment proved to be equally apt for Wilson's national appeal for a Democratic Congress on October 25, 1918. This appeal has long been seen as an act of unabashed partisanship. It is worth noting, though, the extent to which Wilson and his party assistants both developed the idea of the appeal and attempted to craft and deliver it with an eye toward mitigating accusations that the president was inappropriately resorting to party politics during a national crisis.

The genesis of the appeal can be traced to a Tumulty memo in September 1917. Tumulty suggested that Wilson should hold back from giving endorsements to individual Democratic candidates, a course of action that would repeatedly give the impression that the president was concerned more with the fortunes of his party than with his duties as commander in chief. Instead, the president should wait until just before the congressional elections of 1918 and issue a blanket endorsement of all Democrats. Of course, this approach would still be a partisan act on the president's part, but it would be geared directly toward the election and limited to a single instance. Subsequently, in June 1918, Tumulty repeated the need for a general endorsement and suggested that it be combined with a "nonpartisan" speaking tour of the West to bolster support in the region. In September, Wilson decided to forgo the proposed tour to ward off charges that he was politicking on the stump instead of administering the war effort. However, he was persuaded of the need for a general statement supporting the Democratic candidates. In addition to Tumulty, his nervous supporters in Congress also implored him to act on their behalf.[25]

Around October 10, Tumulty gave a highly partisan draft appeal to Wilson. In two revisions over the next week, Wilson muted his secretary's denunciation of the Republicans, allowing that they had been "pro-war" despite being "anti-administration." He cast the appeal not so much as a request for complete command but as an "unmistakable vote of confidence." But Wilson still maintained a sharp partisan tone and singled out Lodge as an obstructionist. He redrafted the appeal yet again with the aid of Democratic National Committee officials Homer Cummings and Vance McCormick, and upon their advice further muted its partisan tenor and dropped the critical reference to Lodge. Despite the numerous revisions, however, the president's final draft remained, in its essence, a partisan document. Cummings and McCormick thought it might backfire because of the apparent political bitterness it projected, and Wilson also admitted that he had reservations along these lines.[26]

Forsaking his doubts, Wilson went ahead and released it to the press on October 25. In the opening paragraph, he told voters that "if you have approved of my leadership and wish me to continue to be your unembarrassed spokesman in affairs at home and abroad, I earnestly beg that you will express yourselves unmistakably to that effect by returning a Democratic majority to both the Senate and the House of Representatives."[27] Wilson tried to diffuse the partisan nature of his appeal by insisting that "I have no thought of suggesting that any political party is paramount in matters of patriotism." He went on to propose that "in ordinary times I would not feel at liberty to make such an appeal to you. In ordinary times divided counsels can be endured without permanent hurt to the country. But these are not ordinary times."[28] What made the times so extraordinary that Wilson believed he could legitimately call for a Democratic Congress? Why was unified counsel so important?

The chief concern in Wilson's mind was not the war, which at that juncture apparently was coming to a close (Germany having approached the West about an armistice), but rather the subsequent peace. Lodge, Roosevelt, and other Republicans had voiced rancorous criticism of Wilson's negotiations with the Germans and his hope of forming a league of nations to enforce the peace. A more or less official statement of the Republican opposition came with Roosevelt's public telegram to Senators Lodge, Poindexter, and Johnson on October 24, one day before Wilson released his appeal. Roosevelt urged the senators to make use of their constitutional prerogatives regarding treaties in order to thwart Wilson's foolish desire to achieve "peace without victory" and to implement his fourteen points. "Let us dictate peace by the hammering guns," the colonel exhorted, "and not chat about peace to the accompaniment of the clicking of typewriters." Roosevelt's rhetoric gave credence to Wilson's claim in the appeal that the Allies "would find it very difficult to believe that the voters of the United States had chosen to support their President by electing to the Congress a majority controlled by those who are not in fact in sympathy with the attitude and the action of the Administration."[29]

As soon as Wilson issued the appeal, it met with the accusations of narrow-minded partisanship that Wilson had feared but in the circumstances had decided to risk. Predictably, Theodore Roosevelt was Wilson's most prominent and vehement critic: "The President's statement is an announcement that he is a partisan leader first and a President of all the people second." His angry rejoinder on behalf of the aggrieved Republicans who were shocked (shocked!) to find Wilson making such a political appeal during the war was wholly disingenuous.[30] But Roosevelt had put a stubby rhetorical finger on one of the major contradictions of Wilson's program, one that Wilson himself was quite sensitive about. Roosevelt's sentiments matched those of many Wilsonians in and outside of the administration, who were pained by their conclusion that the president had demeaned his office, and his authority as a national leader, with the appeal.[31]

In the official Republican Party response, Senator Lodge, House Republican Leader Frederick Gillette, and the chairs of the GOP congressional and senatorial campaign committees took another approach in attacking Wilson. The Republican leaders pointed to the significant gap between, on the one hand, Wilson's pretenses to serving as a national leader and the head of a broad-minded party, and on the other, the more parochial perspectives and activities of the party on whose behalf he was speaking during the war. Unfortunately for Wilson, it was easy to exploit this gap.[32]

IV

The 1918 congressional elections indicated that the voters did not share Wilson's convictions concerning the dangers of divided government, and the Democrats lost control of Congress. When the 66th Congress convened, Wilson would face Republican majorities of fifty seats in the House and two seats in the Senate. The losses were not too severe considering the obstacles that the Democratic Party faced: a well-financed, organized, and united GOP and the typical drop of support in the second midterm election for the president's party.[33] Nevertheless, Wilson now faced the prospect of having to get his peace treaty ratified by a Republican Senate led by Henry Cabot Lodge.

The incoming Senate Majority Leader, partisan and constitutional conservative that he was, was convinced that the outcome of the vote stemmed from fears of usurpation borne of Wilson's appeal: "It came from the popular uprising against [Wilson's] attempt to order a Congress as if he would have ordered a dinner, and the people saw in it instinctively the beginning of a dictatorship and went against it." Democratic analysts were divided on the effect of the appeal. Administration officials such as Interior Secretary Frank Lane thought that such public partisanship in wartime had not only been inappropriate but politically disastrous. Representative Jouett Shouse of Kansas reported that in his state it had "the unfortunate effect of solidifying Republican opposition more strongly than in ten years." On the other hand, a party leader in Massachusetts reported that it had helped tremendously there, and observers from Homer Cummings to the editors of the

New York Times concluded that the appeal had prevented worse losses for the president's party.[34] On balance, it seems doubtful that Wilson's appeal either seriously cut into or increased the Democratic vote.

One explanation for the GOP victories that enjoyed wide credence among disenchanted progressives in 1918 was that the Wilson administration's curtailment of civil liberties had strangled the organs of opinion and the general goodwill on the American left that had sustained the president in 1916. What was more, because of the stilted public debate, Wilson could not carry out the political education that was necessary to build support for his plans for a league of nations abroad and for progressive reconstruction at home. Hence his appeal for a Democratic Congress at the end of the war, essentially an appeal made in the name of these policies, fell on deaf, or at least untutored, ears.[35]

This explanation rests on the assumption that a progressive majority coalition, harmonious, coherent, and national in its outlook, was latent in the U.S. polity and only needed to be drawn out by an astute and visionary leadership. The same assumption figured prominently in Wilson's program. He was continually contemplating ways to bring about such an awakening and a corresponding realignment in the party system. It would have been cruelly ironic if Wilson's failure to preside over a liberal war mobilization killed the realignment that might have sustained his postwar policies.

However, it would have been exceedingly difficult if not impossible for Wilson to have presided over such a war effort. His administration could not command the society and the economy because of administrative weakness and the less than overwhelming popular support for the war; instead, the administration had to resort to exhortation and a shrill war cry in order to buttress the essentially voluntarist principles underlying the mobilization. Hence the administration's emphasis on national morale and the duties of the great mass of citizens rather than the internationalism and rights of the progressive minority.[36] The necessity of this emphasis during the war, furthermore, was quite consistent with the views of Wilson as well as those of more reactionary elements in the Democratic Party, elements that he chose to have represented in the cabinet by Albert Burleson and Thomas Gregory. The conservative reaction against progressive dissenters during the war marked yet another fault line in Wilson's coalition.

Ultimately it was his failure to dissolve these cleavages that led to the Republican victories. Democrats commenting on the elections generally agreed that the party's major problem was the argument (as it was abbreviated and emphasized by a frustrated Joe Tumulty) that "Kitchin, Dent and

Clark are great liabilities. Too much Southern domination. Failure to fix the price of cotton. *We must fight Kitchin. We must fix the price of cotton.*"[37]

Tumulty's analysis has since been affirmed by Seward Livermore and David Burner. They have demonstrated that the Democratic Party lost the crucial seats in the wheat-growing regions of the Midwest and Great Plains, losses that no doubt reflected the resentment of farmers who had to sell their crop for controlled prices while their cotton-growing counterparts in the South were left free to profit. The Republican gains in the wheat belt could also be explained in part by the mass defection of the many German-Americans in the region. Needless to say, after eighteen months of war against their homeland and persecution of similar duration that appeared to be sponsored by the administration, these voters were even less likely to support Wilson and the Democrats than they had been in 1916.[38] But regardless of whether one accepts the wheat or the hyphen thesis for explaining Democratic losses in the Midwest, or some combination thereof, each scenario involves voting behavior based upon sectional or ethnocultural grievances, and thus they both undermine Wilson's programmatic assumptions concerning the responsiveness of the electorate to the issues as the president defined them.

Despite Wilson's attempt to make the congressional elections of 1918 hinge on what he saw as the most pressing and relevant national concerns, especially the shape that the impending peace treaty should take, in the end control of the new Congress turned on the basis of bloody-shirt memories, ethnocultural loyalties, and regional economic grievances, all of which were carefully stoked by the opposition. Wilson failed to animate the voters to respond to his issues, and he was unable to prevent his party from being riven by the sort of centrifugal forces, arising from what he considered malformed public opinion, that had long worked against the construction of durable and harmonious majority coalitions in the American electorate. Wilson himself acknowledged as much a few months later, when he gave his own postmortem of the election to the Democratic National Committee. Citing the divisions and feuding within the Democratic camp during the war, he observed that "in assessing the cause of our defeat we ought to be perfectly frank and admit that the country was not any more sure of us than it ought to be." Only when the Democrats proved themselves to be a party united on policies and underlying principles, Wilson continued, would it again receive the voters' trust.[39]

Perhaps Wilson was judging himself and his compatriots too severely: the demise of the Democrats as a governing party was to be expected, given both the tumultuous circumstances of the war, over which he had little control, and the difficulties that presidents have typically encountered in mid-term elections. Viewed in this light, the Democratic demise in 1918 is unexceptional. However, insofar as Wilson assumed that the president had the power to realign the electorate and to exercise simultaneously party and national leadership without serious complications, the elections of 1918 stood as an overwhelming refutation, not just of his party but also of his program. Worse still, these elections put both the party and the program, along with the policy that Wilson was most concerned with, the establishment of the League of Nations, on the road to even greater ruin.

NINE

Wilson, Lodge, and the Treaty Controversy

During the interbranch struggle over the Versailles Treaty, Wilson took the bad political situation resulting from the 1918 elections and made it worse. Breaking the taboo on sitting presidents traveling abroad, Wilson spent more than six months in Europe heading up the U.S. delegation at the peace negotiations, essentially forsaking all forms of domestic leadership.[1] He also refused to select a senator or an influential member of the Republican Party to accompany him to Paris, even though he eventually would need to secure a two-thirds majority vote for ratification in the Republican-controlled Senate. Despite the pronounced objections of more than a third of the senators, Wilson insisted on including the League of Nations Covenant in the Versailles Treaty. When he finally presented the treaty to the Senate on July 10, 1919, he gave it to them as a fait accompli, asking rhetorically, "Dare we reject it and break the heart of the world?"[2] Thereafter, Wilson would not compromise his demand for unreserved ratification of the treaty by the Senate, even after it was clear that it would not be forthcoming. In the final showdown, he lashed out at his opponents with increasingly strident rhetoric on a monthlong swing across the country, but the tour only hardened the opposition in the Senate. It also decimated Wilson's physical and mental health, ruining any possibility of a constructive resolution to the treaty fight.

Scholars have developed a number of explanations for the abject failure of Wilson's leadership in 1919. Insofar as the clash between Wilson and his Senate opponents was one of foreign policy visions—the president's liberal internationalism versus the more traditional nationalism or isolationism of the senators—Wilson might well have tried to take the nation in a direction that it was not yet prepared to go.[3] Lloyd Ambrosius has refined this argument by pointing out a basic contradiction in Wilson's foreign policy vision, namely, the assumption that the United States could enter into an effective,

universal system of collective security and somehow retain its historical in-
sulation from—and ability to act unilaterally in—world politics.[4] Another
explanation holds that in fact Henry Cabot Lodge and his Republican colleagues in the Senate opposed the president not because of legitimate policy
differences but for reasons of old-fashioned partisanship.[5] Taking a different
tack, Alexander George and Juliette George argue that Lodge was more a
psychological than a partisan tormentor of Wilson, a cunning father figure
whom the president could not slay. The debacle in 1919, they maintain, resulted from the final disintegration of Wilson's insecure psyche.[6] Jeffrey Tulis
argues in contrast that Wilson was brought down not by the contradictions
of his personality but by those of the rhetorical presidency he had created.
The rhetoric that Wilson used to defend his treaty at state fairgrounds and
whistle-stops only produced a backlash in the Senate.[7] Finally, a group of
scholars led by Arthur Link have concluded on the basis of Wilson's medical
records, some of which have only recently come to light, that the problems
in his leadership in 1919 stemmed from his failing health, which affected
him well before and certainly after he suffered the crippling stroke in October.[8]

No doubt all of these factors have to be included in a comprehensive
account of Wilson's downfall in 1919. For the purposes of this book, however, it is worth exploring the extent to which the problematic nature of his
program stands as the common denominator. Although multifaceted in origin, Wilson's demise was hastened considerably by his convictions about the
president's "very absolute" control of U.S. foreign relations, an understanding that was especially bold when it came to the treaty-making power and
that was diametrically opposed to the views of Henry Cabot Lodge and
other opponents of unreserved ratification in the Senate. Wilson's defeat at
the hands of Lodge and his colleagues punctuated his long and increasingly
bitter struggle with Congress over the control of foreign and national security policy.

I

To gain a sense of Wilson's understanding of the president's treaty-making
powers, it is worth going back to his earliest writings, in which the young
political scientist had portrayed the president as little more than the chief
civil servant, one who normally had to approach the Senate as a servant
approached his master. Despite Wilson's low regard for the presidency at this
time, he was nevertheless prepared to argue in *Congressional Government* that
the president could overcome the frequently demonstrated "treaty-*marring*
power" of the Senate and force it to ratify treaties in the form presented by

means of "his initiative in negotiation, which affords him a chance to get the country into such scrapes, so pledged in the view of the world to certain courses of action, that the Senate hesitates to bring about the appearance of dishonor which would follow its refusal to ratify the rash promises or to support the indiscreet threats of the Department of State."[9]

Also, recall that in *Constitutional Government,* having acquired a much fuller appreciation of the need for and power of presidential leadership, particularly in foreign affairs, Wilson affirmed his reading of the executive's power to make treaties in even stronger terms. Although he acknowledged that "the President cannot conclude a treaty with a foreign power without the consent of the Senate," he went on to contend that the president "may guide every step of diplomacy, and to guide diplomacy is to determine what treaties must be made, if the faith and prestige of the government are to be maintained. He need disclose no step of negotiation until it is complete, and when in any critical matter it is completed the government is virtually committed. Whatever its disinclination, the Senate may feel itself committed also."[10]

Wilson's belief that it was both appropriate and possible for the president to control the negotiation and ratification of treaties was only reinforced by the nature of the policy dispute in which he was involved. Over the course of World War I, Wilson had grown more and more convinced of the need for a union of nations that could provide a forum for the peaceful airing and resolution of international disputes, a league resting ultimately upon a mutual pledge among member states to help defend each other from external aggression.[11] In the ratification struggle, Wilson plausibly insisted that if the regime of collective security he envisioned was going to work, it would require the full, resonant support of the nation holding the most power after the ravaging war, namely, the United States. Were the Senate to delimit the extent to and the circumstances in which the United States would rally behind the league, and the issue of reservations essentially boiled down to this, it stood to reason that other member-states would also reduce their commitments, intangibly if not formally. The system of collective security would thus never take root.[12]

Wilson's psychobiographical interpreters point to his refusal to let the senators modify the Versailles Treaty as the best evidence of his irrational behavior in 1919.[13] However, Wilson's unstinting refusal appears reasonable when viewed in light of his long-held convictions about the president's prerogatives in treaty-making and his judgment that the policy he considered essential for the nation's peace and security, not to mention the world's, depended on his exercising those prerogatives to the utmost. This is not to say that the unfortunate stubbornness and self-righteousness that Wilson was prone to did not figure into the treaty fight in 1919, only that their emergence might better be depicted as an effect rather than a cause of his dispute with his Senate opponents. The senators' unstinting and direct challenge to his understanding of his prerogatives and to the imperatives of his foreign policy infuriated him, amplifying aspects of his personality that he had previously been able to keep in check.

The intertwined debates between Wilson and the senators over constitutional powers and foreign policy ultimately hinged on Article 10 of the League of Nations Covenant. It read as follows: "The Members of the League undertake to respect and preserve as against external aggression the territorial integrity and existing political independence of all Members of the League. In case of any such aggression or in case of any threat or danger of such aggression the Council shall advise upon the means by which this obligation shall be fulfilled."[14]

At a White House lunch with Lodge and the members of the Senate Foreign Relations Committee on August 19, 1919, at which Wilson was trying to soften the opposition to the treaty, the president stated that he was essentially the author of the controversial provision. Wilson believed that a mechanism such as that provided by Article 10 was necessary for the success of the system of collective security that he saw the league establishing; indeed, he termed it the "very backbone of the whole Covenant." Were the Senate to modify the provision in any significant way, the league "would be hardly more than an influential debating society."[15]

Lodge and the Senate opponents of the liberal internationalism that Wilson had imparted in the League Covenant likewise focused on Article 10. Speaking for many of his colleagues, Lodge told the Senate on August 12, 1919, of his "gravest objection" to the league: "Congress is granted by the Constitution the right to declare war, and nothing that would take the troops out of the Country at the bidding or demand of other nations should ever be permitted except through congressional action."[16] Article 10, as Lodge described it, would take this momentous choice out of Congress's hands, undermining the Constitution and, more broadly, the nation's sovereignty. Hence the necessity of attaching to the treaty a specific affirmation of the right of Congress to declare war, along with a statement that the United States would assume no military obligation under Article 10 until Congress did so.

Lodge's plan called for the Senate to participate substantively in the process of treaty-making, not simply in an up-or-down vote on ratification, in order to ward off the perceived encroachment on Congress's war power.

This line of attack enabled the senators opposed to unreserved ratification of the Versailles Treaty to seize upon the constitutional issues at stake in order to make their arguments on especially defensible grounds.

Wilson had long known that any treaty that would commit U.S. troops to hostilities without the consent of Congress would be a nonstarter politically and constitutionally.[17] He attempted to explain to Lodge and his committee that the League Covenant did not, on the face of it, contain any such provisions. Wilson pointed out that the United States would always be represented on the council of the league and therefore would be in a position to veto any resolutions by the council recommending the use of force, which required a unanimous vote of the members. Even then, the council could only "advise upon" the moral obligations of member states; while duty bound, the nation was free internally to use its own constitutional procedures as it decided whether or how to meet the obligation. Congress thus retained the power to declare war. Article 10, Wilson proposed, was "binding in conscience only, not in law."[18]

For all the earnestness of Wilson's attempt to calm the constitutional sensitivities of the Senate regarding Congress's war power, it only made matters worse. The U.S. veto on the council would be deployed—or not—by an executive branch official, not a member of Congress. More important, as numerous senators pointed out, the president's easy reconciliation of the U.S. Constitution and the League Covenant seemed to undermine his prediction of the potential impact of the league. For if the United States and other nations were free to decide through their own political and constitutional mechanisms whether they would come to the aid of a beleaguered member-state, then the regime of collective security that Wilson championed already began to look like the mere debating society he warned it would become if reservations were placed on Article 10. Either the United States was obligated (morally or otherwise) to make war upon the advice of the league, in which case the Constitution was being violated (at least in spirit), or the United States had no obligation, in which case Wilson's league would be ineffectual and might well serve only to entangle the nation in an overarching and debilitating set of alliances.[19]

Wilson's insistence that the nation's obligations under Article 10 would be morally but not legally binding allowed him to subscribe to potentially contradictory ideas: that the United States would benefit from being interdependent with other nations in a system of collective security yet at the same time retain the right of independent action in foreign affairs. For his part, Lodge rejected the distinction between a legal and a moral obligation and refused to ignore the contradictions that would arise between the nation's sovereignty and its obligations to the league. Believing that the former should be paramount and secure, he and his allies in the Senate sought to delimit the latter.[20]

And the senators meant to do this formally in the instrument of ratification. In his luncheon with the Foreign Relations Committee, Wilson reversed his announced position and told Lodge and his colleagues that he would be open to Senate "interpretations" that did not qualify but only clarified the meaning of the Covenant, and that were not formally attached to the instrument of ratification.[21] With this announcement, he acknowledged the reality, recognized by Democrats as well as Republicans, that the treaty was not going to pass as it stood. However, the senators who Wilson was attempting to win over were not interested in merely clarifying meanings with informal interpretations but in attaching formal reservations to the treaty in order to specify, among other things, the circumstances in which the United States would assume an obligation under Article 10. The reservationists in the Senate, whether of the mild or strong variety, were not prepared to accept the limitations on their treaty-making prerogative and Congress's war power that Wilson's insistence on unqualified ratification implied.[22] Like Wilson, the Senate opponents of such a ratification were defending what they regarded as their prerogatives as much as they were their foreign policies, not least because they saw the former defense as the key to the latter.

II

It is plausible to conclude that the resort to constitutional arguments by senators opposed to Wilson's league was merely a disguise for their underlying partisan and personal grievances against the Democratic president. These grievances certainly had been stoked by Wilson's dominance during World War I and his appeal for a Democratic Congress at its conclusion. The opposition to unreserved ratification was overwhelmingly Republican, and it was almost exclusively the Republican senators who invoked the specter of constitutional usurpation by the president. What is more, Lodge, the Republican leader, was an inveterate partisan who admitted to friends he hated Wilson.[23]

That Lodge and many of his GOP allies were out to get Wilson goes a long way toward explaining why the treaty was defeated. However, this fact does not discredit the validity or the influence of the constitutional arguments they brought to bear against the president and his league. To propose that arguments that evidently have arisen from underlying political disputes or even personal hatreds are somehow not really "constitutional" is to misconstrue the nature of the Constitution itself. The validity of an executive or legislative interpretation of the separation of powers does not ultimately depend on the motives of the politician making it. Indeed, the Founders intended and hoped that officeholders would be compelled by their own interests and ambitions to perceive and ward off interbranch encroachments on their institutions, i.e., that they would make political use of the separation of powers and in the process defend and preserve the arrangement. Witness the imperative of *Federalist* 51: "Ambition must be made to counteract ambition. The interest of the man must be connected with the constitutional rights of the place."[24]

When the separation of powers is seen in this light, as a constitutional arrangement intended to be thoroughly political in its functioning, accusations of encroachment are no less constitutional if they are generated in part or even completely by narrow partisan motives. In the end, the hearing granted to arguments about the separation of powers depends upon the acts or decisions being questioned and whether they are readily defensible in terms of constitutional precedents and principles. In this respect, the Constitution is a standard that the scoundrel and the man of integrity alike can appeal to with similar resonance in certain circumstances.[25]

Although genuine constitutional convictions are not necessary to make an effective constitutional argument, when the convictions of those upholding a traditional interpretation are real and pronounced, those attempting to reinterpret the Constitution through an expansive reading face a particularly zealous opponent. Such a man was Henry Cabot Lodge, Wilson's nemesis in the treaty fight. Without disregarding the ill will that Lodge had for Wilson, the senator's constitutional conservatism also drove him to stand against the president.

Lodge's concern for the integrity of the Founders' Constitution was unstinting. In 1912, it had led to his denunciation of the program for direct democracy advocated by his close friend, Theodore Roosevelt.[26] Subsequently, over the course of Wilson's presidency, Lodge had grown increasingly alarmed by what he perceived as the president's efforts to override and even disregard the separation of powers. Lodge's constitutional objections to Wilson's leadership figured prominently in the senator's criticism of the administration's shipping bill in 1915 and its exclusive framing of war legislation in 1917. Wilson's October 1918 appeal for a Democratic Congress appeared to Lodge to confirm the worst of his suspicions in this regard: Wilson had finally "thrown off the mask."[27] The reply to Wilson's appeal that Lodge coauthored with the Republican leadership in Congress made a point of promising to check this trend and to reestablish the independence and initiative of the legislature. Reflecting on the subsequent Republican capture of Congress, Lodge wrote to a friend that it was "a great victory for Constitutional Government, as well as for the Republican Party."[28] At long last, he and his party colleagues were in a position to uphold the separation of powers, and on November 26, 1918, he reported with satisfaction and hope to a friend that "the first thing the Republican Conference did when it met the other day was to pass a resolution that Congress should assert and exercise its normal constitutional functions. I think the new Congress will do it and will have some Democratic help in doing it."[29]

Of all the "normal constitutional functions" that Lodge was expecting Congress to exercise, none was more crucial than the Senate's playing an integral role in the upcoming peace negotiations. Lodge laughed at Wilson's assertion in *Constitutional Government* that a president could ignore the Senate during the negotiation of a treaty and then present it with a fait accompli that it would have little choice but to ratify. In the Senate on December 21, 1918, Robert LaFollette, who like Lodge also wanted to expose what he saw as the president's mounting usurpation, quoted derisively from this passage in the book. "Let timid souls then take courage and be cheerful," Lodge declared after LaFollette was finished. "There is nothing either in law or good manners or custom which stands in the way of advice from the Senate to the Executive charged with initiating and carrying on negotiations when the Senate thinks advice desirable." Indeed, Lodge subsequently declared that "in the present unparalleled situation the right of the Senate to advise as to a treaty becomes a solemn, an imperative, duty."[30]

History suggested as much. As Lodge pointed out, several presidents, including Washington, Jackson, and Lincoln, had sought the Senate's advice about treaty negotiations and kept it well informed of their progress. President McKinley had even named three senators, one of them a Democrat, as delegates to the peace conference with Spain. Lodge did not insist, as many senators did, that Wilson was obligated to follow McKinley's example with the Paris peace conference, though he noted that it would certainly be helpful and bode well for ratification (as it was and did in 1898).[31]

What Lodge did insist upon was the Senate's prerogative to participate in the treaty negotiations, if not through senatorial delegates or through advice granted to the president upon his request, then through statements undertaken by senators on their own initiative or through formal resolutions of the whole body as to what sort of peace they would find acceptable as equal holders of the treaty-making power under the Constitution.[32] Indeed, after Lodge discussed the Senate's right to play an independent role in treaty-making in his speech of December 21, 1918, he went on to offer a preliminary critique of the foreign policy goals that Wilson appeared intent upon realizing in Paris. With this speech Lodge fully intended to send a message abroad, a message to the negotiators from other nations who would be sitting down at the table with Wilson, and it no doubt reached them.[33] Just over two months later, in early March 1919, Lodge forced Wilson's hand at the peace table in an even more dramatic fashion by engineering the Round Robin letter, in which thirty-nine Republican senators—more than enough to prevent ratification—publicly announced that the Versailles Treaty as it then stood was unacceptable to them. Significantly, the letter opened with a ringing assertion that it was a constitutional function of the Senate "to advise and consent to, or dissent from, the ratification of any treaty of the United States" and subsequently asserted that the Round Robin itself was understood by its signatories as "a discharge of [the Senate's] constitutional duty of advice in regard to treaties."[34]

Lest Lodge's December 21 speech or the Round Robin be seen as mere partisanship dressed up in constitutional garb, consider the following passage:

> The power of the Senate in making treaties has always been held, as the Constitution intended, to be equal to and co-ordinate with that of the President, except in the initiation of a negotiation. . . . The Senate has the right to amend, and this right it has always exercised largely and freely. It is also clear that any action taken by the Senate is part of the negotiation, just as much so as the action of the President through the Secretary of State. *In other words, the action of the Senate upon a treaty is not merely to give sanction to the treaty, but is an integral part of the treaty making, and may be taken at any stage of a negotiation.*[35]

What makes this passage particularly revealing is that it is taken from an essay that Lodge first published in 1902, in which he had sought to refute the assumption held by John Hay, the Republican secretary of state, among others, that the Senate had no power to take part in the actual making of treaties. During the McKinley, Roosevelt, and Taft administrations, Lodge angered fellow Republicans in the executive branch by insisting on the Senate's prerogatives and working against treaties that he believed did not respect those prerogatives.[36] That Lodge would do likewise with a Democrat in the White House was therefore quite predictable—and not because of the president's party affiliation.

III

Ironically, in *Constitutional Government*, Wilson had written that presidents might very well have to treat the Senate in the fashion that Lodge and his colleagues in the upper house were demanding. Wilson understood that the special constitutional duties of the Senate made the institution more inclined to take issue with the president, especially when it was controlled by the opposition party. At the same time, the senators' staggered, six-year terms made them much less susceptible to any form of presidential pressure. Public appeals from the White House intended to coerce the Senate were likely to backfire.[37]

Therefore, Wilson wrote in 1908, if the president faced a recalcitrant Senate, he might well follow a more conciliatory course,

> which one or two Presidents of unusual political sagacity have followed, with the satisfactory results that were to have been expected. He may himself be less stiff and offish, may himself act in the true spirit of the Constitution, and establish intimate relations of confidence with the Senate on his own initiative, not carrying his plans to completion and then laying them in final form before the Senate, to be accepted or rejected, but keeping himself in confidential communication with the leaders of the Senate while his plans are in course, when their advice will be of service to him and his information of the greatest service to them, in order that there may be veritable counsel and a real accommodation of views instead of a final challenge and contest.[38]

Far from driving Wilson to go over the heads of his Senate opponents, at one level his understanding of the appropriate form of presidential relations with this body bid him to engage it in common counsel.

At various points in time, Wilson sought to act in accordance with his own prescription. When he and Colonel House were considering potential members of the U.S. delegation to the Paris peace talks, for example, they mulled over the selection of some delegates from the Senate and prominent Republicans such as Elihu Root or William Howard Taft.[39] In February 1919, when Wilson returned briefly from Paris, he attempted to duck out of a public speech upon disembarking in Boston—Lodge's home—that Tumulty had lined up; Wilson was concerned about "the impression on the hill" (i.e., in Congress) that such a speech would make.[40] On this visit, Wilson also met with the members of the House and Senate Foreign Relations Committees at the White House for a cordial dinner and an extended discussion of the league. The *New York Times* reported of the meeting that "the course of the President tonight seemed to have removed from the minds of some of those who were present the idea that he was trying to push the campaign for the League without the advice and consent of the Senate."[41] Finally, in July 1919, after returning from his last journey to Europe, Wilson held back from the publicity tour that many were assuming he would undertake immediately. Given the potential backlash that a swing around the circle might generate, he knew that it could only be a last resort, and an uncertain one at that. Over the next few weeks, Wilson conducted over twenty one-on-one meetings with mild reservationists at the White House in the hope of persuading them to drop their plans.[42]

However, these endeavors could not produce any genuine conciliation or consensus because, in the end, Wilson was not prepared to share in any significant way the treaty-making power that he was convinced was rightfully his and upon which his policy depended. Hence no senators served on the peace commission, Wilson's February return to the United States began and ended with highly charged speeches criticizing his Senate opponents,[43] and the attempt at "common counsel" in July and August 1919 was curtailed by the "pitiless publicity" of September's speaking tour.

The self-defeating tour was not the inevitable product of Wilson's rhetorical presidency. Rather, it marked an unsuccessful resolution of a contradiction in his program. His determination to exercise absolute control of the treaty-making power was inconsistent with his recognition that the Senate was in a position and often inclined to thwart such presidential control—and could not be subdued with popular appeals. Wilson nevertheless proceeded with his attempt to set the course for American national security policy, as he had essayed before and during U.S. involvement in World War I. That unqualified American participation in the League of Nations, deemed by Wilson as essential to the nation's well-being, not to mention the world's, depended on his exercising such control only made him that much more determined. The irony, or rather the tragedy, of Wilson's defeat was that he could have predicted it himself.

IV

On September 26, 1919, after having traveled some 8,000 miles and delivered thirty-six major speeches and numerous shorter addresses in little more than three weeks' time, Wilson collapsed under the physical and emotional strain of his tour.[44] With the remainder of the tour canceled, he returned to Washington to convalesce, only to suffer a crippling stroke one week later. From that point forward, Wilson was in the grip of a disease that affected his mind and emotions as well as his body, and he became steadily more recalcitrant. The moment of compromise, if there ever had been one, had passed.[45]

Wilson's stroke raises the question of whether the treaty debacle was not simply a historical accident, the result of the president's incapacitation at the very moment that he might have forged a viable compromise on Capitol Hill, as he had so many times before during his presidency. The editors of *The Papers of Woodrow Wilson* and several medical historians, pointing to recently discovered medical records, conclude that Wilson's health had begun to impinge on his leadership even before the devastating stroke in October 1919. In particular, a viral infection that Wilson suffered in Paris in April 1919, and a minor stroke that evidently befell him in July, in the midst of his meetings with the mild reservationists, are seen by these scholars as having permanently diminished Wilson's emotional and mental capacities, not to mention his physical health.[46]

However, even if Wilson's health was deteriorating before October 1919, it is not easy to blame it for his failure to secure Senate ratification of the Versailles Treaty. Given the policy that he was pushing for, and his understanding of how the president should exercise his treaty-making power, his leadership was understandable and quite consistent with his objectives both before and after his illnesses in April and July. It is highly unlikely, for example, that even a healthy Woodrow Wilson would have made the key compromise that the mild reservationists were demanding—a reaffirmation of Congress's exclusive right to declare war formally attached to the treaty itself—without taking his case to the people. And after the president took his case to the public, the angry reaction in the Senate as much as his collapse effectively ruled out a compromise.

It is also important to recognize how Wilson's own expansive conception of his office contributed to the erosion and eventual devastation of his health. Wilson believed he could personally exercise "very absolute" control of U.S. foreign policy and set up the League of Nations. These were huge objectives, to be sure, but fitting for a man convinced that his office made him "one of the great powers of the world."[47] Wilson's expansive conception of the presidency led to his undertaking the extended journeys abroad to head up the American delegation at the peace negotiations; to his chairing the evening meetings of the commission that would draft the League of Nations Covenant in Paris; to his entering into round after round of frustrating negotiations with the senators; and, finally, to his embarking on a desperate stumping campaign when these negotiations failed. He had quipped in *Constitutional Government* that in light of the mounting demands on the presidency and the multiple roles that the inhabitant of the office had to perform, only wise and well-conditioned athletes could do the job. Even the strongest Olympian would have been hard-pressed to endure unscathed the ordeal that Wilson subjected himself to in 1919.

The bitter end of the treaty fight found the sick and embattled president returning to his earlier, critical judgments on the Founders' separation of powers and the independent executive office it secured. Wilson's remarkable reliance upon and defense of these arrangements during his prosecution of the war effort gave way in peacetime to his old longing for responsible government in the United States. In August 1919, before he began his fateful tour on behalf of the league, he discussed with family members the weaknesses of the presidency that had once again become all too apparent to him. "The office in and of itself is not one of the most powerful of offices," Wilson insisted, especially when compared with that of the British prime minister, who

> can at any time dissolve Parliament and appeal directly back to the British people, and it is this knowledge on the part of Parliament . . . that undoubtedly whips Parliament into supporting the Prime Minister in many things in which they would not otherwise support him. And thus he has a hold on Parliament utterly unlike and superior to the hold which the President has on Congress. Suppose . . . I could dissolve Congress now and appeal to the people to support the Treaty, is there any question that the Treaty would be immediately ratified? I would not have to dissolve Congress. The mere fact that I had the right to do it would bring Congress around at once.[48]

How could the impasse be resolved? How could public opinion be brought to bear on the fifty-three senators who had refused to support unreserved ratification when the treaty was put to a vote on November 19, 1919? From his sickbed in December 1919, Wilson regretted that "the Constitution provides no method or machinery for such a reference." With the help of his wife and Joseph Tumulty, he came up with a proposal that called for the fifty-three senators to resign and run again for their seats in a special election. If, as Wilson was convinced was the case, the vast majority of the voters supported his version of the league, then the deadlock would be broken. On the other hand, if a majority of the offending senators were reelected, Wilson would institute his resignation scheme from 1916: he would appoint a Republican leader as secretary of state, he and Vice President Marshall would resign, and by the rules of succession there effectively would be a new government in the parliamentary sense of the word.[49]

Wilson's far-fetched plan to resolve the impasse with the Senate—which assumed, among other things, that duly elected senators would willingly resign their seats at the president's request—was quickly dropped.[50] The plan that Wilson resorted to next, again with Tumulty's help, was somewhat more practical in design and was put forward in a most conspicuous fashion: a presidential letter to fellow Democrats banqueting on Jackson Day. The Democratic faithful who assembled in two separate halls in Washington on January 8, 1920, heard the president's letter declare that U.S. participation in the league was essential for world peace. "We cannot rewrite this treaty," Wilson argued. "We must take it without changes which alter its meaning, or leave it." Asserting that his opponents in the Senate had defied a popular majority and were responsible for the deadlock, Wilson proposed that the next election be made "a great and solemn referendum" on unreserved ratification of the treaty.[51]

The best analysis of Wilson's Jackson Day appeal can be found in a private memorandum written shortly thereafter by his secretary of state, Robert Lansing. Assuming—which Lansing did not—that Wilson's version of the treaty enjoyed the support of a majority, how could voters, with their own multiplicity of concerns, be expected to concentrate on the one issue that obsessed the president? And the league was not a clear-cut issue given the "several grades of reservations, interpretive, slightly modifying, radical, and nullifying." Moreover, Lansing looked over the list of senators—only one-third of the body—who were up for reelection in 1920 and noted that even "the greatest Democratic landslide in all history would never carry enough seats to give the necessary two-thirds." Therefore, it was "nonsense . . . to talk about a popular decision at the polls." Indeed, attempting to force the Senate to submit to unreserved ratification in such a fashion was akin to butting "one's head against a granite wall." Lansing concluded that if the Democratic Party adopted Wilson's approach, "it is beaten already. . . . whether he wants to or not the President *must* compromise or he will wreck the party."[52] But if there ever had been a possibility that Wilson would come around to this reality, it had collapsed with his health.

Lansing's warning on the need for compromise resonated with the views of congressional Democrats, who had been urging Wilson to soften his stance on the treaty.[53] Circumstances unrelated to the league issue made Wilson's hard line particularly burdensome. Among other things, the administration was no longer dispensing patronage to ease the sting of the party whip. Wilson had stuck to his decision in late 1916 to classify the first-through third-class postmasterships, thereby drying up the chief source of administration patronage. He also had kept his vow to stop letting political considerations dictate appointments in the upper reaches of his administration. It is worth noting, for example, that three men who held perhaps the most powerful positions in Wilson's war machine and who made the most controversial decisions—food administrator Herbert Hoover, fuel administrator Harry Garfield, and chief price-fixer Robert Brookings—were all nominal Republicans.

Wilson's progressivism may have cleared his conscience and halted the criticism of his administration by otherwise supportive reformers, but it rankled the regulars. In December 1919, after hearing that yet another Republican was being considered for a top post in the administration, William Gibbs McAdoo warned against it, reporting what he had learned in his travels across the country since leaving the cabinet a year earlier: "I think the Democratic position has been enormously weakened by the great number of appointments to highly honorable places which the Administration has made of prominent Republicans. . . . they were justified for the war purpose, but the rank and file of the party do not understand this, and they certainly will not understand if the policy is continued in peace time." Neither were the rank and file happy with the classification of postmasterships, which was carried out with an almost spiteful efficiency by the postmaster general. Burleson's newfound zeal as a civil service reformer surprised and alarmed McAdoo, Tumulty, and other prominent Wilsonians, men with whom Burleson once had joined in dividing up the spoils of the administration. One of these men, Robert Woolley, complained to Colonel House in June 1919 that "[Burleson] must resign—or be forced to—if there is to be a shred of the Democratic Party left to go into the campaign of 1920."[54]

It is difficult to estimate the extent to which the new patronage policy contributed to the surge of opposition that Wilson met with from congressional Democrats during the war years or to the electoral demise of the party in 1918 and especially in 1920. But no doubt his sudden adherence to his principles in this regard did not help his ongoing efforts to line up Democratic votes in Congress and the electorate. As the more traditional politicians in Wilson's inner circle—and the president himself, in his more realistic moments—knew, there was a general, albeit rough, correlation between the normal distribution of spoils and party regularity. When it came to patronage, it appears that Wilson was both damned when he did and damned when he did not.

At the same time that Wilson was denying congressional Democrats the spoils that many of them believed were rightfully theirs, he also was forcing on them his exclusive focus on the nation's foreign relations. The Democratic Party, like the nation, was increasingly buffeted by the social and economic turbulence caused by the rapid demobilization. Wilson's evident reluctance to create and maintain administrative bodies that might have assisted with postwar reconstruction of the American economy and the remarkable dearth of domestic policy initiatives by the White House amid the tremendous unrest indicated to observers in and outside of the administration that the president was out of touch with the bread-and-butter issues most important to the masses.[55]

Ironically, Wilson's personal convictions about domestic policy were continuing to shift to the left. He still talked with friends and associates about the need for the government to control, among other things, railroads, mines, and electric power, and he now believed in the need for "industrial democracy" as a prerequisite for "political democracy."[56] Wilson also remained fully aware of the political benefits that would be within reach if the Democratic Party undertook a progressive socioeconomic agenda.[57] But he refused to initiate or oversee domestic legislation that might realign voters.

Wilson was determined to have the treaty ratified first. Just as war legislation took precedence over domestic reform in 1917–1918, now the peace treaty did. Wilson told legislators that the economic problems of the country were primarily due to the unratified treaty and the resulting ambiguity of the nation's foreign relations. By making the treaty the top priority, he was hoping that the increasing demands for domestic action would work to force the Senate to ratify it quickly, if only to get it out of the way.[58] His hope, of course, was not realized, but the political costs of this policy brinkmanship soon would be.

Wilson did everything he could throughout 1920 to bring about the "great and solemn referendum." In March, before the treaty came up for one last vote, Wilson dashed off another resounding public letter in which he ruled out any formal reservation indicating that U.S. fulfillment of its obligations under Article 10 depended on Congress exercising its war power.[59] So long as he held to this position, the Senate would not ratify the treaty, and there the issue stood. Sensing that the president's unyielding stance would not have the beneficial effect in November that he was assuming it would, several party advisers urged him to compromise, as he had done so adeptly with various progressive initiatives before the 1916 election. In his diary, Josephus Daniels paraphrased one such conversation, and Wilson's response to it, at a cabinet meeting on April 20: "Burleson wanted W. W. to send treaty to Senate and say what reservations he would accept. Otherwise people thought it was his stubbornness that killed the treaty. . . . Burleson said three issues would outweigh treaty—Liquor, Taxes, Cost of Living. Meredith thought it would be good tactics. So did Palmer. WW said he would not play for position. No time for tactics, time to stand square."[60]

Of course, the man who was determined to "stand square" was sick; a healthy Wilson might well have been more apt to consider the electoral situation, as he had in endorsing direct democracy in 1910–1911 and social welfare and labor legislation in 1916. But even if healthy, Wilson may have been just as unyielding. At no time in his presidency had he hesitated in forcing his strongly held diplomatic views upon his party, disregarding their protests and pointing to the inescapable imperatives of world politics as he did so.

The Versailles Treaty fight thus laid bare a problem in Wilson's ideal of interpretive statesmanship. Three factors, he believed, should push a statesman to alter his positions: changes in or a better grasp of public opinion, the unfolding logic of reform ideas, and the leader's experience in power. Wilson's unstated assumption was that these three factors would always push in the same direction. With his conversion to direct democracy in 1910–1911, and to advanced progressivism in 1916, they generally did; i.e., with these shifts Wilson was simultaneously "fishing for a majority," to use his phrase, following certain premises to their conclusions, and reconciling his views with the lessons he had learned while in office. With the league, trends in public opinion pointed toward a compromise, but Wilson could not or would not acknowledge this because his grasp of the logic of collective security, and his experience as chief diplomat and commander in chief, both pointed in the direction of unqualified American participation.

Much to Wilson's ire, James Cox, the Democratic Party's presidential candidate in 1920, bowed to the public's increasing dissatisfaction with the president's stance on unreserved ratification and adopted a supportive but decidedly ambiguous position on the issue. Cox's waffling frustrated Wilson's hope of making the election a clean vote on the league. That being said, in light of Cox's retreat and his nonetheless massive defeat at the hands of the Republican Party and its candidate, Warren Harding, who were clearly opposed to the unaltered Article 10, the returns of 1920 amounted to a resounding "no" on the question of whether the majority of the people were behind Wilson on this issue.[61] Secretary of State Robert Lansing's warning that Wilson's quest for a solemn referendum on the league was the political equivalent of beating one's head on a granite wall proved to be all too prophetic.

᙭ Conclusion

Wilson's party and foreign policy may have suffered a massive setback in the 1920 elections, but his theoretical program for responsible government emerged unscathed, at least judging by its long-standing influence on American political science. Throughout the twentieth century, political scientists have evaluated the workings of American government by measuring them against Wilson's ideal, in which a responsible party, led by a masterful president, integrates the separated legislative and executive powers and brings coherence and effectiveness to the policy-making process. Only in the past decade or so has Wilson's program been seriously called into question. The growing doubts have been prompted by the fact that it cannot account very well for divided government, in which the two parties split control of the executive and legislative branches. Since Eisenhower, this pattern has been the norm rather than the exception. To Charles O. Jones, a professed Madisonian, the possibility and even the normality of divided government is but one more piece of evidence demonstrating that the dominant "presidency-centered, party government perspective" is a hindrance to understanding and evaluating the dynamics of what he terms "the separated system." Even James Sundquist, long a vocal Wilsonian, acknowledges that "those who still cherish the idea of party government have an obligation," namely, to retool the theory first developed by Wilson so that it can better account for the persistent realities of American politics.[1] But if Wilsonians hope to succeed in crafting their new synthesis, they will need to come to better terms with the political fortunes of Wilson's program from his day to our own.

As the preceding chapters indicate, Wilson's program began to falter not at midcentury, but much earlier, in his own presidency. To be sure, he established a highly effective method for the presidential leadership of legislation during the New Freedom period, in which he used carefully timed speeches on Capitol Hill to call forth each measure and focus public opinion on the key principles at stake, all the while working with and through legislative leaders to draw the bills out of Congress. But Wilson's skillful blending of public rhetoric and persuasion behind the scenes was not enough. He also had to rely on the dispensation of spoils and the legislative caucus, even though he had condemned these practices and predicted, rightly it turned out, that presidents could not sustain their use. And despite the impressive sweep of Wilson's interpretive statesmanship, the diversity of his coalition and the strains of the war kept him from fostering the realignment he had long deemed essential.

The war also brought to the fore the problems with Wilson's conception of "the two presidencies." While he believed in common counsel with his party's legislators in domestic affairs, he held that necessity dictated the executive could and should exercise "very absolute" control of the nation's foreign relations. He sought to do this amid the crisis of the World War. However, members of Congress, including, most significantly, many of the leaders and rank and file of his own party, were not prepared to cede to Wilson the control he presumed. He fought back against what he regarded as legislative encroachments on his office, using all the energy and independence and prerogatives of diplomacy and command that the separation of powers secured for him. He prevailed, at least during the hostilities, and American national security policy was the better for it. But as Wilson used and defended the separation of powers in this way, he repudiated the parliamentary ideal of responsible party government. He also spurred the institutional rivalry and jealousy between the presidency and Congress, thereby endangering Senate ratification of the Versailles Treaty. Desperate to maintain his exclusive grip on the nation's foreign affairs, Wilson lashed out at his Senate opponents on an extended speaking tour, destroying all hope for ratification in the process.

One of the many prices that Wilson had to pay for this failed rhetorical strategy, which amounted to a rejection of his own teaching and the example of his first term, was that it enabled his critics—then and now—to paint unbalanced portraits of his leadership. The defining moment in this regard came on July 22, 1920, when Senator Henry Cabot Lodge formally invited Warren Harding to be the Republican Party's candidate for president. After Lodge condemned Wilson's "scheme which would turn the Government of the United States into an autocracy based upon a plebiscite," he warned Harding in no uncertain terms that "the makers of the Constitution . . . strove to guard against either usurpation or trespass by one branch at the expense of the other two. In that spirit, we all know well, you will enter upon your great responsibility." Harding, the junior senator, accepted the implicit conditions on the nomination. As president, he would be an agent, not the principal, of a Republican Party dominated by legislators. "I believe in party government," Harding responded in his own inimitable way, "as distinguished from personal government, individual, autocratic, or what not."[2]

Of course, the irony is that Wilson's program—in its essence, before it was confounded by the alternative logic of the separation of powers—was fully aligned with Harding's premise that "party government" was superior to "personal government." That is why Wilson had come out against Albert Stickney's program in 1879 and Theodore Roosevelt's in 1912. That being said, the respective presidencies of Wilson and Harding made clear that they meant different things by "party government." For Wilson, this allowed, indeed required, the president to take an active leadership role in interpreting the party's principles and coordinating the legislative agenda. For Harding and for the Republican presidents who followed him into office in the 1920s, these concepts essentially meant deferring to their party brethren in Congress. As a result, Harding's defeat of Wilson led directly to what Wilfred Binkley termed a "renaissance of Congressional Government."[3]

It was left to Woodrow Wilson's assistant secretary of the navy to reassert the powers of the presidency. Political scientists have generally agreed that while the modern presidency was more or less fully developed by Franklin Roosevelt during the crises of the Great Depression and World War II, this development had its origins in the presidencies of Theodore Roosevelt and Woodrow Wilson. Franklin Roosevelt completed the augmentation and institutionalization of presidential power that his progressive predecessors had initiated.[4]

In the realms of foreign and national security policy, there is indeed great continuity across these three presidencies. Theodore Roosevelt, Woodrow Wilson, and Franklin Roosevelt held to the same expansive interpretation of presidential prerogatives in this regard. If Wilson's use of these prerogatives was more controversial, it was primarily because unlike Theodore Roosevelt he led the nation amid the turbulence of a global conflict, and unlike Franklin Roosevelt he did so before this expansive interpretation was legitimated in constitutional and political terms.[5]

But Wilson did not use a unilateral, presidentialist approach in his domestic leadership; the same cannot be said of the Roosevelts. Franklin Roosevelt used his cousin's model to drive the domestic agenda, having most of the key measures of the New Deal drawn up by the "brains trust" in his administration, after which he simply sent them down for ratification, frequently without warning, to the Democratic leadership in Congress. Franklin Roosevelt was more blatant, however, not always bothering with his cousin's pretense of covertly submitting administration bills via an ally in Congress. Also like Theodore Roosevelt, FDR came to conclude that the best way to line up votes for his domestic agenda was appealing over the heads of his party's legislators to the people at large. Indeed, as Sidney Milkis has demonstrated, in the wake of FDR's failed purge campaign in 1938, he gave up altogether on the idea of governing through his party, relying more and more exclusively on the personal aides, administrative experts, and ideological allies that had played such a crucial role in his presidency. Roosevelt's push for the establishment of the Executive Office of the President in 1939 made this strategy more feasible. So did a number of policies enacted during the New Deal (e.g., Social Security and agricultural subsidies) that transferred the loyalties and attention of voters from political parties to the administrative state over which Roosevelt presided.[6]

As a result of these changes, circumstances that Woodrow Wilson had long warned against—a government dominated by an executive unconstrained by any sense of collective responsibility—had for all practical purposes been established by Franklin Roosevelt's second term. Just as Warren Harding's presidency amounted to a practical repudiation of Wilson's program, so too did Franklin Roosevelt's, albeit from another direction.

Perhaps the best evidence that Franklin Roosevelt departed from Wilson's program is found in the Wilsonian critiques of Roosevelt's presidency that began to circulate in the early 1940s. Political scientists and reformers wasted little time in expressing dissatisfaction with the political order that Roosevelt established. On the one hand, despite the power that the president had aggrandized in the executive branch and in his own person, his estrangement from Congress, worsened by the retreat from party government, meant that the nation's legislative machinery remained adrift at a crucial moment in history. On the other hand, the concentration of power in the president was not combined with a more exacting accountability. Indeed, insofar as Roosevelt had consolidated his power by giving up on party government and a good working relationship with Congress, the president was less accountable than ever before, a situation that portended a dictatorship in the eyes of some observers.[7]

This critique produced two different kinds of remedies, both of which Woodrow Wilson had advocated at various points in his own career as a reformer. The first remedy called for instituting parliamentary-style cabinet government in the United States by amending the Constitution. This solution was advocated, in one form or another, by Harvard professor and New Deal adviser William Yandell Elliot, the journalist Henry Hazlitt, and State Department official Thomas K. Finletter. (Political scientist Edward Corwin issued a similar call for the creation of a joint executive-legislative cabinet, though he argued that this could be done without amending the Constitution.)[8]

The second remedy focused not on formal changes in presidential-congressional relations but rather on the development of more principled and programmatic political parties, which could then informally unite the separation of powers in a parliamentary fashion. The informal, party-based approach to responsible government quickly gained ascendance, no doubt because it was more in keeping with the movement toward behaviorialism that was then emerging in American political science, a movement that downplayed the importance of formal constitutional arrangements. E. E. Schattschneider's *Party Government,* published in 1942, emerged as an early treatise in the new line of political science. Schattschneider also had a hand in the most renowned presentation of the party government argument when he served on the drafting committee that produced "Toward a More Responsible Two-Party System," the 1950 report of the American Political Science Association's Committee on Political Parties.[9]

Schattschneider and his colleagues on the committee made no call for constitutional amendments to bring about responsible government in the United States, deeming such fundamental changes to be at once too difficult to attain and essentially unnecessary. Instead, the members of the committee held that the prospect of more responsible government ultimately hinged on an intellectual and cultural conversion on the part of the American people, arguing in their foreword that "the weaknesses of the American two-party system can be overcome as soon as a substantial part of the electorate wants it overcome." The committee proposed that the moment of conversion could be hastened by a series of party reforms designed to democratize the party organizations and sharpen the parties' focus on national issues and programs. These reforms would prepare the parties to serve as responsible instruments for translating majority will into national policy, on the one hand, and stimulate the voters' trust in and desire for programmatic party government, on the other.[10]

Evron Kirkpatrick and Austin Ranney have demonstrated that the Committee on Political Parties let its hopes for reform and normative judgments drift into and confound its empirical analysis. Among the resulting unsteady assumptions of this analysis were that a party system consisting of two ideologically coherent, programmatic parties could thrive amid the diversity of Madison's extended republic; that citizens would vote on the basis of well-reasoned judgments about what the alternative programs of two parties entailed for the future; and that the American people would eventually recognize and embrace the merits of responsible party government.[11]

The Committee on Political Parties thus relied on several assumptions that had been embodied in Wilson's program and demonstrated to be problematic during his presidency. Perhaps the committee might have reached different conclusions had it scrutinized the difficulty that Wilson experienced in his efforts to have the various factions of the Democratic Party adopt a coherent stand on national issues; to persuade citizens to transcend family traditions, ethnocultural concerns, and sectional grievances in the voting booth; and to dispel the criticism of the party discipline imposed by the Democratic Caucus during the New Freedom. But given the dedication of the Committee on Political Parties to the ideal of party government, its members more likely would have concluded that in Wilson's day the parties had yet to be sufficiently reformed. At midcentury, the potential power and legitimacy of democratic, national, and issue-oriented parties appeared to reformers to be untapped and closer at hand.

The ensuing decades, however, have indicated that no matter how "responsible" political parties are, they cannot galvanize the powers separated by the Constitution in the manner that Wilsonians desire. The shortcomings of the informal approach to constitutional change, which hamstrung Wilson as he sought to implement his program, have also limited contemporary reformers. Not that the party system has not been reformed. Indeed, many of the changes called for by the American Political Science Association (APSA) Committee on Political Parties, most notably the spread of the primary system, have since been adopted. The two major parties are now more democratic, homogeneous in their principles, and animated by issues of national policy than ever before.[12] However, by freeing up the candidates from the influence of party organizations and by increasing the ideological temper of the parties, party reform has in some ways worsened the collective action problem in American politics, bringing politicians into office who are simultaneously more individualistic and zealous.[13] Perhaps because of these ironic developments, Americans are no more convinced of the need to put the presidency and Congress into the hands of a group of like-minded officeholders than they were in Wilson's day. Indeed, in recent decades, the voters have tended to do the opposite, to divide control of the government between the increasingly polarized parties, leading some political scientists to suggest that rationally or not, voters have internalized the Madisonian model.[14]

In the wake of the failure of party reform to establish more responsible government in the United States, the other strand in the Wilsonian tradition, emphasizing the need to amend the Constitution's separation of powers, has enjoyed more prominence in the past two decades. The shift from party to constitutional remedies is reflected in the name of the organization that now serves as the redoubt for Wilsonians: the Committee on the Constitutional System. Political scientists James Sundquist and James MacGregor

Burns, former Secretary of the Treasury C. Douglas Dillon, and Lloyd Cutler, counsel to Presidents Carter and Clinton, are a few of the members who have been active in driving the committee's agenda. The committee's "Bicentennial Analysis of the American Political Structure," published in 1987, provides a common platform of changes that have been proposed elsewhere by its members. Although advocating further party and campaign finance reforms, the crux of the committee's recommendations involves the establishment of such parliamentary mechanisms as legislators serving in the cabinet and coincidental electoral terms for Congress and the president. Some members of the committee go so far as to advocate mechanisms that would allow for the calling of new elections in the face of an impasse between the branches.[15]

The Committee on the Constitutional System has returned to the amendments that the young Woodrow Wilson proposed, thus following the logic of the Constitution to its conclusion. Committee members recognize that the Constitution prevents the government and politics that they desire, so they are seeking to amend it. However, while the theoretical rigor of the committee is commendable, it is less than complete, and it runs into serious political difficulties.

The separation of powers, after all, is only one obstacle to responsible government in the United States. The various ethnocultural, regional, and economic fault lines in the American electorate—the historical precursors of which frustrated Woodrow Wilson's quest for a sustaining realignment—make it unlikely that a disciplined and programmatic two-party system will follow in the wake of the imposition of parliamentary mechanisms in Washington. Even though the earlier APSA Committee on Political Parties never came up with a feasible solution to this problem, it was correct in observing that the constitutional amendment of the separation of powers "would make sense only when the parties have actually demonstrated the strength they now lack . . . the experience of foreign countries suggests that the adoption of the cabinet system does not automatically result in an effective party system."[16]

Recent research in comparative politics validates this claim. When a parliamentary system of government is combined with a heterogeneous society, the result is often a multiparty system, coalition government, and an informal though nonetheless effective system of veto points among elites struggling to foster the modicum of consensus needed to govern. Leaders in parliamentary regimes of this sort experience many of the same difficulties in setting policy priorities, targeting resources, and imposing losses on organized interests that leaders attempting to govern in the United States have struggled with, Woodrow Wilson among them.[17]

Furthermore, the members of the Committee on the Constitutional System have yet to come to terms with the suspicion of centralized power, the antipartisanship, and the dislike of balancing individual rights against the public interest that continue to distinguish American political culture.[18] Here the members of the committee have followed the precedents of the APSA committee and Woodrow Wilson himself. The curious staying power of the resistance to responsible government, notwithstanding the best arguments of Wilson and subsequent reformers, indicates that the resistance is more than an artifact from a bygone era or the result of false consciousness, a dependent variable that can be swept away if the right reform program is found. Rather, the American aversion to responsible government is embodied in and emanates from one of the foremost independent variables in American politics, the Constitution itself. American political culture might thus be seen as the first line of defense of the Founders' Constitution against reforms imported from Great Britain.[19]

Sooner or later, the Committee on the Constitutional System, which continues to push the need for systematic change, has to confront the political impossibility of amending the separation of powers. While citizens are no doubt concerned about gridlocked government and irresponsible partisanship, the prospects for marshaling the tremendous amount of political capital needed to secure a series of constitutional amendments designed to centralize power in a majority party in Washington are now more remote than ever. Indeed, the one fundamental reform to enjoy support in recent years, term limits for members of Congress, is a whiggish measure intended to level, not enhance, political power in the national government.[20] The debate over constitutional reform thus comes full circle, back to the dilemma that Wilson first faced as a graduate student and was never able to resolve fully: formal amendment of the separation of powers appears to be a necessary precondition for the full establishment of responsible government in the United States, but barring an unforseen crisis, such a change is out of the question politically.

If it is not possible to amend the forms of the separation of powers, then Wilsonians might draw some solace from the evidence pointing to the drawbacks of doing so. The first is age-old: while the separation of powers might keep what one wants to happen from happening, it can also put a stop to what one opposes. Consider the example of a reformer who in 1993 reported that he was supportive of President Clinton's initiatives in reaching out to the 103d Congress. Yet he still held that constitutional reform was needed "to encourage cooperation between the branches, so that platforms can be enacted and implemented and the government held accountable for the results at the ensuing election." Two years later, however, during the 104th Congress, in which the House was controlled by a Republican majority that had presented a clear platform to the voters, this same Wilsonian acknowledged that there was something to be said for a system that "checks power" and "protects the poor and the vulnerable, as well as the environment, from the mean-spirited and reckless legions in the House of Representatives." [21]

It is also worth noting that the arguments of Wilson's formidable opponent, Sir Henry Maine, still echo in Westminster. Reformers in the United Kingdom, the polity long regarded as the model of responsible government by American reformers, also look across the Atlantic for their model. They hold up the autonomy of Congress, the independence of American politicians, and the constitutional guarantee of rights in the United States as remedies for the government ministry's domination of Parliament, the tight party discipline, and the unwritten constitution that they see as stifling debate and threatening freedom in the British system. [22]

The separation of powers, moreover, can be defended not only as protective of liberty but also, in some key respects, as conducive to efficient government. Many Wilsonians have made a point of arguing that the eighteenth-century arrangement is especially obsolete, even dangerous, in the face of the international challenges of the twentieth century. [23] This critique certainly has not been validated here—quite the opposite, in fact. Woodrow Wilson discovered for himself during the war that there is much to be said for the "Newtonian Constitution" and the independent, energetic executive it provides for when governing in an emergency. The Framers of the Fifth French Republic acknowledged as much when framing their constitution amid the crisis of 1958. They self-consciously sought to create such a president, one with special responsibilities for foreign and defense policy, in order to prevent the turbulence and indecisiveness that had plagued government after government in the purely parliamentary Fourth Republic. [24] Contemporary Wilsonians need to acknowledge that the separation of powers is not the hindrance to effective national security policy that they have made it out to be.

Wilson's inability to secure Senate ratification of the Versailles Treaty does not disprove this point. Unlike the diplomatic and military crises of the war, in which Wilson needed to and could act quickly and unilaterally, the ratification issue allowed for, indeed, required, full deliberation and the establishment of a broad, bipartisan consensus before action was taken. Without this consensus, the nation's support for the new, extensive, and ongoing commitments required by the treaty would have been in doubt, and, by Wilson's own logic, the regime of collective security he envisioned would have been weakened. Lloyd Cutler is a Wilsonian wont to complain about how the separation of powers undermines foreign policy effectiveness, but even he admits that "there is merit to the view that treaties should indeed require the careful bi-partisan consultation essential to win a two-thirds majority."[25]

It is of course no easy thing to assemble a two-thirds majority in the Senate for treaty ratification, or, for that matter, to combine the presidential endorsement and simple majorities in both the House and Senate that are required for everyday legislation. The difficulty in assembling coalitions for action across the House, Senate, and presidency stems from the different political interests, electoral imperatives, constitutional powers, and policy perspectives of officeholders in these institutions. And, of course, in an age of divided government, partisanship does not solve but rather exacerbates this difficulty. It is certainly a cumbersome system, but the Founders designed it to ensure, insofar as they could, that any national policy emerging from it would be backed by a thoughtful and general consensus as is appropriate for an expansive and diverse republic.[26] When there is a sustaining consensus behind a policy agenda, as there was during the New Freedom, the separation of powers does not stand in the way. When, as in the case of the Versailles Treaty, the requisite support does not exist, the separation can and probably should lead to further debate or, if it comes to it, even outright gridlock.[27]

In light of the preceding discussion, the challenge for Wilsonians attempting to develop a more workable synthesis of "responsible government *under* the Constitution" is to accept the emphasis of Wilson's phrase in a way that he never completely did. The goal, that is, should be to develop a program that fully comes to terms with the entrenched logic of the separation of powers and the benefits accruing under it, and that as a result seeks to complement and improve rather than supplant it.

For this synthesis to take form, Wilsonians may well need to reconsider one of the key assumptions of their traditional model, namely, that the president is the American prime minister, *the* legislative leader of the majority party. Wilson's celebratory introduction of these roles in *Constitutional Government,* as we have seen, coincided with an unmistakable theoretical ambivalence. His presidency proved the ambivalence was justified. The prime ministerial conception of presidential leadership is completely confounded by divided government, which presidents have usually confronted in recent decades, and which Wilson faced after 1918. But even before the end of Wilson's first term, in which he worked with Democratic majorities, he was reaffirming the Congress-centered program for responsible government that he had put forward in his early writings, admitting in private conversations that he lacked the direct influence over the legislators to be the prime ministerial leader for which he had long called.[28] Then there is the great difficulty prime ministerial presidents face in reconciling their party leadership with the national leadership roles assigned to the president in the Constitution. Partisan action, as Wilson knew, does not become the chief of state, chief executive, chief diplomat, and commander in chief. Time and again, on issues ranging from patronage to his participation in congressional elections, he was torn between the imperatives of national and party leadership. And he pleased no one: by the end of his term his supporters believed him to be wrecking the party, while his opponents saw him as a zealous partisan.

The point here is not that presidents should forgo legislative leadership or party action. The Constitution bids the executive to play a legislative role, and as Wilson demonstrated, a skillful president can have great impact. And so long as presidents campaign on a party ticket and use the party to bolster their administration, it will be a partisan office. That being said, presidents and political scientists need to recognize that the executive leadership of the legislative branch in the United States cannot match the efficiency that prevails in the Westminster model. There is also a need to acknowledge the stark tradeoffs between the party leadership role that Wilson essayed and the more fundamental national leadership roles that the Founders assigned to the office. Those wanting to bolster the authority of the presidency might return to the example of the early presidents, who sought to raise their administrations above the appearance (if not always the reality) of partisanship.[29] A president, for example, could follow Wilson's general method of blending public rhetoric and private persuasion in working for a bill's adoption while abstaining from his open declarations that he was doing so as a party leader. Indeed, in a divided government, that option is the only one; in a united government, it still might be the best one.

If the presidency-centered conception of party government has all too often undermined the authority of the office when vigorously pursued by executives, it has not done much for the parties either. The powers, incentives, and nonpartisan ideals accompanying the president's national leadership roles give him the means and the inclination to go his own way—with or without his party, as Wilson did in his diplomatic and wartime leadership. This tendency has been strengthened in the twentieth century by the dramatic increase in the administrative power under the executive's command, the spread of the direct primary, and the development of electronic media. Sidney Milkis and Theodore Lowi have persuasively argued that insofar as presidents beginning with Franklin Roosevelt have been able to govern administratively without depending on the regular support of their partisans in the legislature and to pursue their ambitions by appealing directly to voters rather than relying on their parties to mobilize the electorate, the modern office is antithetical to the idea of party government.[30]

As Wilsonians reconsider the basics of their model, they might recognize that in contrast to the presidency, Congress is hospitable to partisanship. The presence of multiple officeholders with divergent views and ample opportunity to express them allows and even calls for party action. The Founders expected partisans in their legislature and did not see this prospect as necessarily undesirable. In *Federalist* 70, Publius contrasted the different purposes of the sole—and thus energetic—executive and the more numerous—and thus deliberative—legislature. Speaking of the workings of the legislature, he observed that "the differences of opinion, and the jarrings of parties . . . though they may sometimes obstruct salutary plans, yet often promote deliberation and circumspection, and serve to check excesses in the majority."[31]

That ample room is given to party government in the workings of Congress is especially true for the House of Representatives, the most majoritarian body in the Founders' design, the body that they intended to be most responsive to public opinion. Wilson deemed these general elements as essential components of responsible government. The same holds true for the unmistakable interdependence of leaders and followers and the regular and clear confrontation of opposing parties that characterize the House. Its leaders are selected by the members of the majority party, who delegate power to their leadership in order to realize common party goals more efficiently. These leadership posts are coveted by the more ambitious and proven legislators because they carry the power to exercise significant if not compelling control over what Congress does. At the same time, however, if the leaders want to maintain the power that has been delegated to them, they must serve the purposes of their supporters in the majority.[32] One of the challenges the majority leadership confronts in this regard is defending their party against criticism from their counterparts in the minority. If debate between the parties in the House of Representatives does not always produce the eloquence and high drama of the House of Commons, it nevertheless does provide a forum in which the two parties regularly raise and debate the issues facing the nation.

What is more, developments in recent decades have revealed a potential for party action and leadership in the House that many political scientists, subscribing to Wilson's depiction of a decentralized and parochial Congress, have long assumed was impossible. Students of these trends have taken to calling the collective result "conditional party government." "The 'condition' in conditional party government," John Aldrich and David Rohde state, "is that there is reasonable cohesion on policy preferences within each party and differentiation between the two."[33] This condition has largely prevailed in the 1980s and 1990s. Following broad changes in the electorate, most notably the drift of conservative southerners into the GOP, which made the Democratic Party more liberal and the Republican Party more conservative, the parties in the House have become more ideologically coherent and polarized. This change has led both Democratic and Republican majorities to limit the ability of committees to thwart common party goals and to empower party leaders to achieve them. As a result, Democratic Speakers Jim Wright and Tom Foley and Republican Speaker Newt Gingrich have been able to exercise a real agenda-setting power.[34] The rise to power of Gingrich is especially interesting, demonstrating that a legislator with great ambition and a vision that resonates with his fellow partisans can facilitate a transformation in the goals of the party's delegation. Gingrich was not simply an agent empowered by a unified group of partisans in the 104th Congress; he helped bring about that unity.[35]

The new possibilities of party action and leadership in the House allow for a sharper and more focused debate over the means and ends of government. These possibilities also cut away at the common but problematic expectation that party and legislative leadership can only be exercised from the White House. And they do so within the context of the separation of powers. Gingrich and his Republican majority, for example, for all of their initial revolutionary momentum, could only start the debate and present their legislation to the other institutions in the lawmaking nexus; they could not dictate the outcome. House majorities that want to retain their power and sustain their agenda have no choice but to work with senators and presidents to frame policies backed by a sustaining consensus in the large and diverse American nation.[36]

This concluding sketch of possibilities for a new Wilsonian synthesis does not provide for responsible government of the sort that Wilson always held up as the ideal. Rather, it is offered as a closer approximation—and no doubt others can be developed—of what responsible government must be under the Constitution. Woodrow Wilson traveled a good way down this intellectual road. American political scientists, with the benefit of his example, the insight of his teachings, and the lessons of his presidency, can and should go further.

In the final paragraph of *Congressional Government*, Woodrow Wilson made a point of saluting "the sound sense and practical genius of the great and honorable statesmen of 1787." He challenged his fellow citizens to live up to their example of statesmanship not through "blind worship" of the Constitution but rather through critical scrutiny of how it had come to work in their own day. "When we shall have examined all its parts without sentiment," Wilson argued, "and gauged all its functions by the standards of practical common sense, we shall have established anew our right to the claim of political sagacity."[37] To honor the example of Wilson's statesmanship, we must submit his program for responsible government to the same unsentimental examination.

✿ Notes

INTRODUCTION

1. Arthur Link et al., eds., *The Papers of Woodrow Wilson*, 69 vols. (Princeton: Princeton University Press, 1966–1993), 31:95–96 (hereafter cited as *PWW*).

2. Ibid.

3. "Government by Debate," ca. December 4, 1882, ibid., 2:257–59.

4. "Responsible Government Under the Constitution," ca. February 10, 1886, ibid., 5:122.

5. On the definition of statesmanship, see Morton Frisch and Richard Stevens, "Introduction," in Frisch and Stevens, eds., *American Political Thought*, 2d ed. (Itasca, Ill.: F. E. Peacock, 1983), pp. 3–8, and Paul Eidelberg, *A Discourse on Statesmanship: The Design and Transformation of the American Polity* (Urbana: University of Illinois Press, 1974), p. 3.

6. Alexander George and Juliette George, *Woodrow Wilson and Colonel House: A Personality Study* (1956; New York: Dover Publications, 1964); James David Barber, *Presidential Character: Predicting Performance in the White House* (Englewood Cliffs, N.J.: Prentice Hall, 1972); William Bullitt and Sigmund Freud, *Thomas Woodrow Wilson: Twenty-Eighth President of the United States: A Psychological Study* (Boston: Houghton Mifflin, 1967). See also Robert Tucker, "The Georges' Wilson Reexamined: An Essay on Psychobiography," *American Political Science Review* 71 (June 1977): 606–18, and Dorothy Ross, "Woodrow Wilson and the Case for Psychohistory," *Journal of American History* 69 (December 1982): 659–68.

7. Niels Thorsen, *The Political Thought of Woodrow Wilson, 1875–1910* (Princeton: Princeton University Press, 1988), pp. 240–44; John Mulder, *Woodrow Wilson: Years of Preparation* (Princeton: Princeton University Press, 1978), pp. xii; Henry Bragdon, *Woodrow Wilson: The Academic Years* (Cambridge, Mass.: Belknap Press, 1967), pp. vii.

8. W. Wilson to E. L. Axson, October 30, 1883, *PWW*, 2:499–502.

9. An address to the Princeton alumni of New York, February 23, 1886, ibid., 5:141.

10. Ibid., 22:269–71.

11. Robert Wiebe, *The Search for Order, 1877–1920* (New York: Hill and Wang, 1967); Stephen Skowronek, *Building a New American State: The Expansion of National Administrative Capacities, 1877–1920* (New York: Cambridge University Press,

1982); Samuel Hays, "Political Parties and the Community-Society Continuum," in William Nisbet Chambers and Walter Dean Burnham, eds., *The American Party Systems: Stages of Political Development* 2d ed. (New York: Oxford University Press, 1975), pp. 152–81; Richard L. McCormick, *The Party Period and Public Policy: American Politics from the Age of Jackson to the Progressive Era* (New York: Oxford University Press, 1986).

12. For an extended review of the debate between traditionalists and revisionists, see Stephen Skowronek and Terri Bimes, "Woodrow Wilson's Critique of Popular Leadership: Reassessing the Modern-Traditional Divide in Presidential History," *Polity* 29 (Fall 1996): 33–39.

13. Arthur Link, *Wilson,* 5 vols. (Princeton: Princeton University Press, 1947–1965), quotation from 2:145; John Milton Cooper, *The Warrior and the Priest: Theodore Roosevelt and Woodrow Wilson* (Cambridge, Mass.: Belknap Press, 1983); August Heckscher, *Woodrow Wilson* (New York: Scribner's Sons, 1991); Robert Dallek, "Woodrow Wilson, Politician," *Wilson Quarterly* 15 (Autumn 1991): 106–14; Kendrick Clements, *The Presidency of Woodrow Wilson* (Lawrence: University Press of Kansas, 1992); Wilfred Binkley, *President and Congress,* 3d ed. (New York: Random House, 1962), pp. 247–64; Arthur MacMahon, "Woodrow Wilson as Legislative Leader and Administrator," *American Political Science Review* 50 (September 1956): 641–75; Marshall Dimock, "Woodrow Wilson as a Legislative Leader," *Journal of Politics* 19 (February 1957): 3–19.

14. James Ceaser, Glen Thurow, Jeffrey Tulis, and Joseph Bessette, "The Rise of the Rhetorical Presidency," *Presidential Studies Quarterly* 11 (Spring 1981): 158–71, quotation from p. 170; James Ceaser, *Presidential Selection: Theory and Development* (Princeton: Princeton University Press, 1979); Jeffrey Tulis, *The Rhetorical Presidency* (Princeton: Princeton University Press, 1987); Robert Eden, *Political Leadership and Nihilism: A Study of Weber and Nietzsche* (Tampa: University of South Florida Press, 1983); Eidelberg, *Discourse on Statesmanship.*

1: TOWARD "POWER AND STRICT ACCOUNTABILITY FOR ITS USE"

1. *PWW* (*The Papers of Woodrow Wilson,* ed. Arthur Link et al., 69 vols. [Princeton: Princeton University Press, 1966–1993]), 1:493.

2. Alexander Hamilton, John Jay, and James Madison, *The Federalist* (New York: Random House, 1937), p. 320.

3. Wilson, *Congressional Government* (Boston: Houghton Mifflin, 1885), pp. 284, 332–33.

4. Vernon Parrington, *Main Currents in American Thought,* 3 vols. (New York: Harcourt, Brace, 1927), 3:22–26; *PWW,* 1:619.

5. Arthur Link, *The Higher Realism of Woodrow Wilson* (Nashville, Tenn.: Vanderbilt University Press, 1971), pp. 21–37; John Mulder, *Woodrow Wilson: Years of Prepa-*

ration (Princeton: Princeton University Press, 1978), pp. 3–29; Wilson to A. B. Hart, June 3, 1889, *PWW,* 6:243.

6. Wilson, "The Union," November 11, 1876, *PWW,* 1:226–28.

7. Wilson shorthand diary, ibid., 1:142, 147, 221; for a contemporary analysis that influenced Wilson's views, see "The Democratic Party in the United States," *Gentleman's Magazine,* April 1875, pp. 429–40; Ray Stannard Baker, *Woodrow Wilson: Life and Letters,* 8 vols. (Garden City, N.Y.: Doubleday, Page, 1927–1939), 1:88; for Tilden's reputation and views, see Robert Kelley, *The Transatlantic Persuasion: The Liberal-Democratic Mind in the Age of Gladstone* (New York: Knopf, 1969), pp. 238–92.

8. Wilson diary, *PWW,* 1:208, 222–26; J. Wilson to W. Wilson, November 15, 1876, ibid., 1:228–29.

9. These views are readily apparent in essays that Woodrow Wilson, then nineteen years old, wrote for a church newsletter, the *North Carolina Presbyterian,* edited by his father: "Christ's Army," August 17, 1876, *PWW,* 1:180–81, and "Christian Progress," December 12, 1876, ibid., 1:234–35. See also Arthur Link, "Wilson the Diplomatist," in Earl Latham, ed., *The Philosophies and Policies of Woodrow Wilson* (1958; Chicago: University of Chicago Press, 1975), pp. 153–54; Merle Curti, "Woodrow Wilson's Concept of Human Nature," *Midwest Journal of Political Science* 1 (May 1957): 1–29; and Mulder, *Years of Preparation,* pp. 29–37.

10. "A Christian Statesman," September 1, 1876, *PWW,* 1:188–89.

11. Henry Bragdon, *Woodrow Wilson: The Academic Years* (Cambridge, Mass.: Belknap Press, 1967), p. 10; Parrington, *Main Currents,* 3:154–68. When a cousin asked the sixteen-year-old Wilson who the figure above his desk was, Wilson proclaimed, "That is Gladstone, the greatest statesman that ever lived" (Baker, *Life and Letters,* 1:57, 87).

12. Wilson, "Mr. Gladstone, A Character Sketch," April 1880, *PWW,* 1:624–42, quotations from pp. 626–27. See also Wilson, "John Bright," March 1880, ibid., 1:608–21. For an analysis that shaped Wilson's impressions of the two leaders and heightened his admiration of them, see Baker, *Life and Letters,* 1:87–88, and the Member for the Chiltern Hundreds, "The Orator," *Gentleman's Magazine,* April 1874, pp. 466–77.

13. The phrase is from "The Orator," p. 467.

14. Baker, *Life and Letters,* 1:37–39, 46, 92–93; *PWW,* 1:255, 274–75, 294–96, 343–44, quotation from p. 244.

15. *PWW,* 1:49–50, 245–49, 256–57, 688–702.

16. Ibid., 1:352–53.

17. Ibid., 1:148–49.

18. Walter Bagehot, *The English Constitution* (1867; Ithaca, N.Y.: Cornell University Press, 1966), esp. pp. 59–81; Wilson draft of a letter to W. M. Sloane, December 5, 1881, *PWW,* 2:567; editorial note, *PWW,* 1:492–93.

19. Wilson to E. L. Axson, January 1, 1884, *PWW,* 2:641–42; for the intellectual milieu at the university and Wilson's experience there, see Niels Thorsen, *The Po-*

litical Thought of Woodrow Wilson, 1875–1910 (Princeton: Princeton University Press, 1988), pp. 68–88; Wilson to E. L. Axson, November 9, 1884, *PWW,* 3:417–18.

20. On this point, see R. H. S. Crossman's introduction to *The English Constitution,* pp. 5–27.

21. Wilson to R. H. Dabney, October 28, 1885, *PWW,* 5:37–38 (Wilson's emphasis). See also Wilson, *Congressional Government,* pp. 332–33.

22. Wilson, *Congressional Government,* pp. 307–11.

23. Hamilton, Jay, and Madison, *The Federalist,* p. 322.

24. Wilson, *Congressional Government,* pp. 44–52.

25. James Bryce, *The American Commonwealth,* 3 vols. (New York: Macmillan, 1888), 1:93–110; James Ceaser, *Presidential Selection: Theory and Development* (Princeton: Princeton University Press, 1979), pp. 157–68.

26. Wilson discussed these dynamics at length in chapters 2–4 of *Congressional Government.* It is worth noting that he reserved most of his criticism for the House, to which he devoted two chapters. In his single chapter on the Senate, Wilson argued that the smaller numbers, less business-like organization, longer terms, and freer debates made it a somewhat more functional legislative body, although in its dealings with the president on matters of appointments and treaties, it, too, had shown itself to be detrimentally presumptive of executive prerogatives.

27. "Cabinet Government in the United States," August 1879, *PWW,* 1:498–99; "Committee or Cabinet Government?" January 1, 1884, ibid., 2:627–31.

28. "Cabinet Government in the United States," ibid., 1:499–504, quotation from p. 501.

29. Ibid., 1:505–7; "Committee or Cabinet Government?" ibid., 2:632–35.

30. John G. Sproat, *The Best Men: Liberal Reformers in the Gilded Age* (New York: Oxford University Press, 1968), pp. 257–71; see also Stephen Skowronek, *Building a New American State: The Expansion of National Administrative Capacities, 1877–1920* (New York: Cambridge University Press, 1982), chap. 3.

31. *PWW,* 5:359–80, quotation from p. 371; see also Paul Van Riper, ed., *The Wilson Influence on Public Administration: From Theory to Practice* (Washington, D.C.: American Society for Public Administration, 1990).

32. Wilson, *Congressional Government,* pp. 285–91.

33. Albert Stickney, *A True Republic* (New York: Harper, 1879), pp. 154–244, quotation from p. 104; Richard L. McCormick, *The Party Period and Public Policy: American Politics from the Age of Jackson to the Progressive Era* (New York: Oxford University Press, 1986), pp. 228–59. The discussion of Stickney is adapted from Daniel Stid, "Woodrow Wilson and the Problem of Party Government," *Polity* 26 (Summer 1994): 556–57.

34. Wilson to R. Bridges, February 5, 1883, *PWW,* 2:298–99 (Wilson's emphasis); editorial note, ibid., 2:153; Wilson, marginal notes to Albert Stickney's *A True Republic,* ca. October 1, 1879, ibid., 1:546–47; "Congressional Government," ca. October 1, 1879, ibid., 1:548–79.

35. See "Government by Debate," December 4, 1882, ibid., 2:203–15; "Commit-

tee or Cabinet Government," January 1, 1884, ibid., 2:622–35; Wilson, *Congressional Government,* 97–98.

36. Harvey C. Mansfield, Jr., *Statesmanship and Party Government: A Study of Burke and Bolingbroke* (Chicago: University of Chicago Press, 1965).

37. Edmund Burke, "Thoughts on the Present Discontents," in *The Writings and Speeches of Edmund Burke,* ed. Paul Langford (Oxford: Clarendon Press, 1981), 2:314–22, quotations from pp. 318–19.

38. *PWW,* 1:618 (Wilson's emphasis).

39. Stickney, *A True Republic,* pp. 206–16, quotations from pp. 41, 107.

40. *PWW,* 2:155 (Wilson's emphasis).

41. "Shall the Cabinet Have Seats in Congress?" *Nation,* April 3, 1873, pp. 233–34; "The President and Party Responsibility," *Nation,* May 17, 1877, pp. 288–89; "Cabinet Officers in Congress," *Nation,* April 10, 1879, pp. 243–44; "The Admission of Cabinet Officers to Seats in Congress," *Nation,* February 17, 1881, pp. 107–9; Gamaliel Bradford, "The Progress of Civil Service Reform," *International Review* 13 (September 1882): 271–73; George Pendleton, 46th Cong., 3d sess., February 4, 1881, S. Rept. 837; Arthur Link, *Wilson* (Princeton: Princeton University Press, 1947–1965), 1:17–19.

42. "Cabinet Government in the United States," August 1879, *PWW,* 1:498; Gamaliel Bradford's review of *Congressional Government,* February 12, 1885, ibid., 4:236–40; Bradford to Wilson, February 14, 1885, ibid., 4:250; Pendleton, S. Rept. 837. Two otherwise insightful studies of Wilson's program that fail to grasp this basic point are A. J. Wann, "The Development of Woodrow Wilson's Theory of the Presidency: Continuity and Change," in Latham, *Woodrow Wilson,* pp. 48–54, and George A. Curran, "Woodrow Wilson's Theory and Practice Regarding the Relations of the President and Congress" (Ph.D. diss., Fordham University, 1948), pp. 7–8.

43. "Government by Debate," *PWW,* 2:227–28.

44. Wilson to R. Bridges, February 5, 1883, ibid., 2:298 (Wilson's emphasis).

45. Wilson to R. Bridges, November 19, 1884, ibid., 3:465.

46. Wilson to E. L. Axson, February 15, 1885, ibid., 4:255.

47. Ibid., 4:236–40.

48. Wilson to E. L. Axson, February 15, 1885, ibid., 4:254–55; Wilson to R. H. Dabney, October 28, 1885, ibid., 5:38.

49. Bragdon, *The Academic Years,* p. 135; Wilson to E. L. Axson, March 14, 1885, *PWW,* 4:363–65.

50. Henry Maine, *Popular Government* (London: John Murray, 1885), pp. 212–13, 234–38.

51. A. Lawrence Lowell, "Ministerial Responsibility," *Atlantic Monthly,* February 1886, pp. 189–93.

52. On the Founders' intentions regarding the executive, see Hamilton, Jay, and Madison, *Federalist* 70–74; David Epstein, *The Political Theory of the Federalist* (Chicago: University of Chicago Press, 1984), pp. 171–76; Ralph Ketcham, *Presidents Above Party: The First American Presidency, 1789–1829* (Chapel Hill: University of

North Carolina Press, 1984), pp. 76–85; and Louis Fisher, "The Efficiency Side of Separated Powers," *Journal of American Studies* 5 (August 1971): 113–31.

53. "Responsible Government," *PWW*, 5:116–17.

54. Maine, *Popular Government,* pp. xi–xii; Lowell, "Ministerial Responsibility," pp. 180–81.

55. Lowell, "Ministerial Responsibility," pp. 180–88, quotation from p. 181.

56. "Responsible Government," *PWW*, 5:109–111, quotation from p. 111.

57. On this point, see Austin Ranney, *The Doctrine of Responsible Party Government* (Urbana: University of Illinois Press, 1954), pp. 28–30, and Thorsen, *Political Thought of Woodrow Wilson,* p. 233.

58. For Wilson's first thoughts on the value of expediency and his interest in exploring it further, see Wilson, memorandum for "The Modern Democratic State," ca. December 1–20, 1885, *PWW*, 5:59; Wilson to H. E. Scudder, May 12, 1886, ibid., 5:219. For his mature reflections, see Wilson, lecture notes, July 2, 1894, ibid., 8:606–7. See also John Milton Cooper, *The Warrior and the Priest: Theodore Roosevelt and Woodrow Wilson* (Cambridge, Mass.: Belknap Press, 1983), pp. 55–56.

2: POLITICAL DEVELOPMENT, INTERPRETIVE LEADERSHIP, AND THE PRESIDENCY

1. *PWW* (*The Papers of Woodrow Wilson,* ed. Arthur Link et al., 69 vols. [Princeton: Princeton University Press, 1966–1993]), 5:61–92. See also editorial note, ibid., 5:54–58. For Wilson's academic career, see Henry Bragdon, *Woodrow Wilson: The Academic Years* (Cambridge, Mass.: Belknap Press, 1967).

2. Wilson to H. E. Scudder, May 12, 1886, *PWW*, 5:218–20; Wilson to A. Shaw, May 29, 1887, ibid. 5:512.

3. Wilson, *The State: Elements of Historical and Practical Politics* (Boston: D. C. Heath, 1889).

4. Walter Bagehot, *Physics and Politics, or Thoughts on the Application of the Principles of "Natural Selection" and "Inheritance" to Political Society* (New York: D. Appleton, 1873). Wilson would later say of *Physics and Politics:* "There is more stimulation in this book than in any other modern writing on the history of political development" (*PWW*, 7:281–82). See also Wilson, "Notes for Four Lectures on the Study of History," ca. September 24, 1885, ibid., 5:18–23, essentially a summary outline of Bagehot's study that Wilson used to orient his students. On the general intellectual movement, see Richard Hofstadter, *Social Darwinism in American Thought* (Boston: Beacon Press, 1955). On Wilson's exposure to the German historical school and social Darwinism at Johns Hopkins, see editorial note, *PWW*, 5:19, and Niels Thorsen, *The Political Thought of Woodrow Wilson 1875–1910* (Princeton: Princeton University Press, 1988), pp. 68–76.

5. Bagehot, *Physics and Politics,* pp. 36–37, 64.

6. Wilson review of Burgess, *A System of Political Science and Law,* May 1891, *PWW,* 7:201.

7. Wilson, *The State,* pp. 575–76, quotation from p. 667.

8. Wilson, *Congressional Government* (Boston: Houghton Mifflin, 1885), pp. 311–12; Wilson, *The State,* pp. 467–69; Wilson, "Bryce's *American Commonwealth,*" ca. January 31, 1889, *PWW,* 6:72.

9. Wilson, "Bryce's *American Commonwealth,*" ca. January 31, 1889, *PWW,* 6:72.

10. Wilson, *The State,* p. 576.

11. Christopher Wolfe has argued that Wilson's change in views regarding the imperative of amendments and the possibility of adaptation reflected a historicist shift in Wilson's constitutional thinking, i.e., he came to see it as a document whose meaning changed with time; "Woodrow Wilson: Interpreting the Constitution," *Review of Politics* 41 (January 1979): 121–42. However, Wilson had exhibited a historicist understanding from the beginning. A basic theme of the writings that culminated in *Congressional Government* was that through informal changes the meaning of the document had changed considerably, and Wilson held to the idea of a "living constitution" right from the start: see pp. 7–10, 242–43. Wilson's dropping his advocacy of formal amendments was largely a function of his bow to political expediency; his subsequent stress on the adaptability of the Constitution originated in his newfound belief in the generally progressive direction of political development.

12. Critique of Bagehot's *Physics and Politics, PWW,* 6:335 (I have transposed the first and second quotations).

13. Editorial note, ibid., 6:644–46. For a recent formulation of this general understanding of leadership, see James MacGregor Borns, *Leadership* (New York: Harper and Row, 1978).

14. James Ceaser, *Presidential Selection: Theory and Development* (Princeton: Princeton University Press, 1979), pp. 188–92; Jeffrey Tulis, *The Rhetorical Presidency* (Princeton: Princeton University Press, 1987), pp. 124–30; David Marion, "Alexander Hamilton and Woodrow Wilson on the Spirit and Form of a Responsible Government," *Review of Politics* 42 (July 1980): 309–28.

15. *PWW,* 6:658 (Wilson's emphasis).

16. See Wilson, "Democracy," December 5, 1891, ibid., 7:350–51.

17. "Leaders of Men," ibid., 6:650.

18. Ibid., 6:232–33 (Wilson's emphasis).

19. Stephen Skowronek and Terri Bimes, "Woodrow Wilson's Critique of Popular Leadership: Reassessing the Modern-Traditional Divide in Presidential History," *Polity* 29 (Fall 1996): 41–48.

20. "Nature of Democracy," *PWW,* 6:224–28, 233–35.

21. Ibid., 6:235–37; Wilson, "The Modern Democratic State," ca. December 1–20, 1885, ibid., 5:86–87.

22. Ceaser, *Presidential Selection,* pp. 170–212; Skowronek and Bimes, "Woodrow Wilson's Critique," pp. 59–63.

23. *PWW,* 6:462 (Wilson's emphasis).

24. Ibid., 6:463 (Wilson's emphasis).

25. Albert Bushnell Hart, "The Speaker as Premier," *Atlantic,* March 1891, pp. 380–86. See also Richard Pious, "A Prime Minister for America?" *Constitution* 4:3 (Fall 1992): 4–12.

26. *PWW,* 7:210–11, 370–71.

27. W. Wilson to E. Wilson, February 17, 1898, ibid., 10:399; Webb diary, April 25, 1898, ibid., 10:525.

28. Mr. Cleveland's Cabinet," March 17, 1893, ibid., 8:173.

29. Ibid., 8:172, 175–76.

30. Ibid., 8:175–78.

31. "Mr. Cleveland as President," January 15, 1897, ibid., 10:102–19, quotation from pp. 102–3.

32. Ibid., 1:684; for the reformers' positions, see John G. Sproat, *The Best Men: Liberal Reformers in the Gilded Age* (New York: Oxford University Press, 1968).

33. *PWW,* 2:68.

34. Wilson to E. Wilson, July 22 and November 7, 1884, ibid., 3:259, 410–11; Wilson, "Responsible Government Under the Constitution," ibid., 5:116–17; "Wanted—A Party," ibid., 5:342–46, quotation from p. 346; Wilson to E. Wilson, March 15, 1889, ibid., 6:151–52.

35. "Mr. Cleveland as President," ibid., 10:105.

36. Ibid., 10:118–19.

37. Ibid., 10:109–13 (the quotations have been transposed).

38. E. L. Godkin, "Mr. Cleveland's Presidency," *Nation,* March 4, 1897, pp. 156–57; Carl Schurz, "Grover Cleveland's Second Administration," *McClure's Magazine* 9 (May 1897): 633–44.

39. *PWW,* 10:103, 109.

40. The quotation is from a letter that Turner wrote to William E. Dodd on October 7, 1919. It is printed in Wendell H. Stephenson, "The Influence of Woodrow Wilson on Frederick Jackson Turner," *Agricultural History* 19 (October 1945): 249–53. See also Wilson to Turner, August 23, 1889, *PWW,* 6:369, Turner to Wilson, December 20, 1893, ibid., 8:417, and Thorsen, *Political Thought of Woodrow Wilson,* pp. 144–47.

41. "The Course of American History," May 16, 1895, *PWW,* 9:257–74; quotations from "The Making of the Nation," April 15, 1897, ibid., 10:219–20.

42. "Nature of Democracy in the United States," May 10–16, 1889, ibid., 6:231–35; "The Making of the Nation," ca. April 15, 1897, ibid., 10:217–36, quotation from p. 230.

43. Ibid., 10:301 (the quotations have been transposed). See also "The Making of the Nation," ibid., 10:219.

44. "Leaderless Government," ibid., 10:292–93, 303–4; "The Making of the Nation," ibid., 10:231–33.

45. "Leaderless Government," ibid., 10:294–95, 301–4.

46. "What Ought We to Do?" August 1, 1898, ibid., 10:575.

47. Wilson, *Congressional Government,* 49–52, and Wilson, "Responsible Government Under the Constitution," February 10, 1886, *PWW,* 5:113–14.

48. See *Federalist* 70 and 74–75, and "Pacificus Number 1," in *The Works of Alexander Hamilton,* ed. Henry Cabot Lodge, 2d ed. (New York: G. P. Putnam's Sons, 1904), 4:432–44.

49. Wilson, *Congressional Government,* pp. 43–44. In his revised preface in 1900 (p. xii), Wilson adjusted this theory to include Lincoln's dominance in the Civil War.

50. "Democracy and Efficiency," *PWW,* 12:11.

51. Wilson, *Congressional Government,* pp. xii–xiii; "The Ideals of America," December 26, 1901, *PWW,* 12:226–27.

52. Henry Jones Ford, *The Rise and Growth of American Politics* (New York: Macmillan, 1898; reprint, New York: De Capo Press, 1967), pp. 275–93, quotation from p. 279.

53. "Hide and Seek Politics," March 2, 1910, *PWW,* 20:198; Wilson to C. Boyer, July 15, 1902, ibid., 14:13–14; Wilson to H. Garfield, April 10, 1908, ibid., 18:259; Wilson to H. Ford, April 9, 1908, ibid., 18:294; Edward Corwin, "Woodrow Wilson and the Presidency," *Virginia Law Review* 6 (October 1956): 764. The late H. Douglas Price helped me to understand the importance of Ford's influence on Wilson during the course of several conversations in his office.

54. John Milton Cooper, *The Warrior and the Priest: Theodore Roosevelt and Woodrow Wilson* (Cambridge, Mass.: Belknap Press, 1983), pp. 130–35; Corwin, "Woodrow Wilson," pp. 765–66.

55. Of course, Roosevelt's decision in 1912 to break with his party and lead many enemies of partisanship in the Bull Moose movement would throw an ironic light on Wilson's praise, but it was genuine when initially bestowed; "Why Office Seeks Roosevelt," *Chicago Daily Tribune,* May 6, 1903, in *PWW,* 14:454–55. For similar remarks, see Wilson, speech on patriotism in Worcester, Massachusetts, January 30, 1902, ibid., 12:262–63.

56. David Lawrence, *The True Story of Woodrow Wilson* (New York: George Doran, 1924), p. 39.

57. Theodore Roosevelt, *Autobiography* (New York: Scribner's, 1913), p. 352.

58. "Hide and Seek Politics," March 2, 1910, *PWW,* 20:202. See also Cooper, *Warrior and the Priest,* pp. 131–32.

59. It should be noted here that despite the impact of the Spanish-American War on Wilson's thinking, he devoted surprisingly little attention to McKinley, apparently subscribing to the traditional view of him, i.e., a president who was essentially beholden to the Republican barons in Congress. See Wilson, *A History of the American People,* 10 vols. (New York: Harper, 1918), 10:158, and "Leaderless Government," August 5, 1897, *PWW,* 10:295. For a different view, see Lewis Gould, *The Presidency of William McKinley* (Lawrence, Kans.: Regents Press, 1980).

192 THE PRESIDENT AS STATESMAN

3: *CONSTITUTIONAL GOVERNMENT* AND PRESIDENTIAL POWER

1. Butler to Wilson, April 26, 1906, *PWW* (*The Papers of Woodrow Wilson,* ed. Arthur Link et al., 69 vols. [Princeton: Princeton University Press, 1966–1993]), 16:373–74; Wilson to Butler, April 26, 1906, ibid., 16:375–76; announcement, January 11, 1907, ibid., 16:554; Wilson, *Constitutional Government in the United States* (New York: Columbia University Press, 1908).

2. Wilson, *Constitutional Government,* pp. 54–57, 198–202. Henry Jones Ford, *The Rise and Growth of American Politics* (New York: Macmillan, 1898; reprint, New York: De Capo Press, 1967), pp. 51, 334–42.

3. Alexander Hamilton, John Jay, and James Madison, *The Federalist* (New York: Random House, 1937), p. 204; David Epstein, *The Political Theory of the Federalist* (Chicago: University of Chicago Press, 1984), pp. 1–2; Arthur M. Schlesinger Jr., *The Cycles of American History* (Boston: Houghton Mifflin, 1986), pp. 6–14.

4. Wilson, *Constitutional Government,* p. 56.

5. James Ceaser, *Presidential Selection: Theory and Development* (Princeton: Princeton University Press, 1979), quotations from p. 38. This section is adapted from Daniel Stid, "Woodrow Wilson and the Problem of Party Government," *Polity* 26 (Summer 1994): 559–66.

6. Wilson, *Constitutional Government,* pp. 206–20. Wilson quoted from Ford's *Rise and Growth* twice (setting off the quotes with marks but not citing Ford directly), on pp. 210 and 213 (from pp. 299 and 326 of *Rise and Growth,* respectively). For Ford's analysis of party politics, see ibid., pp. 294–333, and Austin Ranney, *The Doctrine of Responsible Party Government* (Urbana: University of Illinois Press, 1954), pp. 70–91.

7. See, for example, Wilson, *Constitutional Government,* pp. 188, 191, 207–9; Wilson to J. Calloway, October 30, 1907, *PWW,* 17:461; J. M. Taylor to W. Wilson, November 23, 1909, *PWW,* 19:532–33; an address on political reform to the City Club of Philadelphia, November 18, 1909, *PWW,* 19:511. Wilson was a prominent advocate of one progressive reform in this period, the short ballot, but only because he believed that this measure would concentrate, instead of bypassing or undermining, the competition between the parties, therefore making it more responsible; *Constitutional Government,* pp. 221–22; R. S. Child to Wilson, October 25, 1909, *PWW,* 19:446–47; "Hide and Seek Politics," *PWW,* 20:192–207; Arthur Link, *Wilson,* 5 vols. (Princeton: Princeton University Press, 1947–1965), 1:124–26.

8. *PWW,* 18:384.

9. Wilson, *Constitutional Government,* pp. 220–21.

10. Richard L. McCormick, *The Party Period and Public Policy: American Politics from the Age of Jackson to the Progressive Era* (New York: Oxford University Press, 1986), pp. 257–59, 311–56.

11. "Cabinet Government in the United States," August 1879, *PWW* 1:507 (Wilson's emphasis).

12. Ceaser, *Presidential Selection,* pp. 203–5.

13. Edmund Burke, "Thoughts on the Present Discontents," in *The Writing and Speeches of Edmund Burke,* ed. Paul Langford (Oxford: Clarendon Press, 1981), 2:317–20; Anthony Downs, *An Economic Theory of Democracy* (New York: Harper, 1957), pp. 103–12.

14. Wilson, *Constitutional Government,* pp. 220–21.

15. J. Allen Smith, *The Spirit of American Government* (New York: Macmillan, 1907; Cambridge, Mass.: Belknap Press, 1965), pp. 51–52, 185, 203–29.

16. Grant McConnell, *Private Power and American Democracy* (New York: Knopf, 1966), pp. 36–38, quotation on p. 47.

17. Ralph Ketcham, *Presidents Above Party: The First American Presidency, 1789–1829* (Chapel Hill: University of North Carolina Press, 1984), pp. 231–35; Paul Eidelberg, *A Discourse on Statesmanship: The Design and Transformation of the American Polity* (Urbana: University of Illinois Press, 1974), pp. 304–7.

18. Robert Wiebe, *The Search for Order, 1877–1920* (New York: Hill and Wang, 1967), pp. 159–63.

19. Richard Hofstadter, *The Idea of a Party System* (Berkeley: University of California Press, 1964), chaps. 2–4.

20. Wilson, *Constitutional Government,* p. 203; on the necessity of party as an integrating device in the Newtonian Constitution, see pp. 210–17.

21. *PWW,* 17:76. The quotation comes from a revealing tribute that Wilson delivered (during the same period in which he was lecturing at Columbia) at a seventieth birthday celebration for Grover Cleveland.

22. Wilson, *Constitutional Government,* p. 68.

23. Ibid., p. 71.

24. Ibid., pp. 60–66, quotation from p. 66.

25. Ibid., pp. 70–72. Here Wilson's whig theory reads very much like (but should not be confused with) the whig theory of the presidency as it was formulated by Andrew Jackson's opponents in the Whig Party and that had predominated in Whig and Republican circles throughout the nineteenth century. The traditional whig theory, it should be noted, in response to the vetoes of Jackson and Tyler, called for even more presidential restraint vis-à-vis Congress than did Wilson's. See Wilfred Binkley, *President and Congress,* 3d ed. (New York: Random House, 1962), pp. 106–7, 117–21.

26. Wilson, *Constitutional Government,* pp. 72–73.

27. These passages, which I have transposed, are from the same sentence in ibid., p. 70.

28. Ibid., pp. 70–71, 108, quotation from p. 139.

29. Edward Corwin, *The Presidency: Office and Powers, 1787–1984,* 5th rev. ed. (New York: New York University Press, 1984), p. 201.

30. Aaron Wildavsky's seminal article, first published in 1966, is reprinted in *The Beleaguered Presidency* (New Brunswick, N.J.: Transaction Publishers, 1991), 29–46.

4: PROGRESSIVISM AND POLITICS IN NEW JERSEY AND
THE NATION

1. *PWW* (*The Papers of Woodrow Wilson,* ed. Arthur Link et al., 69 vols. [Princeton: Princeton University Press, 1966–1993]), 17:322.

2. Ibid., 18:535.

3. An old-fashioned Democrat to the editor of the *Indianapolis News,* May 1, 1902, ibid., 12:356–58; Wilson to E. Wilson, June 1, 1902, ibid., 12:390–91; "Strong Appeal to the South," *New York Sun,* November 30, 1904, in *PWW,* 15:547–48; Arthur Link, *Wilson,* 5 vols. (Princeton: Princeton University Press, 1947–1965), 1:97–100; Wilson to G. Harvey, December 16, 1906, *PWW,* 16:531–32; Wilson, "A Credo," August 6, 1907, *PWW,* 17:335–38; Wilson to St.C. McKelway, March 11, 1906, *PWW,* 16:330.

4. Wilson to M. Peck, November 2, 1908, *PWW,* 18:479–80.

5. Ibid., 17:500.

6. See, e.g., "The Banker and the Nation," September 30, 1908, ibid., 18:424–34; "Conservatism: True and False," December 9, 1908, ibid., 18:535–40; "The Tariff Make Believe," September 5, 1909, ibid., 19:359–80; Niels Thorsen, *The Political Thought of Woodrow Wilson* (Princeton: Princeton University Press, 1988), pp. 188–89. See also Link, *Wilson,* 1:120–23, 128–32.

7. Link, *Wilson,* 1:133–40.

8. See the recollections of William O. Inglis, Harvey's assistant, which are printed in David Hirst, *Woodrow Wilson, Reform Governor: A Documentary Narrative* (Princeton, N.J.: D. Van Nostrand, 1965), p. 7. See also Wilson to D. B. Jones, June 27, 1910, *PWW,* 20:543–44.

9. Wilson to J. Harlan, June 23, 1910, *PWW,* 20:540–41; Hirst, *Reform Governor,* pp. 15–24.

10. *PWW,* 21:94. See also Joseph Tumulty, *Woodrow Wilson as I Knew Him* (Garden City, N.Y.: Doubleday, Page, 1921), pp. 15–22; James Kerney, *The Political Education of Woodrow Wilson* (New York: Century, 1926), pp. 49–55.

11. *PWW,* 21:338–47; Tumulty, *Wilson,* pp. 38–39.

12. Wilson to G. Harvey, August 8, 1910, *PWW,* 21:41–42; G. Harvey to Wilson, August 12, 1910, ibid., 21:52–53; Wilson to G. Harvey, October 11, 1910, ibid., 21:297; Kerney, *Political Education,* pp. 69–71.

13. *PWW,* 21:407–10.

14. Record quoted in Hirst, *Reform Governor,* p. 106, vote totals from p. 113, and Scudder quoted on p. 115.

15. Ibid., pp. 7–8, 40; Tumulty, *Wilson,* pp. 46–55; E. Wilde to Wilson, November 11, 1910, *PWW,* 22:41–42; J. Wescott to Wilson, November 11, 1910, *PWW,* 22:42–43.

16. Wilson to G. Harvey, November 15, 1910, *PWW,* 22:46–48.

17. Kerney, *Political Education,* pp. 89–93; Tumulty, *Wilson,* pp. 56–71. See also

Wilson, statement on the senatorship, December 8, 1910, *PWW,* 22:153–54; statement on the senatorship, December 23, 1910, ibid., 22:248–52; address in Jersey City, January 5, 1911, ibid., 22:295–307.

18. *PWW,* 22:297.

19. Statement on the senatorship, December 23, 1910, ibid., 22:251–52.

20. January 5, 1911, ibid., 22:307. See also Link, *Wilson,* 1:235–36.

21. Wilson to M. Peck, April 9, 1911, *PWW,* 22:545 (Wilson's emphasis).

22. Quoted in David Sarasohn, *Party of Reform: Democrats in the Progressive Era* (Jackson: University of Mississippi, Press, 1989), p. 127. For the conservative opposition to the initiative, referendum, and recall, see Link, *Wilson,* 1:339–42.

23. Wilson to S. Thompson, March 27, 1911, *PWW,* 22:521; Kerney, *Political Education,* pp. 97–99, 101–3.

24. Kerney, *Political Education,* pp. 135–37, Wilson's remarks quoted on p. 136.

25. Wilson to R. Dabney, November 16, 1911, *PWW,* 23:551–52.

26. Address to the Jefferson Club of Los Angeles, May 12, 1911, ibid., 23:34–35, 37.

27. "Money Monopoly Is Most Menacing, Wilson Warns," *Philadelphia North American,* June 15, 1911, in *PWW,* 23:156–57; Wilson to G. Harvey, January 11, 1912, ibid., 24:31; John Blum, *Joe Tumulty and the Wilson Era* (Boston: Houghton Mifflin, 1951), pp. 41–42; Tumulty, *Wilson,* pp. 82–89.

28. Wilson to A. Joline, April 29, 1907, *PWW,* 17:124; Wilson to A. Dunlap, April 1, 1908, ibid., 18:219–20; Tumulty, *Wilson,* pp. 94–95.

29. *PWW,* 24:10.

30. There are some perils in attempting to understand and evaluate Wilson's gubernatorial experience as a trial of his program for responsible government—a program that was, as Wilson conceived it, national in character. See, e.g., "Toast Wilson as President," *Newark Evening News,* April 27, 1911, in *PWW,* 22:588–89. Nevertheless, because Wilson self-consciously sought to use his program in New Jersey, and because the results he met with are revealing, his attempt to do so will be analyzed here.

31. Campaign address in Trenton, New Jersey, October 3, 1910, ibid., 21:229–30.

32. Kerney, *Political Education,* pp. 100–101, 103–6; memorandum of Ray Stannard Baker interview with George Record, April 6, 1926, Baker Papers, Library of Congress.

33. See, for example, Wilson's speeches during January and February 1911, which are compiled in Hirst, *Reform Governor,* pp. 165–87.

34. "Wilson Confident He'll Get Reform," *Trenton Evening Times,* March 7, 1911, in *PWW,* 22:481–82.

35. Kerney, *Political Education,* pp. 108–9; Burton Hendrick, "Woodrow Wilson: Political Leader," *McLure's Magazine,* December 1911, pp. 229–30; "Governor Wins Conference Again," *Trenton Evening Times,* March 14, 1911, in *PWW,* 22:504–5.

36. Record interview, Baker Papers, Library of Congress; Kerney, *Political Educa-*

tion, pp. 104–11; Tumulty, *Wilson*, pp. 72–75; Wilson to M. Peck, March 5, 1911, *PWW*, 22:477; "Wilson Confident He'll Get Reform," *Trenton Evening Times*, March 7, 1911, in *PWW*, 22:481; Wilson to M. Peck, April 2, 1911, *PWW*, 22:532.

37. Link, *Wilson*, 1:271–74.

38. Wilson to M. Peck, April 23, 1911, *PWW*, 22:582 (Wilson's emphasis).

39. Wilson, *Constitutional Government*, p. 71; campaign address in Trenton, October 3, 1910, *PWW*, 21:230.

40. Wilson, statement about an altercation with James Richard Nugent, March 20, 1911, *PWW*, 22:512; Wilson to M. Peck, March 26, 1911, ibid., 22:518; Blum, *Tumulty*, p. 28.

41. Wilson to O. Villard, January 2, 1911, *PWW*, 22:288; Tumulty, *Wilson*, pp. 1–64; Blum, *Tumulty*, pp. 3–26.

42. Blum, *Tumulty*, p. 28; Kerney, *Political Education*, pp. 116–18.

43. Kerney, *Political Education*, p. 118; E. Grosscup to J. Gifford, May 23, 1912, *PWW*, 24:429; Link, *Wilson*, 1:270–71.

44. Blum, *Tumulty*, pp. 30–40.

45. Record interview, Baker Papers, Library of Congress; Link, *Wilson*, 1:285–87.

46. Quoted in Hirst, *Reform Governor*, pp. 225–26.

47. Link, *Wilson*, 1:294–95.

48. Wilson to C. Grasty, November 10, 1911, *PWW*, 23:546–47; Wilson, a statement, November 8, 1911, ibid., 23:544.

49. Link, *Wilson*, 1:297–306; Hirst, *Reform Governor*, p. 233.

50. Theodore Roosevelt, "A Remedy for Some Forms of Selfish Legislation," *Outlook*, August 6, 1910, pp. 759–63; Herbert Croly, *Progressive Democracy* (New York: Macmillan, 1914), pp. 349–77; Walter Lippmann, *Drift and Mastery* (Englewood Cliffs, N.J.: Prentice Hall, 1961), pp. 38–44; Kirk H. Porter and Donald Bruce Johnson, eds., *National Party Platforms* (Chicago: University of Illinois Press, 1956), pp. 178, 180–81.

51. See, e.g., Wilson, "Law or Personal Power," April 13, 1908, *PWW*, 18:263–69; address in Sioux City, Iowa, September 17, 1912, ibid., 25:149–54; address in Kansas City, October 8, 1912, ibid., 25:386–87.

52. Henry F. Pringle, *The Life and Times of William Howard Taft*, 2 vols. (Hamden Conn.: Archon Books, 1964), 2:766, 770, quotation from p. 772; George Mowry, *Theodore Roosevelt and the Progressive Movement* (Madison: University of Wisconsin Press, 1946), pp. 226–27. This section is adapted from Daniel Stid, "Woodrow Wilson and the Problem of Party Government," *Polity* 26 (Summer 1994): 566–70.

53. Taft to O. Bannard, January 22, 1912, in Pringle, *Life and Times*, 2:764; Lodge to Roosevelt, February 28, 1912, in *Selections from the Correspondence of Theodore Roosevelt and Henry Cabot Lodge, 1884–1918*, ed. Henry Cabot Lodge, 2 vols. (New York: Scribner's, 1925), 2:423–24; Root to P. Jessup, September 13, 1930, in Philip C. Jessup, *Elihu Root*, 2 vols. (New York: Dodd, Mead, 1938), 2:191. The opening statement of the Republican platform included a sustained defense of "an untrammeled and independent judiciary" (Porter and Johnson, *National Party Platforms*, pp. 183–

84). See also William A. Schambra, "Elihu Root," in Morton Frisch and Richard Stevens, eds., *American Political Thought,* 2d ed. (Itasca, Ill.: F. E. Peacock, 1983), pp. 237–65.

54. Roosevelt to W. Glasscock, February 24, 1912, *The Letters of Theodore Roosevelt,* ed. Elting E. Morison, 8 vols. (Cambridge: Harvard University Press, 1952–1954), 7:511; Roosevelt to H. Croly, February 29, 1912, ibid., 7:512; Roosevelt to J. Dixon, March 8, 1912, ibid., 7:521–24, quotation from p. 524; Roosevelt to J. Reynolds, June 11, 1912, ibid., 7:561.

55. Porter and Johnson, *National Party Platforms,* pp. 175–76; Sidney Milkis and Daniel Tichenor, "'Direct Democracy' and Social Justice: The Progressive Party Campaign of 1912," *Studies in American Political Development* 8 (Fall 1994): 282–340, quotation from p. 335. On the "state of courts and parties," see Stephen Skowronek, *Building a New American State: The Expansion of National Administrative Capacities, 1877–1920* (New York: Cambridge University Press, 1982), pp. 39–42.

56. Address in Minneapolis, September 18, 1912, *PWW,* 25:175. For variations, see Wilson, campaign address in Detroit, September 19, 1912, ibid., 25:187–88; campaign speech on new issues in Hartford, Connecticut, September 25, 1912, ibid., 25:244.

57. A campaign speech in Montclair, New Jersey, October 29, 1912, ibid., 25:468.

58. Ibid., 24:480. No such plank on party organization, it should be noted, appeared in the Democratic platform. See also, e.g., Wilson, address to the General Assembly of Virginia and the city council of Richmond, February 1, 1912, ibid., 24:110; address to the General Assembly of Maryland, March 7, 1912, ibid., 24:232–34.

59. Ibid., 25:144–45.

60. William Howard Taft, *Our Chief Magistrate* (New York: Columbia University Press, 1916), pp. 139–40.

61. Theodore Roosevelt, *Autobiography* (New York: Scribner's, 1913), p. 357.

62. Herbert Croly, *Promise of American Life* (New York: Macmillan, 1909; reprint, Boston: Northeastern University Press, 1989), pp. 167–75, quotation from p. 174; Walter Lippmann, *A Preface to Politics* (Ann Arbor: University of Michigan Press, 1962), pp. 78–79; John Milton Cooper, *The Warrior and the Priest: Theodore Roosevelt and Woodrow Wilson* (Cambridge, Mass.: Belknap Press, 1983), pp. 161–62, 172–74, 213–15.

63. *PWW,* 24:512. The best account of the Democratic Convention in 1912 is found in Link, *Wilson,* 1:431–65.

64. See note 14 in the Introduction.

65. Sarasohn, *Party of Reform,* chaps. 1–4.

66. *PWW,* 22:555.

67. Ibid., 23:7.

68. An address to the New York Press Club, September 9, 1912, ibid., 25:127–28, quotation from p. 127. See also, e.g., Wilson's remarks in the following: "Great Reception Greets Governor Wilson Today," *Ann Arbor Daily Times,* January 19, 1912, in ibid., 24:57–58; "House Gives Him Warm Welcome," *Richmond Times Dispatch,* Feb-

ruary 2, 1912, in ibid., 24:122; "Governor Wilson Addresses Two Big Audiences," *Milwaukee Journal*, March 24, 1912, in ibid., 24:260–61.

69. Several representative examples of Wilson's campaign speeches are compiled in *The New Freedom: A Call for the Emancipation of the Generous Energies of a People*, ed. William Bayard Hale (New York: Doubleday, 1913; reprint, Englewood Cliffs, N.J.: Prentice Hall, 1961). For Wilson's evaluation of the future shape of the two-party system in the electorate and the impending Democratic realignment, see "The Democratic Opportunity," ca. November 1, 1909, *PWW*, 19:465–71; a news report of two addresses in Kansas City, Missouri, May 6, 1911, ibid., 23:6–7; a news report of a campaign address in Boston, April 27, 1912, ibid., 24:364–65; evening address in Buffalo, New York, September 2, 1912, ibid., 25:85–86; address in New Haven, Connecticut, September 25, 1912, ibid., 25:246–47.

70. *PWW*, 27:148.

71. Walter Dean Burnham, "The System of 1896," in Paul Kleppner, ed., *The Evolution of American Electoral Systems* (Westport, Conn.: Greenwood, 1981), pp. 148, 188; James Sundquist, *Dynamics of the Party System: Alignment and Realignment of Political Parties in the United States* (Washington, D.C.: Brookings Institution, 1973), pp. 165–66; Cooper, *Warrior and the Priest*, p. 207; Arthur Link, *Woodrow Wilson and the Progressive Era* (New York: Harper and Row, 1963), p. 24.

72. David Sarasohn marshals impressive evidence supporting this point in *Party of Reform*, pp. 142–54. He contrasts the high degree of unity among the leading Democrats—such as William Jennings Bryan, Wilson, Champ Clark, and Oscar Underwood—on matters of policy with the divisions among the Republicans and progressives. He also notes that in five states where the Taft and Roosevelt supporters jointly nominated a candidate for governor, the Democratic candidate for governor received a significantly higher percentage of the vote than did Wilson, indicating that many Republican and progressive voters were more ready to vote for a Democrat than to join in a cooperative effort with the rival faction. See also Louis H. Bean, *How to Predict Elections* (New York: Alfred Knopf, 1948), pp. 68–69. On the fundamental differences between the progressives and the GOP regulars and the crucial respects in which the former were not simply a vehicle for Roosevelt, see Milkis and Tichenor, "The Progressive Party Campaign of 1912."

73. For expositions of this view, see Jerome Clubb, William Flanigan, and Nancy Zingale, *Partisan Realignment: Voters, Parties and Government in American History* (Beverly Hills, Calif.: Sage, 1980), and Richard L. McCormick, *The Party Period and Public Policy: American Politics from the Age of Jackson to the Progressive Era* (New York: Oxford University Press, 1986), pp. 64–88.

74. Link, *Wilson*, 2:147–49; Wilfred Binkley, *President and Congress*, 3d ed. (New York: Random House, 1962), pp. 257, 259; Walter Oleszek, "John Worth Kern: Portrait of a Floor Leader," in Richard Baker and Roger Davidson, eds., *First Among Equals* (Washington, D.C.: Congressional Quarterly Press, 1991), pp. 19–21; on the legislative conditions for realignment, see David Brady, *Critical Elections and Congressional Policy-Making* (Stanford, Calif.: Stanford University Press, 1988).

5: WILSON'S PROGRAM AND THE NEW FREEDOM

1. Wilson to A. Palmer, February 5, 1913, *PWW* (*The Papers of Woodrow Wilson,* ed. Arthur Link et al., 69 vols. [Princeton: Princeton University Press, 1966–1993]), 27:98–101. Wilson drafted this letter to head off a move by congressional Democrats to act on a favorite platform plank of Bryan's—a constitutional amendment limiting the president to a single six-year term. Stressing the importance of preserving a degree of electoral responsibility in such a powerful office, Wilson wrote to Palmer, of the House Judiciary Committee, to argue against going forward with it. The amendment had already passed the Senate. Following Wilson's advice, the Democratic leaders buried the amendment, but they decided not to release the letter, lest it antagonize Bryan. It was released before the 1916 election, though, to show Wilson's early and consistent opposition to the second-term ban at the start of his reelection campaign. A. Palmer interview with Ray Stannard Baker, January 22, 1929, Baker Papers, Library of Congress; Arthur Link, *Wilson,* 5 vols. (Princeton: Princeton University Press, 1947–1965), 1:472; Walter Lippmann, "The Palmer Letter," *New Republic,* January 15, 1916, p. 268.

2. Wilson, *The State: Elements of Historical and Practical Politics* (Boston: D. C. Heath, 1889), pp. 565–66. Jefferson's reasoning is analyzed by Jeffrey Tulis, *The Rhetorical Presidency* (Princeton: Princeton University Press, 1987), p. 56.

3. David Houston, *Eight Years with Wilson's Cabinet,* 2 vols. (New York: Doubleday, Page, 1926), 1:52–54; Josephus Daniels, *The Wilson Era,* 2 vols. (Chapel Hill: University of North Carolina Press, 1944), 1:101; "President's Visit Nettles Senators," *New York Times,* April 8, 1913, p. 1; "Congress Cheers Wilson," *New York Times,* April 9, 1913, p. 1; "President Wilson on Capitol Hill," *Harper's Weekly,* April 19, 1913, pp. 3–4; Henry Fountain Ashurst, *A Many-Colored Toga: The Diary of Henry Fountain Ashurst,* ed. George Sparks (Tucson: University of Arizona Press, 1962), pp. 25–26; Wilson, address on the tariff, *PWW,* 27:269–70.

4. James Miller Leake, "Four Years of Congress," *American Political Science Review* 11 (May 1917): 254; Daniels, *Wilson Era,* 1:99–101; "Wilson Revisits Capitol on Tariff," *New York Times,* April 10, 1913, p. 1; "President Visits Capitol Again," *New York World,* April 10, 1913, in *PWW,* 27:278–80.

5. Remarks to the Gridiron Club of Washington, April 12, 1913, *PWW,* 27:294–96.

6. "The President and Legislation," *Nation,* April 10, 1913, p. 350; A. Maurice Low, "The New Bossism," *Harper's Weekly,* April 19, 1913, p. 8.

7. Address on tariff reform to a joint session of Congress, April 8, 1913, *PWW,* 27:269–72; address on banking and currency reform to a joint session of Congress, June 23, 1913, ibid., 27:570–73; address on antitrust legislation to a joint session of Congress, January 20, 1914, ibid., 29:153–58; "The Spoken Message," *New Republic,* December 5, 1914, pp. 11–12; Elmer Cornwell, *The Presidential Leadership of Public Opinion* (Bloomington: Indiana University Press; Westport, Conn.: Greenwood Press, 1979), pp. 45–47; George Juergens, *News from the White House: The Presidential-*

Press Relationship in the Progressive Era (Chicago: University of Chicago Press, 1981), pp. 154–57.

8. *PWW,* 27:573.

9. See Link, *Wilson,* 2:177–240, 417–44; Lawrence Chamberlain, *The President, Congress, and Legislation* (New York: Columbia University Press, 1946), pp. 33–46, 109–19, 313–21; Leake, "Four Years of Congress," pp. 254–61; David Sarasohn, *Party of Reform: Democrats in the Progressive Era* (Jackson: University of Mississippi Press, 1989), pp. 155, 167–70.

10. Remarks at a press conference, November 3, 1913, *PWW* 28:487.

11. Henry Jones Ford, "The Record of the Administration," *Atlantic Monthly,* May 1916, p. 580; Wilson, a statement on the tariff lobbyists, May 26, 1913, *PWW,* 27:473. See Link, *Wilson,* 2:185–91, and Juergens, *News from the White House,* pp. 152–53, for details of the controversy.

12. For an analysis of the obstructionists' motivations, see Charles Willis Thompson, "Revolt Against President Wilson Ends in a Fiasco," *New York Times Magazine,* November 16, 1913, p. 1, and Link, *Wilson,* 2:228.

13. Link, *Wilson,* 2:230; "Wilson May Stump for Currency Bill," *New York Times,* October 3, 1913, p. 1; "O'Gorman's Ire Up over Money Bill," *New York Times,* October 9, 1913, p. 5; Wilson to M. A. H. Peck, September 28, 1913, *PWW,* 28:336; Wilson, remarks at a press conference, October 9, 1913, *PWW,* 50:268; Wilson, letter to the editor of the *Washington Post,* October 8, 1913, *PWW,* 28:373. For a similar categorical disavowal of such a rumor in a subsequent controversy, see Wilson, remarks at a press conference, April 2, 1914, *PWW,* 29:397–98.

14. Ray Stannard Baker, "Wilson," *Collier's,* October 7, 1916, pp. 6, 41; Samuel G. Blythe, "Wilson in Washington," *Saturday Evening Post,* November 8, 1913, pp. 8, 45; Link, *Wilson,* 2:154–55; House diary, *PWW,* 29:59.

15. "Wilson and Legislation," *Nation,* August 10, 1913, p. 136; "President Wilson's Record," *London Times,* September 13, 1913, p. 7; Lindsay Rogers, "President Wilson's Theory of His Office," *Forum,* February 1914, pp. 174–86; "A Congress with a Record," *New York Times,* October 23, 1914, p. 10; "Team-Work," *Nation,* January 21, 1915, pp. 69–70; "The Spoken Message," *New Republic,* December 5, 1914, pp. 11–12.

16. Wilfred Binkley, *President and Congress,* 3d ed. (New York: Random House, 1962), p. 262. See also Edward Corwin, "Woodrow Wilson and the Presidency," *Virginia Law Review* 6 (October 1956): 170–71; Chamberlain, *President, Congress, and Legislation,* pp. 17–18; Norman Small, *Some Presidential Interpretations of the Presidency* (Baltimore: Johns Hopkins University Press, 1932), pp. 171–75.

17. Wilson to T. W. Hardwick, March 15, 1915, *PWW,* 32:375–76. See also Wilson to J. R. Thorton, July 15, 1913, ibid., 28:35. Caucus rule among the Democrats worked essentially as follows. Meeting in private, the delegations debated the measures then pending on the floor and voted to determine whether they, as party members, should be required to vote in a particular way. If two-thirds of those present and voting agreed that party discipline should be enforced, then all members were so bound (provided that the two-thirds vote among those present in the caucus

amounted to a majority of the entire delegation). The only exceptions were if the measure hinged on matters of constitutional interpretation or if legislators had pledged before the election, or been formally instructed by their electors, to support the defeated position. If members otherwise defied the caucus, an observer remarked in 1915, they ran the risk of being read out of the party and denied the "three necessities of congressional existence—perquisites, patronage, and 'pork'" (Wilder Haines, "The Congressional Caucus of Today," *American Political Science Review* 9 [November 1915]: 696–706, quotation on p. 701). The caucus rules of the House Democrats, adopted in 1909, are reprinted in George B. Galloway, *The Legislative Process in Congress* (New York: Thomas Y. Crowell, 1953), pp. 328–29. The Senate Democrats had adopted a similar two-thirds binding rule back in 1903; Randall B. Ripley, *Majority Party Leadership in Congress* (Boston: Little, Brown, 1969), p. 65.

18. Ripley, *Majority Party Leadership*, pp. 61–62, 143–44; James S. Fleming, "Reestablishing Leadership in the House of Representatives: The Case of Oscar W. Underwood," *Mid-America* 54 (October 1972): 234–50.

19. Wilson, remarks at a press conference, April 7, 1913, *PWW*, 50:11; "House Democrats Reject Open Caucus," *New York Times*, April 9, 1913, p. 1; Fleming, "Oscar Underwood," p. 242.

20. Wilson to J. R. Thorton, July 15, 1913, *PWW*, 28:35; F. M. Simmons to Wilson, September 4, 1913, ibid., 28:253; Wilson to F. M. Simmons, September 4, 1913, ibid., 28:254. Carter Glass gave an example of Wilson's doubts in his memoir of the passage of the Federal Reserve Act. Glass recalled that when the bill was reported out to the Senate in late November 1914, Wilson "was disposed to assert vigorously his established aversion to 'rule by caucus' . . . [but] the practical politicians finally convinced the President that there must be a caucus or an abandonment of all hope for legislation" (*An Adventure in Constructive Finance* [New York: Doubleday, Page, 1927], p. 195).

21. Ripley, *Majority Party Leadership*, pp. 61–67; Fleming, "Oscar Underwood," pp. 239–41; Walter Oleszek, "John Worth Kern: Portrait of a Floor Leader," in Richard Baker and Roger Davidson, eds., *First Among Equals* (Washington, D.C.: Congressional Quarterly Press, 1991), pp. 28–30.

22. Alexander George and Juliette George, *Woodrow Wilson and Colonel House: A Personality Study* (1956; New York: Dover Publications, 1964), pp. 135–41; James Sundquist, *Decline and Resurgence of Congress* (Washington, D.C.: Brookings Institution, 1981), pp. 171–74.

23. See, for example, remarks at a press conference, January 26, 1915, *PWW*, 32:123.

24. On this point, see Stephen Balch, "Party Government in the U.S. House of Representatives, 1911–18" (Ph.D. diss., University of California, Berkeley, 1973), pp. 214–25.

25. Remarks in Trenton to the New Jersey electors, January 13, 1913, *PWW*, 32:40; Ray Stannard Baker interview with Albert Burleson, March 17, 1927, Ray Stannard Baker Papers, Library of Congress. This section is adapted from Daniel

Stid, "Woodrow Wilson and the Problem of Party Government," *Polity,* 26 (Summer 1994): 569–74.

26. Burleson interview, Baker Papers, Library of Congress; Link, *Wilson,* 2:160–73; John Blum, *Joe Tumulty and the Wilson Era* (Boston: Houghton Mifflin, 1951), pp. 72–83.

27. William Dudley Foulke, *Fighting the Spoilsmen: Reminiscences of the Civil Service Reform Movement* (New York: G. P. Putnam's Sons, 1919), pp. 228–29; 233–37; Stephen Skowronek, *Building a New American State: The Expansion of National Administrative Capacities, 1877–1920* (New York: Cambridge University Press, 1982), pp. 195–96.

28. Burleson interview, Baker Papers, Library of Congress; Link, *Wilson,* 2:158–59; Skowronek, *New American State,* p. 194 (citing Link); August Heckscher, *Woodrow Wilson* (New York: Scribner's Sons, 1991), p. 286. Burleson's oft repeated story has aged well, not least because of the teller's efforts to establish his place in the historical record as the tough-minded politician who cleared the way for the many accomplishments of Wilson's administration. Burleson was a notorious self-promoter. One cabinet colleague, after having dinner with him, recounted, "I spent most of the evening hearing the Postmaster General tell of the great burden that it was to have a Congress on his hands. Bernard Shaw writes of the Superman, and so does, I believe, the crazy Philosopher of Germany. I was convinced last night that I had met one in the flesh" (Franklin Knight Lane to his wife, February 5, 1916, in *The Letters of Franklin Knight Lane,* ed. Anne Wintermute Lane and Louise Herrick [New York: Houghton Mifflin, 1922], p. 201).

29. House diary, December 18, 1912, in *PWW,* 25:610.

30. Wilson to E. B. Galt, August 28, 1915, ibid., 34:351–52; House diary, November 16, 1912, ibid., 25:550; T. B. Love to Wilson, December 27, 1912, ibid., 25:624–66; O. W. Underwood to Wilson, January 13, 1913, ibid., 27:44–45; House Diary, February 14, 1913, ibid., 27:111.

31. House diary, February 19, 1913, ibid., 27:119–20; Wilson, "A Warning to Office Seekers," ibid., 27:153; House diary, December 14, 1916, ibid., 40:239, 241; Houston, *Wilson's Cabinet,* 1:40–41, 89; Daniels, *Wilson Era,* 1:139, 146–47.

32. Foulke, *Fighting the Spoilsmen,* 229–32; Paul Van Riper, *History of the United States Civil Service* (New York: Row, Peterson, 1958), pp. 231, 237–38; C. W. Eliot to Wilson, September 10, 1913, *PWW,* 28:272; Bryan to Wilson, June 25, 1913, *PWW,* 28:4–5; Bryan to Wilson, August 4, 1913, *PWW,* 28:111–12; Link, *Wilson,* 1:97–107.

33. For the criticism generated by Wilson's position, and his awkward attempts to defend his administration in this regard, see O. Villard to Wilson, July 21, 1913, *PWW,* 28:60–61; M. Storey, W. Dubois, and O. Villard to Wilson, August 15, 1913, ibid., 28:163–65; Wilson to O. Villard, July 23, August 21, 1913, ibid., 28:65, 202; remarks by Wilson and a dialogue, November 12, 1914, ibid., 31:301–8; *New Republic,* November 21, 1914, p. 5.

34. Kendrick Clements, *The Presidency of Woodrow Wilson* (Lawrence: University Press of Kansas, 1992), chap. 4; Link, *Wilson,* pp. 119–22, 137–40.

35. A campaign address, October 17, 1916, *PWW*, 38:363. See also Burleson interview, Baker Papers, Library of Congress; Joseph Tumulty, *Woodrow Wilson as I Knew Him* (Garden City, N.Y.: Doubleday, Page, 1921), p. 101.

36. D. Breckinridge to W. McCombs, March 7, 1914, *PWW*, 29:343; W. McAdoo to Wilson, October 29, 1914, ibid., 31:252–54; Link, *Wilson*, 2:160–73.

37. "Unregenerate Democracy," *New Republic*, February 5, 1916, p. 18. See also C. Eliot to Wilson, September 10, 1913, *PWW*, 28:272; Foulke, *Fighting the Spoilsmen*, pp. 226–27; Skowronek, *New American State*, p. 196.

38. Wilson to J. Tumulty, January 4, 1914, *PWW*, 29:100; Wilson to Burleson, May 29, 1913, ibid., 27:487; Wilson interview with Samuel Blythe, December 5, 1914, ibid., 31:400–401.

39. Wilson to S. S. Wise, June 4, 1914, ibid., 30:144.

6: TOWARD PARTY REFORM AND REALIGNMENT

1. *PWW* (*The Papers of Woodrow Wilson*, ed. Arthur Link et al., 69 vols. [Princeton: Princeton University Press, 1966–1993]), 27:98–101.

2. Ibid.; Arthur Link, *Wilson*, 5 vols. (Princeton: Princeton University Press, 1947–1965), 2:22–23.

3. *PWW*, 29:7–8.

4. Wilson to O. W. Underwood, January 23, 1914, ibid., 29:163; Underwood to Wilson, January 24, 1914, ibid., 29:170; Wilson, remarks at a press conference, January 15, 1914, ibid., 50:340; "Wilson Primary Hits Republicans," *New York Times*, February 12, 1914, p. 1.

5. Wilson, remarks at a press conference, October 5, 1914, *PWW*, 50:591–92; "No Primaries for 1916," *New York Times*, October 6, 1914, p. 7; House diary, November 9 and 25, 1914, *PWW*, 31:281–82, 355; "Drops National Primary," *New York Times*, March 25, 1915, p. 5; W. L. Stoddard, "The Presidential Primary," *New Republic*, June 12, 1915, pp. 145–46;

6. F. J. Heney to Wilson, July 1, 1916, *PWW*, 37:338–39; Wilson to F. J. Heney, July 4, 1916, ibid., 37:358.

7. James Ceaser, *Presidential Selection: Theory and Development* (Princeton: Princeton University Press, 1979); James Ceaser, Glen Thurow, Jeffrey Tulis, and Joseph Bessette, "The Rise of the Rhetorical Presidency," *Presidential Studies Quarterly* 11 (Spring 1981): 166–68; Robert Eden, *Political Leadership and Nihilism: A Study of Weber and Nietzche* (Tampa: University of South Florida Press, 1983), pp. 13–15.

8. For the background to the controversy, see "The Senate Against Mr. Wilson," *Independent*, January 4, 1915, pp. 10–11. See also Wilfred Binkley, *President and Congress*, 3d ed. (New York: Random House, 1962), pp. 194–204.

9. "Senate Accepts Wilson's Challenge," *New York Times*, December 19, 1914, p. 1.

10. House diary, December 17, 1914, *PWW*, 31:481–82; "Wilson-Senate Row May Split Party," *New York Times*, December 21, 1914, p. 1; "Senate Renews Patron-

age Fight," *New York Times,* January 5, 1915, p. 1; *New Republic,* December 26, 1914, pp. 3–4; Henry Jones Ford, "Usurpation by the Senate," *New Republic,* January 9, 1915, pp. 17–18; Wilson, remarks at a press conference, December 22, 1914, *PWW,* 31:507.

11. "Senate Unanimous in Rejecting Bid," *New York Times,* January 7, 1915, p. 11.
12. *PWW,* 32:33.
13. "Wilson and the Senate Near Compromise," *New York Times,* January 13, 1915, p. 1.
14. Wilson to Bland, March 5, 1913, *PWW,* 32:325; "Won't Name Men Rejected," *New York Times,* March 7, 1915, p. 8.
15. *New Republic,* January 16, 1915, p. 4.
16. Wilson to O. Underwood, October 17, 1914, *PWW,* 31:168–74; Roger Davidson and Walter Oleszek, *Congress and Its Members,* 5th ed. (Washington, D.C.: Congressional Quarterly Press, 1996), p. 436; David Sarasohn, *The Party of Reform: Democrats in the Progressive Era* (Jackson: University of Mississippi Press, 1989), pp. 172–77; John Blum, *Joe Tumulty and the Wilson Era* (Boston: Houghton Mifflin, 1951), pp. 85–86; House diary, November 4, 1914, *PWW,* 31:265.
17. *PWW,* 32:29–40, quotation from p. 38. See also *Nation,* January 14, 1915, p. 41. Election data from Margaret Thompson, ed., *Presidential Elections Since 1789,* 3d ed. (Washington, D.C.: Congressional Quarterly Press, 1983), p. 102.
18. Link, *Wilson,* 2:206–18.
19. Wilson to H. Hollis, June 2, 1914, *PWW,* 30:134; Thomas K. McGraw, *Prophets of Regulation* (Cambridge, Mass.: Belknap Press, 1984), pp. 115–17.
20. Brandeis to Wilson, June 14, 1913, *PWW,* 27:520–21; N. Hapgood to Wilson, April 21, 1914, ibid., 29:481–82; Wilson to H. Hollis, June 2, 1914, ibid., 30:134; Link, *Wilson,* 2:212, 438; Arthur M. Schlesinger Jr., *The Age of Roosevelt,* 3 vols. (Boston: Houghton Mifflin, 1957), 1:34.
21. Wilson to C. Kitchin, January 24, 1916, *PWW,* 35:510–12; J. Tumulty to Wilson, January 25, 1916, ibid., 35:524; Wilson to C. Kitchin, January 26, 1916, ibid., 35:526–27; R. Owen to Wilson, January 5, 1916, Wilson Papers, Library of Congress; David Houston, *Eight Years With Wilson's Cabinet,* 2 vols. (New York: Doubleday, Page, 1926), 1:196–98; "President Asks for Tariff Board," *New York Times,* January 26, 1916, p. 1.
22. "The Democrats as Legislators," *New Republic,* September 2, 1916, pp. 103–4; Walter Lippmann, "The Case for Wilson," *New Republic,* October 14, 1916, p. 263; Herbert Croly, "The Two Parties in 1916," *New Republic,* October 21, 1916, pp. 286, 290–91.
23. "The Democrats as Legislators," *New Republic,* September 2, 1916, pp. 103–4; Sarasohn, *Party of Reform,* pp. 184–89; Arthur Link, *The Higher Realism of Woodrow Wilson* (Nashville, Tenn.: Vanderbilt University Press, 1971), pp. 306–7. Even the origins and formulation of the two exceptions, the tariff commission measure and the Adamson Act, were significantly influenced by congressional Democrats, most no-

tably Robert Owen. It was Owen who brought home to Wilson the political and policy arguments for a tariff commission, the legislation for which was drafted in the administration at the request of Majority Leader Claude Kitchin; Link, *Wilson,* 4:342–45. Then, in June 1916, again on the advice of Owen, Wilson endorsed the principle of the eight-hour-day clause that was central to the Adamson Act in the draft platform that he sent out to the Democratic Convention. Later, at the behest of congressional leaders, Wilson considerably shortened the list of what he was prepared to ask Congress to do to avert a railroad strike. In this case the bill was drafted by Representative William Adamson and Majority Leader Claude Kitchin; Link, *Wilson,* 5:88–90.

24. Wilson to J. Tumulty, January 24, 1914, *PWW,* 29:170; Wilson to C. Glass, May 12, 1914, ibid., 30:24; "Threatens Wilson Unless He Agrees to Exempt Labor," *New York Times,* April 30, 1914, in ibid., 29:537–38.

25. Wilson to A. Pomerene, May 12, 1916, ibid., 37:25.

26. On this point, see Lippmann, "The Case for Wilson," p. 263; Croly, "The Two Parties in 1916," pp. 286, 290–91; Link, *Wilson,* 4:323.

27. See the following exchange of letters: Owen to Wilson, June 2, 3, 8, 1916, *PWW,* 37:151, 162, 174–75, and Wilson to Owen, June 5, 12, 1916, ibid., 37:162, 207; see also Wilson, a draft of the National Democratic Platform of 1916, ca. June 10, 1916, ibid., 37:198–99.

28. Ibid., 37:195–96. For the political reasoning behind Wilson's discussion of international relations, see House to Wilson, May 29, 1916, ibid., 37:121; Wilson to House, July 2, 1916, ibid., 37:345; Thomas Knock, *To End All Wars* (New York: Oxford University Press, 1992), pp. 85–86.

29. Wilson to W. Kent, July 18, 1916, ibid., 37:432. Among the prominent members were journalists Norman Hapgood and Ray Stannard Baker and Jewish leader Jacob Schiff. See Ray Stannard Baker, *Woodrow Wilson: Life and Letters,* 8 vols. (Garden City, N.Y.: Doubleday, Page, 1927–1939), 6:266; McCormick interview, Baker Papers, Library of Congress; "Wilson Welcomes Independents," *New York Times,* July 20, 1916, p. 5.

30. Wilson to V. McCormick, August 4, 1916, *PWW,* 37:523–24; memorandum by Bainbridge Colby, ca. 1932, Baker Papers, Library of Congress; "Moose, Associates in Wilson Campaign," *New York Times,* August 11, 1916, p. 3.

31. *PWW,* 37:432.

32. Link, *Wilson,* 5:124; Knock, *To End All Wars,* p. 94; "Progressive Voice Raised for Wilson," *New York Times,* November 1, 1916, p. 5.

33. Wilson, address on Commodore John Barry, May 16, 1914, *PWW,* 30:35–36; address to the Daughters of the American Revolution, October 11, 1915, ibid., 35:50–51.

34. H. Munsterberg to Wilson, November 7, 1914, ibid., 31:276–78; D. Malone to Wilson, January 18, 1915, ibid., 32:86; P. Husting to Wilson, January 5, 1915, ibid., 32:19–20; Blum, *Tumulty,* pp. 88–95, 105–9; "Appeal to Foreign Born," *New York*

Times, October 1, 1916, p. 2. On the appearance of American diplomacy favoring Great Britain, see Kendrick Clements, *The Presidency of Woodrow Wilson* (Lawrence: University Press of Kansas, 1992), pp. 117–23.

35. Annual message, *PWW,* 35:307; platform cited in editor's note, ibid., 37:200. See also Palmer interview, Baker Papers, Library of Congress; O'Leary to Wilson, Wilson to O'Leary, September 29, 1916, *PWW,* 38:285–86; House to Wilson, September 30, October 1, 1916, ibid., 38:317–18; Joseph Tumulty, *Woodrow Wilson as I Knew Him* (Garden City, N.Y.: Doubleday, Page, 1921), pp. 213–15; Link, *Wilson,* 5:104–5.

36. Because of this predicament Wilson initially had vetoed and in 1916 was holding off a bill that proposed a literacy test to restrict immigration. Wilson admitted to John Sharp Williams, a supporter of restriction, that he was opposing the provision in order to appease the leadership of the various ethnic groups; *PWW,* 32:26; Lawrence Chamberlain, *The President, Congress, and Legislation* (New York: Columbia University Press, 1946), pp. 364–65.

37. Link, *Wilson,* 5:135; H. Wallace to House, September 3, 1916, *PWW,* 38:139–41; "Appeal to Foreign Born," *New York Times,* October 1, 1916, p. 2.

38. Thompson, *Presidential Elections,* pp. 103, 168; Woolley interview, Baker Papers, Library of Congress.

39. Sarasohn, *Party of Reform,* 219–28; Knock, *To End All Wars,* pp. 101–3; Link, *Wilson,* 5:160–64.

40. On this point, see Link, *Wilson,* 5:161; "How the Hyphen Voted," *New York Times,* November 12, 1916, p. 6; William Leary, Jr., "Woodrow Wilson, Irish-Americans, and the Election of 1916," *Journal of American History* 54 (June 1967): 57–72.

41. Sarasohn, *Party of Reform,* 228–38; Meyer Nathan, "The Presidential Election of 1916 in the Middle West" (Ph.D. diss., Princeton University, 1965), pp. 258–61; *New Republic,* November 11, 1916, p. 31.

42. Figures compiled from Department of Commerce, Bureau of the Census, *Historical Statistics of the United States: Colonial Times to 1970,* 2 vols. (Washington, D.C.: Government Printing Office, 1975), 2:1084, and Thompson, *Presidential Elections,* p. 103. In his study of the 1916 election, S. D. Lovell notes that in almost every state Wilson ran ahead of the Democratic candidates for governor and senator (*The Presidential Election of 1916* [Carbondale: Southern Illinois University Press, 1980], pp. 178–79).

43. Davidson and Oleszek, *Congress and Its Members,* p. 436; W. Adamson to Wilson, November 16, 1916, *PWW,* 38:666–67; George C. Roberts, "Woodrow Wilson, John Worth Kern, and the 1916 Indiana Election: Defeat of a Senate Majority Leader," *Presidential Studies Quarterly* 10 (Winter 1980): 63–73.

44. Wilson to J. Hopkins, November 16, 1916, *PWW,* 38:663. For an insightful analysis of the mixed message of the returns, see "The Two Parties After the Election," *New Republic,* November 18, 1916, pp. 63–64.

45. Toy diary, *PWW,* 32:9–10; Ray Stannard Baker, memorandum of a conver-

sation at the White House, May 12, 1916, ibid., 37:33–34; House diary, November 15, 1916, ibid., 38:660–61; House diary, April 29, 1917, ibid., 42:162.

46. Toy diary, ibid., 32:9–10.

47. House diary, October 19, 1916, and House to Wilson, October 20, 1916, ibid., 38:493–94; Wilson to Lansing, November 5, 1916, ibid., 38:617–18.

48. Ibid.

7: DIPLOMACY, WAR, AND EXECUTIVE POWER

1. Quotation from "Wilson to Address Congress on Tolls," *New York Times,* March 4, 1914, p. 1; "Clark Hotly Denies Aim to Split Party," *New York Times,* April 1, 1914, p. 2; Stephen Balch, "Do Strong Presidents Really Want Strong Legislative Parties? The Case of Woodrow Wilson and the House Democrats," *Presidential Studies Quarterly* 7 (Fall 1977): 235. For the background on the dispute, see Arthur Link, *Wilson,* 5 vols. (Princeton: Princeton University Press, 1947–1965), 2:304–6. American ships going from coast to coast were exempted from the toll altogether; those heading abroad enjoyed a lower rate than was charged to ships from other nations.

2. Wilson to J. Tumulty, February 19, 1914, *PWW* (*The Papers of Woodrow Wilson,* ed. Arthur Link et al., 69 vols. [Princeton: Princeton University Press, 1966–1993]), 29:271.

3. James Miller Leake, "Four Years of Congress," *American Political Science Review* 11 (May 1917): 262–63; Link, *Wilson,* 2:311–14; Wilson, interview with Ida Minerva Tarbell, October 3, 1916, *PWW,* 38:328–29; Herbert Croly, *Progressive Democracy* (New York: Macmillan, 1914), p. 346.

4. *PWW,* 29:312–13.

5. William Gibbs McAdoo, *Crowded Years* (New York: Houghton Mifflin, 1931), pp. 295–96; David Kennedy, *Over Here: The First World War and American Society* (New York: Oxford University Press, 1980), p. 301; Wilson, "An Annual Message," *PWW,* 31:415–16, 418.

6. Lodge to T. Roosevelt, January 15, 1915, in *Selections from the Correspondence of Theodore Roosevelt and Henry Cabot Lodge, 1884–1918,* ed. Henry Cabot Lodge, 2 vols. (New York: Scribner's, 1925), 2:451–52. See Lodge's speech in the Senate on January 22, 1915, "The Ship Purchase Bill" (Washington, D.C.: Government Printing Office, 1915); Root's speech in the Senate, bearing the same title, January 25, 1915 (Washington, D.C.: Government Printing Office, 1915); Link, *Wilson,* 3:147–48.

7. Wilson to W. G. McAdoo, November 8, 1914, *PWW,* 31:279–80; R. L. Lansing to Wilson, November 23, 1914, ibid., 31:347–49; W. J. Bryan to Wilson, January 23, 1915, ibid., 32:114–15; Wilson, remarks at a press conference, January 26, 1915, ibid., 32:123; Wilson to C. W. Eliot, February 18, 1915, ibid., 32:244–45.

8. Wilson, Jackson Day address in Indianapolis, January 8, 1915, ibid., 32:32–34; Wilson to W. J. Stone, January 27, 1915, ibid., 32:134; "Ship Bill Session Lasts 37 Hours," *New York Times,* January 31, 1915, p. 1; "Offer to Modify Ship Bill," *New*

York Times, February 3, 1915, p. 1; "Democrats Move Ship Bill Cloture," February 10, 1915, *New York Times,* p. 1; Henry Fountain Ashurst, *A Many-Colored Toga: The Diary of Henry Fountain Ashurst,* ed. George Sparks (Tucson: University of Arizona Press, 1962), p. 38; Root, "Ship Purchase Bill," pp. 7–9, 31–32; Lodge to T. Roosevelt, February 4, 1915, *Correspondence,* 2:453; Wilson, remarks at a press conference, January 26, 1915, *PWW,* 32:122–23.

9. "Mr. Wilson's Congress," *Nation,* September 14, 1916, p. 252; "Senate Democrats Unite on Ship Bill," *New York Times,* July 29, 1916, p. 6; Link, *Wilson,* 4:339–41.

10. Wilson to L. Garrison, Wilson to J. Daniels, July 21, 1915, *PWW,* 34:4–5.

11. Ibid., 35:171.

12. F. K. Lane to A. Miller, December 12, 1915, in *The Letters of Franklin Knight Lane,* ed. Anne Wintermute Lane and Louise Herrick (New York: Houghton Mifflin, 1922), p. 189; "Bryan Assails President's Plan," *New York Times,* November 11, 1915, p. 1; "Fails to Win Kitchin," *New York Times,* November 9, 1915, p. 4; Richard Bensel, *Sectionalism and American Political Development* (Madison: University of Wisconsin Press, 1984), pp. 124–27.

13. Address in New York on preparedness, January 27, 1916, *PWW,* 36:8.

14. Address in Pittsburgh on preparedness, January 29, 1916, ibid., 36:35.

15. "Unregenerate Democracy," *New Republic,* February 5, 1916, pp. 18–19.

16. George Herring, "James Hay and the Preparedness Controversy," *Journal of Southern History* 30 (November 1964): 388–402; Link, *Wilson,* 4:329–32, 334–38.

17. "A Costly Resignation," *New Republic,* February 19, 1916, pp. 56–57; Lindley M. Garrison interview, Baker Papers, Library of Congress.

18. Ray Stannard Baker, *Woodrow Wilson: Life and Letters,* 8 vols. (Garden City, N.Y.: Doubleday, Page, 1927–1939), 6:157–64; "House in Revolt over Armed Liners," *New York Times,* February 24, 1916, pp. 1–2; W. J. Stone to Wilson, February 24, 1916, *PWW,* 36:209–11.

19. "President's Stand Halts Congress," *New York Times,* February 26, 1916, p. 1; J. P. Tumulty to Wilson, February 24, 1916, *PWW,* 36:211–13; Wilson to W. J. Stone, February 24, 1916, *PWW,* 36:213–14; Link, *Wilson,* 3:175–78.

20. *PWW,* 36:231–32.

21. "Washington Notes," *New Republic,* March 18, 1916, pp. 181–82.

22. "President or Prime Minister," *Nation,* March 9, 1916, p. 272.

23. *PWW,* 37:33–35.

24. David Houston, *Eight Years with Wilson's Cabinet,* 2 vols. (New York: Doubleday, Page, 1926), 1:233–36.

25. Lodge, *Correspondence,* 2:497; "Extra Session Fight in Senate," *New York Times,* February 24, 1917, pp. 1, 4; see also "The President to Congress and the People," *Nation,* March 6, 1917, p. 228.

26. *PWW,* 41:285–86. For Wilson's attitude toward his Senate opponents at this point, see an unpublished statement, February 26, 1917, ibid., 41:287.

27. Link, *Wilson,* 5:354, 359; *Congressional Record,* 64th Cong., 2d sess., March 3, 1917, p. 4912; Thomas W. Ryley, *A Little Group of Willful Men* (Port Washington, N.Y.:

Kennikat Press, 1975), 103–31; "Bitter Wrangle as Senate Closes," *New York Times,* March 5, 1917, pp. 1–2.

28. *PWW,* 41:318–20.

29. R. Lansing to Wilson, March 6, 1917, ibid., 41:341–44; Daniels diary, March 6, 1917, ibid., 41:346; R. Lansing to Wilson, March 8, 1917, ibid., 41:360–61; Daniels diary, March 8, 1917, ibid., 41:364.

30. Baker, *Life and Letters,* 6:486–504; Barbara Tuchman, *The Zimmermann Telegram* (New York: Ballantine Books, 1985), pp. 184–96.

31. Houston, *Wilson's Cabinet,* 1:89; House diary, June 24, 1915, *PWW,* 33:449; Wilson to A. Palmer, February 5, 1913, *PWW,* 27:100; Link, *Wilson,* 5:viii; Richard Fenno, *The President's Cabinet* (Cambridge: Harvard University Press, 1959), pp. 44, 120–21; Alexander George and Juliette George, *Woodrow Wilson and Colonel House: A Personality Study* (1956; New York: Dover Publications, 1964), pp. 128–29.

32. Memorandum by Robert Lansing, March 20, 1917, *PWW,* 41:444. See also Baker, *Life and Letters,* 6:502–3, and Fenno, *President's Cabinet,* 122–23.

33. "A Proclamation," March 21, 1917, *PWW,* 41:446; F. Lane to G. Lane, April 4, 1917, *Letters of Franklin Knight Lane,* pp. 242–43; Brahany diary, March 30, 1917, *PWW,* 41:506–7; House diary, April 2, 1917, ibid., 41:529.

34. R. Lansing to Wilson, with enclosure, March 26, 1917, *PWW,* 41:471–72; Wilson to R. Lansing, March 27, 1917, ibid., 41:475.

35. House diary, March 27, 1917, ibid., 41:482–83.

36. Ibid., 41:521.

37. Ibid., 41:522.

38. Richard Watson Jr., "A Testing Time for Southern Congressional Leadership: The War Crisis of 1917–18," *Journal of Southern History* 44 (February 1978): 20; E. Pou to J. Tumulty, April 11, 1917, *PWW,* 42:42–43; C. Caldwell to Wilson, April 19, 1917, *PWW,* 42:103–4; P. Husting to Wilson, April 27, 1917, *PWW,* 42:146–50; "Congress Again Shows Leaning to Volunteers," *New York Times,* April 10, 1917.

39. "Senators See Peril in Espionage Bill," *New York Times,* April 15, 1917; "Senate Riddles Espionage Bill," *New York Times,* April 19, 1917; "Anti-Censorship Tide Floods House," *New York Times,* May 4, 1917; J. Tumulty to Wilson, May 8, 1917, Wilson Papers, Library of Congress.

40. *Congressional Record,* 65th Cong., 1st sess. June 14, 1917, p. 3597, and June 29, 1917, pp. 4459–61. See also Tom G. Hall, "Wilson and the Food Crisis: Agricultural Price Control During World War One," *Agricultural History,* 48 (January 1973): 40–42.

41. Seward Livermore, *Politics Is Adjourned: Woodrow Wilson and the War Congress, 1917–18* (Seattle: University of Washington Press, 1968), pp. 35–36.

42. *Congressional Record,* 65th Cong., 1st sess., April 27, 1917, p. 1376.

43. Ibid., May 16, 1917, pp. 2383–85. See also ibid., May 4, 1917, p. 1785; "Senators Close Doors to Attack Administration," *New York Times,* May 17, 1917; "Senators Despair of Secret Session," *New York Times,* May 18, 1917; H. Hollis to J. Tumulty, June 1, 1917, Wilson Papers, Library of Congress.

44. Wilfred Binkley, *President and Congress,* 3d ed. (New York: Random House, 1962), chap. 6.

45. Republican Senator John Weeks of Massachusetts was the first to propose such a committee, which he did on April 9, 1917, but it was quickly tabled. The more serious initiatives, sponsored by Democrats, would come later. See *Congressional Record,* 65th Cong., 1st sess., April 9, 1917, p. 459; Baker, *Life and Letters,* 7:24; Seward Livermore, *Woodrow Wilson and the War Congress, 1916–18* (Seattle: University of Washington Press, 1968), pp. 15–16, 53–57, 91–94.

46. A. Lever to Wilson, July 21, 1917, *PWW,* 43:242; *Congressional Record,* 65th Cong., 1st sess., July 17 and 21, 1917, pp. 5176–77 and 5363–64. The final vote on the Owen Amendment was 53–31 in favor; the Senate then voted 81–6 to approve the amended bill. Voting data from ibid.; Michael Wormser, ed., *Congressional Quarterly's Guide to Congress,* 3d ed. (Washington, D.C.: Congressional Quarterly Press, 1982), appendix B; "Food Bill Passed by Senate," *New York Times,* July 22, 1917.

47. *PWW,* 43:348–50.

48. Ibid., 43:245. See also Wilson to R. Owen, August 3, 1917, ibid., 43:357–58.

49. "May Veto Food Bill Because of War Board Rider," *New York Times,* July 24, 1917; "President Wins, Hoover to Be Sole Food Controller," *New York Times,* July 31, 1917; Livermore, *War Congress,* p. 56; Carl Swisher, "The Control of War Preparations in the United States," *American Political Science Review* 34 (December 1940): 1090, 1092.

50. Daniel Beaver, *Newton D. Baker and the American War Effort, 1917–1919* (Lincoln: University of Nebraska Press, 1966), pp. 88–91; Wilson to G. Chamberlain, January 11, 1918, *PWW,* 45:566–67; "Moves to Add New Cabinet Member," *New York Times,* January 4, 1918; "Bill Before Senate for Munitions Chief," *New York Times,* January 5, 1918; "President Opposes Munitions Secretary," *New York Times,* January 12, 1918.

51. "Press of the Country Condemns Garfield's Action," *New York Times,* January 17, 1918; House diary, January 17, 1918, *PWW,* 46:23; "Senate Wanted Time to Reconsider," *New York Times,* January 18, 1918. The text of the Chamberlain bill was printed in the *New York Times* on January 21, 1918.

52. "President Assails Critics," *New York Times,* January 22, 1918; Daniels diary, January 22, 1918, *PWW,* 46:78–79; Wilson, a statement, January 21, 1917, *PWW,* 46:55–56; Livermore, *War Congress,* pp. 87–97.

53. *Congressional Record,* 65th Cong., 1st sess., July 21, 1917, p. 5364. After serving as the point man in the Senate on preparedness, Chamberlain had gone on to be the leading Democratic proponent of conscription (when virtually all of the Democratic leaders were set against the draft) and had taken over Senate sponsorship of the food bill when T. P. Gore, the Agriculture Committee Chair, refused to accept it.

54. Even after Wilson had issued his attack on Chamberlain and begun his lobbying of the Democratic senators, forcing at least ten of them to turn against the plan, four of the eight Democratic members of the Military Affairs Committee

were reported as being prepared to defy the president and support the bill. "Moves for a War Cabinet," *New York Times*, January 19, 1918; "Senate Ready for War Cabinet Fight," *New York Times*, January 23, 1918; Livermore, *War Congress*, p. 100.

55. Terry Eastland, *Energy in the Executive: The Case for the Strong Presidency* (New York: Free Press, 1992), pp. 139–53. See also Richard Nathan, *The Administrative Presidency* (New York: John Wiley, 1983), pp. 7–14, for the origins of the quoted phrases.

56. Newton Baker and Josephus Daniels interviews, Baker Papers, Library of Congress; Harry Garfield interview, Bragdon Collection, Princeton University; Daniels diary, January 16, 1918, *PWW*, 46:12; Baker, *Life and Letters*, 8:182–83; Fenno, *President's Cabinet*, pp. 120, 123; David Lawrence, *The True Story of Woodrow Wilson* (New York: George Doran, 1924), pp. 223–24; W. McAdoo to Wilson, May 16, 1917, and B. Baruch to Wilson, June 4, 1917, Wilson Papers, Library of Congress; House diary, July 4, 1917, *PWW*, 43:99–100; House diary, August 7, 1917, *PWW*, 43:390–91; House diary, January 17, 1917, *PWW*, 46:23–24.

57. Link, *Wilson*, 2:15–16, 18, 122–25; Beaver, *Newton D. Baker*, pp. 1–8.

58. "Baker Opposes Munitions Chief," *New York Times*, January 13, 1918.

59. Quoted in Robert Cuff, *The War Industries Board: Business-Government Relations During World War One* (Baltimore: Johns Hopkins University Press), p. 139.

60. For an astute analysis of the situation Wilson faced, see Colonel House's diary entry for January 17, 1917, *PWW*, 46:23.

61. "President Seeks Blanket Powers for War Period," *New York Times*, February 7, 1918.

62. Wilson to L. Overman, March 21, 1918, *PWW*, 47:94; *New Republic*, February 16, 1918, p. 69.

63. N. Baker to Wilson, with enclosure, February 2, 1918, *PWW*, 46:215–17.

64. Wilson to B. Baruch, March 4, 1918, ibid., 46:520–22; Bernard Baruch, *Baruch: The Public Years* (New York: Holt, Rinehart, and Winston, 1960), pp. 41–72; Kendrick Clements, *The Presidency of Woodrow Wilson* (Lawrence: University Press of Kansas, 1992), pp. 88–89; Cuff, *War Industries Board*, pp. 145–47.

65. Baruch, *Public Years*, pp. 85–86; House diary, February 25, 1918, *PWW*, 46:444–45; Wilson to B. Baruch, March 16, 1918, *PWW*, 47:43; Baker, *Life and Letters*, 8:36–37; Vance McCormick interview, Baker Papers, Library of Congress; Baker quoted in Beaver, *Newton D. Baker*, p. 173.

66. Edward Corwin, *The Presidency: Office and Powers, 1787–1957* (New York: New York University Press, 1957), p. 514.

67. Wilson's remarks were recorded by his visitor, the historian William H. Dodd, and are quoted in Samuel Flagg Bemis, *Diplomatic History of the United States*, 5th ed. (New York: Holt, Rinehart, and Winston, 1965), p. 630.

68. For the GOP responses, see "Not Wilson's War, Republicans Say," *New York Times*, October 26, 1918; William Howard Taft, "President's Stand Autocratic," ibid. For the calls of Theodore Roosevelt, William Howard Taft, and party chair Will Hays for a GOP Congress in 1918, see the reports of the New York State Republican

Convention in ibid., July 19–20, 1918. Roosevelt and Henry Cabot Lodge had made similar appeals on behalf of their party and President McKinley in 1898; "World Peace Plan Chief Issue Now," ibid., October 27, 1918.

69. The *Outlook* also explored this implication of Wilson's appeal: "In the other self-governing countries with which we allied not only is the action of the executive subject to the control of the legislative body, but its continued existence depends upon the will of the legislative body. . . . It is curious, possibly alarming, that at the very time when Germany is loudly proclaiming her purpose to abandon a Constitution in which the legislative body is subject to the control of the executive, our President should propose that we abandon a policy in which the Executive is subject to the control of the legislative" ("The President Re-Enters Politics," November 6, 1918, p. 338).

70. *PWW,* 53:364–65.

8: PARTY AND NATIONAL LEADERSHIP IN WORLD WAR I

1. See J. Hopkins to V. McCormick, November 14, 1916, *PWW (The Papers of Woodrow Wilson,* ed. Arthur Link et al., 69 vols. [Princeton: Princeton University Press, 1966–1993]), 38:642–44; J. Gavit to Wilson, November 22, 1916, ibid., 40:40–42; A. Riker to E. House, April 25, 1918, ibid., 47:437–39; "The Two Parties After the Election," *New Republic,* November 18, 1916, pp. 63–64.

2. C. Eliot to Wilson, November 21, 1916, *PWW,* 40:28; J. Gavit to Wilson, November 22, 1916, ibid., 40:41; House diary, November 26, 1916, ibid., 40:86; House diary, November 28, 1916, ibid., 40:97; House diary, January 4, 1917, ibid., 40:408; "All Postmasters Under Civil Service," April 1, 1917, *New York Times,* p. 13. This discussion is adapted from Daniel Stid, "Woodrow Wilson and the Problem of Party Government," *Polity* 26 (Summer 1994): 574–75.

3. Clark quoted in "Fight Civil Service Order," *New York Times,* March 9, 1917, p. 6. See also "Civil Service Order Angers Congressman," ibid., March 8, 1917, p. 7; H. Rainey to J. Tumulty, March 9, 1917, J. Small to Wilson, March 13, 1917, F. Simmons to Wilson, March 15, 1917, Wilson Papers, Library of Congress; Aldrin Norris Anderson, "Albert Sidney Burleson: A Southern Politician in the Progressive Era" (Ph.D. diss., Texas Technological College, 1967), p. 158.

4. Anderson, "Burleson," pp. 159–60; William Dudley Foulke, *Fighting the Spoilsmen: Reminiscences of the Civil Service Reform Movement* (New York: G. P. Putnam's Sons, 1919), pp. 255–57; David Burner, *The Politics of Provincialism: The Democratic Party in Transition* (New York: Alfred Knopf, 1967), p. 53; "The American Way," *Nation,* March 15, 1917, p. 302; Keyes quoted in "All Postmasterships Under Civil Service," *New York Times,* April 1, 1917, p. 13.

5. Wilson, address to the Senate, January 22, 1917, *PWW,* 40:533–39; war message to Congress, April 2, 1917, ibid., 41:526–27; Thomas Knock, *To End All War* (New York: Oxford University Press, 1992), pp. 105–22.

6. Knock, *To End All War*, pp. 134–37, 158–60; "Wilson Demands Press Censorship," *New York Times,* May 23, 1917, p. 1; Seward Livermore, *Woodrow Wilson and the War Congress, 1916–18* (Seattle: University of Washington Press, 1968), pp. 32–37.

7. House diary, February 24, 1918, *PWW,* 46:436.

8. Wilson to the Democrats of New Jersey, March 20, 1918, ibid., 47:82–84; a platform for the Indiana Democratic Party, June 15, 1918, ibid., 48:318–19; J. Tumulty to E. House, May 23, 1918, E. House to J. Tumulty, ca. June 22, 1918, Tumulty Papers, Library of Congress; John Blum, *Joe Tumulty and the Wilson Era* (Boston: Houghton Mifflin, 1951), p. 160; *New Republic,* March 30, 1918, p. 246.

9. *New Republic,* March 30, 1918, p. 246; J. Tumulty to Wilson, April 4, 1918, *PWW,* 47:253–54; platform for the Indiana Democratic Party, *PWW,* 48:318; Wilson to J. Daniels, November 28, 1917, *PWW,* 45:148; Wilson to F. Lane, May 14, 1918, *PWW,* 48:11.

10. Arthur Link, *Wilson,* 5 vols. (Princeton: Princeton University Press, 1947–1965), 2:259–60; Wilson to J. Tumulty, December 12, 1917, *PWW,* 45:275; Wilson to M. Sheppard, March 22, 1918, *PWW,* 47:106–7; Wilson to J. Cannon, June 29, 1917, *PWW,* 43:42–43; J. Tumulty to Wilson, September 7, 1918, *PWW,* 49:476–78; A. Burleson to Wilson, *PWW,* September 17, 1918, 51:28–30; House diary, September 24, 1918, *PWW,* 51:105; Livermore, *War Congress,* pp. 181–82.

11. A press release, October 6, 1915, *PWW,* 35:28; D. Malone to Wilson, September 7, 1917, ibid., 44:167–69; Sally Hunter Graham, "Woodrow Wilson, Alice Paul, and the Woman Suffrage Movement," *Political Science Quarterly* 98 (Winter 1983–1984): 665–79; a news report, *New York Times,* October 3, 1918, in *PWW,* 51:189; Richard L. Watson, "A Testing Time for Southern Congressional Leadership: The War Crisis of 1917–18," *Journal of Southern History* 44 (February 1978): 34–35; Wilson, remarks to a group of suffragists, October 3, 1918, *PWW,* 51:190; William Gibbs McAdoo, *Crowded Years* (New York: Houghton Mifflin, 1931), p. 498; Livermore, *War Congress,* pp. 183–84.

12. In the 65th Congress, of the following committees in the two houses—Rules, Military Affairs, Foreign Affairs/Relations, Ways and Means/Finance, Judiciary, Commerce, Appropriations, Post Office and Post Roads, and Agriculture—southerners chaired all but the Appropriations Committee in the House and all but Foreign Relations, Agriculture, and Military Affairs Committees in the Senate; I. A. Newby, "State's Rights and Southern Congressman During World War I," *Phylon* 24 (Spring 1963): 36.

13. David Kennedy, *Over Here: The First World War and American Society* (New York: Oxford University Press, 1980), pp. 243–44; Thomas Gore, "The Wheat Farmers' Dilemma," *Forum,* September 1918, pp. 257–65; S. Ferris to Wilson, May 16, 1918, *PWW,* 48:42; Wilson to S. Ferris, May 20, 1918, *PWW,* 48:74; S. Ferris to Wilson, July 9, 1918, *PWW,* 48:576; a veto message, July 12, 1918, *PWW,* 48:595–97; Wilson to J. Tumulty, July 16, 1918, *PWW,* 48:628.

14. R. Brookings to Wilson, March 22, 1918, *PWW,* 47:117–18; Kennedy, *Over Here,* p. 244; Wilson to W. Harris, September 6, 1918, *PWW,* 49:461; White House

staff to Wilson, September 14, 1918, *PWW,* 51:5; "President to Fix Price for Cotton," *New York Times,* September 21, 1918, p. 13; "Break in Cotton," *New York Times,* September 22, 1918, p. 24; "Cotton Rises Sharply on Good War News," *New York Times,* September 28, 1918, p. 18.

15. For a friendly account of Kitchin's stance regarding the war, which nevertheless establishes the extent of his opposition to the administration, as well as the reaction that Kitchin generated, see Alex Arnett, *Claude Kitchin and the Wilson War Policies* (Boston: Little, Brown, 1937). See also Claude Kitchin, "Who Will Pay the New Taxes?" *Forum,* August 1918, pp. 149–54.

16. Livermore, *War Congress,* pp. 31, 122, quotation on p. 153.

17. Wilson to F. Doremus, September 4, 1914, *PWW,* 30:475–78; Wilson to O. Underwood, October 10, 1914, ibid. 31:168–74.

18. Wilson to A. Burleson, March 13, 1918, *PWW,* 47:8; Wilson to J. Davies, March 18, 1918, ibid., 47:52–53; Wilson to T. Marshall, March 15, 1918, ibid., 47:40–41; "Politics During War," *New Republic,* April 13, 1918, pp. 309–10; "Parties in Wartime," *Nation,* March 28, 1918, pp. 338–39.

19. "Parties in Wartime," *Nation,* March 28, 1918, pp. 338–39; G. McNab to E. House, April 20, 1918, *PWW,* 47:388–90; a memorandum by Franklin Knight Lane, November 6, 1918, ibid., 51:616; Livermore, *War Congress,* pp. 121–22.

20. Woodrow Wilson, address to a joint session of Congress, May 27, 1918, *PWW* 48:162–65.

21. Wilson to M. Dunaway, March 9, 1918, ibid., 46:583–84. For Wilson's discussion of the dangers of intervening in the primaries and his hesitance to take any action, see also Wilson to A. Burleson, January 19, 1918, ibid., 46:38; Wilson to J. Wilson, March 13, 1918, ibid., 47:6; Wilson to J. Wilson, March 15, 1918, ibid., 47:37; Wilson to E. Brown, March 29, 1918, ibid., 47:192; Wilson to J. Watkins, June 3, 1918, ibid., 48:229–30.

22. For examples of Wilson's various covert interventions, see Wilson to W. McAdoo, March 13, 1918, ibid., 47:6–7; Wilson to E. Brown, March 29, 1918, ibid., 47:192; Wilson to J. Bankhead, May 5, 1918, ibid., 48:30–31; Wilson to J. Tumulty, June 5, 1918, ibid., 48:241; Wilson to J. Lewis, June 13, 1918, ibid., 48:603–4.

23. Daniels diary, July 30, 1918, ibid., 49:137; a memorandum by Franklin Knight Lane, November 7, 1918, ibid., 51:616; Wilson to M. McNeil, August 5, 1918, ibid., 49:180; Wilson to C. Howell, August 7, 1918, ibid., 49:205–6; J. Tumulty to Wilson, August 28, 1918, ibid., 49:369; F. Glass to Wilson, August 13, 1918, ibid., 49:245; *Nation,* September 21, 1918, p. 308.

24. *Nation,* August 24, 1918, p. 189; Wilson to F. Glass, July 31, 1918, *PWW,* 49:138; Wilson to F. Glass, August 9, 1918, *PWW,* 49:224. In the Texas case, again at Postmaster General Burleson's request, an unwitting Wilson signed a letter denouncing James Slayden, an eleven-term representative from Texas, who promptly dropped out of the race. Slayden's biggest mistake appears not to have been his record of support for the administration's war policies, which was no worse than that of many other Democrats in the House, but rather that he was running against one Carlos Bee—

Burleson's brother-in-law! Wilson to H. Beach, July 24, 1918, *PWW,* 49:73; Daniels diary, July 30, 1918, ibid., 49:137; a memorandum by Franklin Knight Lane, November 6, 1918, ibid., 51:616; Livermore, *War Congress,* pp. 162–63.

25. J. Tumulty to A. Burleson, September 15, 1917, *PWW,* 44:204–5; Wilson to E. House, September 17, 1917, ibid., 44:203; J. Tumulty to Wilson, June 18, 1918, ibid., 48:346–49; J. Tumulty to Wilson, September 4, 1918, ibid., 49:439; House diary, September 8, 1918, ibid., 49:489–90; a statement, September 9, 1918, ibid., 49:490; J. Tumulty to Wilson, September 18, 1918, ibid., 51:63. Vance McCormick later told Ray Stannard Baker that the Democratic legislators had "descended like an avalanche upon the Democratic Committee, and it was agreed by everyone concerned that some sort of an appeal had to be made" (Ray Stannard Baker, *Woodrow Wilson: Life and Letters,* 8 vols. [Garden City, N.Y.: Doubleday, Page, 1927–1939], 8:487).

26. A draft of an appeal to voters by J. Tumulty, ca. October 11, 1918, *PWW,* 51:304–6; Wilson, fragment of the first draft of an appeal to voters, ca. October 13, 1918, ibid., 51:317; second draft of an appeal to voters, ca. October 15, 1918, ibid., 51:343–44; Wilson to J. Tumulty, with enclosure, ca. October 17, 1918, ibid., 51:353–55; a memorandum by H. Cummings, October 18, 1918, ibid., 51:380–81; a memorandum by H. Cummings, October 20, 1918, ibid., 51:389–93; McCormick interview, Baker Papers, Library of Congress; Baker, *Life and Letters,* 8:510.

27. An appeal for a Democratic Congress, October 19, 1918, *PWW,* 51:381.

28. Ibid., 51:381–82.

29. "Roosevelt Assails 14 Peace Points," *New York Times,* October 25, 1918, p. 2; Knock, *To End All War,* pp. 168, 170; an appeal for a Democratic Congress, October 19, 1918, *PWW,* 51:382.

30. "Roosevelt Calls Wilson a Partisan," *New York Times,* October 26, 1918, p. 2.

31. A memorandum by F. Lane, November 1, 1918, *PWW,* 51:548; C. Eliot to Wilson, November 5, 1918, ibid., 51:599; Baker, *Life and Letters,* 8:513–14; Livermore, *War Congress,* pp. 220–22.

32. The letter is reprinted in "Not Wilson's War, Republicans Say," *New York Times,* October 26, 1918, pp. 1–2.

33. Roger Davidson and Walter Oleszek, *Congress and Its Members,* 5th ed. (Washington, D.C.: Congressional Quarterly Press, 1996), p. 436; a memorandum by Homer S. Cummings, November 11, 1918, *PWW,* 51:627–33.

34. Lodge to Lord Bryce, November 16, 1918, Lodge Papers, Massachusetts Historical Society; a memorandum by Franklin Knight Lane, November 8, 1916, *PWW,* 51:616; J. Shouse to Wilson, November 7, 1918, *PWW,* 51:623–24; A. Peters to Wilson, November 7, 1918, *PWW,* 51:624; H. Cummings to Wilson, with enclosure, November 7, 1918, *PWW,* 51:629–30; "Republican Responsibility," *New York Times,* November 7, 1918, p. 14.

35. *New Republic,* November 9, 1918, p. 26; G. Creel to Wilson, November 8, 1918, *PWW,* 51:645–46; O. Villard to J. Tumulty, November 8, 1918, ibid., 51:646. For a persuasive and well buttressed restatement of this view, see Knock, *To End All War,* pp. 185–87.

36. Kennedy, *Over Here;* Eldon Eisenach, *The Lost Promise of Progressivism* (Lawrence: University Press of Kansas, 1994), pp. 243–48.

37. A memorandum by J. Tumulty, November 9, 1918, *PWW,* 53:25. See also J. Burke to J. Tumulty, November 17, 1919, Wilson Papers, Library of Congress; *New York Sun* editorial quoted in *Literary Digest,* November 16, 1918, p. 15; "Republican Responsibility," *New York Times,* November 7, 1918, p. 14.

38. Livermore, *War Congress,* 242–45; Burner, *Politics of Provincialism,* 35–39. On the German defections, many of which were to the Nonpartisan League, see Samuel Lubell, *The Future of American Politics,* 3d rev. ed. (New York: Harper and Row, 1965), pp. 138–40; and La Vern Rippley, *The German Americans* (Boston: Twayne, 1976), p. 190.

39. Remarks to members of the Democratic National Committee, February 28, 1919, *PWW,* 55:309–12.

9: WILSON, LODGE, AND THE TREATY CONTROVERSY

1. John Michael Pyne, "Woodrow Wilson's Abdication of Domestic and Party Leadership: Autumn 1918 to Autumn 1919" (Ph.D. diss., Notre Dame University, 1979).

2. *PWW* (*The Papers of Woodrow Wilson,* ed. Arthur Link et al., 69 vols. [Princeton: Princeton University Press, 1966–1993]), 61:434.

3. The classic treatment of the foreign policy debate is Robert Osgood, *Ideals and Self-Interest in America's Foreign Relations* (Chicago: University of Chicago Press, 1964). For defenses of each of the leading camps in the GOP, see Herbert Margulies, *The Mild Reservationists and the League of Nations Controversy* (Columbia: University of Missouri Press, 1989); William Widenor, *Henry Cabot Lodge and the Search for an American Foreign Policy* (Berkeley: University of California Press, 1980); Ralph Stone, *The Irreconcilables: The Fight Against the League of Nations* (Lexington: University Press of Kentucky, 1970).

4. Lloyd Ambrosius, *Woodrow Wilson and the American Diplomatic Tradition* (New York: Cambridge University Press, 1987).

5. W. Stull Holt, *Treaties Defeated by the Senate* (Baltimore, Johns Hopkins University Press, 1933), pp. 249–307. See also Dana Frank Fleming, "Lodge the Partisan Republican," in *Wilson and the League of Nations,* ed. Ralph Stone (Huntington, N.Y.: Robert E. Kreiger, 1978), pp. 83–91. Even Thomas Bailey, who presents a relatively complex explanation of Wilson's defeat, still argues that "blind partisanship, as much as any other single factor, ruined the League of Nations in the United States" (*Woodrow Wilson and the Great Betrayal* [New York: Macmillan, 1945], p. 38).

6. Alexander George and Juliette George, *Woodrow Wilson and Colonel House: A Personality Study* (1956; New York: Dover Publications, 1964), pp. 268–315.

7. Jeffrey Tulis, *The Rhetorical Presidency* (Princeton: Princeton University Press, 1987), pp. 147–61.

8. See, e.g., *PWW,* 58:607–40, 64:494–513. See also Thomas Krattenmaker, "New Medical Evidence Reshapes View of Wilson's Presidency," *Princeton Alumni Weekly,* January 23, 1991, p. 7.

9. Wilson, *Congressional Government* (Boston: Houghton Mifflin, 1885), pp. 50 (Wilson's emphasis), 233–34.

10. Wilson, *Constitutional Government in the United States* (New York: Columbia University Press 1908), pp. 77–78.

11. On the balance in the League Covenant between peaceful discussion and armed force, termed by Wilson the "last resort," see Wilson, address to the Paris Peace Conference, February 14, 1919, *PWW,* 55:174–75.

12. On this point, see Tulis, *Rhetorical Presidency,* pp. 153–57.

13. George and George, *Woodrow Wilson,* pp. 291–315.

14. Covenant of the League of Nations, April 28, 1919, *PWW,* 58:191.

15. Ibid., 62:343, 403.

16. Lodge's remarks are reprinted in his *The Senate and the League of Nations* (New York: Scribner's, 1925), pp. 403–4.

17. See, for example, remarks at a press conference, January 15, 1917, *PWW,* 40:470–71, and Wilson to E. House, March 22, 1918, ibid., 47:105.

18. Ibid., 62:343.

19. Ibid., 62:353–56, 360–64.

20. See Ambrosius, *Woodrow Wilson,* especially chap. 6, and Widenor, *Henry Cabot Lodge,* 336–41.

21. *PWW,* 62:343–44.

22. See, e.g., the interchange between Senator McCumber and Wilson on a reservation to Article 10 in ibid., 62:355–56. Wilson drew up a list of interpretations just before leaving on his tour and gave it to his spokesperson in the Senate, Gilbert Hitchcock, with the instructions that the senator was not to attribute authorship to Wilson but was otherwise free to use the list as he saw fit to reach an agreement. A comparison of Wilson's interpretations with the reservations that the mild reservationists proposed in early August is particularly revealing on the gap between the president and the senators who were the least opposed to the league. Wilson's list is described by George and George as being virtually identical to that of the mild reservationists and thus as evidence that Wilson was only, and unreasonably, splitting hairs (*Woodrow Wilson,* pp. 292–93, 350). In fact, there were key differences in the respective documents; for one thing, the Republicans proposed that their reservations "be made a part of the treaty by the instrument of ratification," while Wilson proposed that the president would only "communicate these interpretations to the several States signatory to said treaty at the same time that he deposits the formal instrument of ratification." More important, the senators' reservations included the following specific affirmation vis-à-vis Article 10: "That any undertaking under the provisions of article 10, the execution of which may require the use of American military or naval forces or economic measures can under the constitution be carried out only by the action of the Congress, and that the failure of the Congress to adopt

the suggestions of the council of the league, or to provide such military or naval forces or economic measures, shall not constitute a violation of the treaty." In contrast, Wilson's interpretation of Article 10 read: "The advice of the Council of the League with regard to the employment of armed force contemplated in Article Ten of the Covenant of the League is to be regarded only as advice and leaves each Member State free to exercise its own judgment as to whether it is wise or practicable to act upon that advice or not." From the standpoint of constitutional interpretation, the terms of which framed the treaty fight, the assertion of the Senate's treaty power and the affirmation of Congress's war power that were manifested in the mild reservationist program posed a fundamental challenge to Wilson's policy and prerogatives. See Wilson, a memorandum, September 3, 1919, *PWW,* 62:621, and Margulies, *Mild Reservationists,* pp. 88. For the mild reservationists' proposals, see a news report, *Washington Post,* August 2, 1919, in *PWW,* 62:112–14.

23. For Lodge's attitudes toward Wilson, see the following, all in the Lodge Papers, Massachusetts Historical Society: Lodge to J. Bishop, December 23, 1918; A. Beveridge to Lodge, November 27, 1918; Lodge to A. Beveridge, December 3, 1918; Lodge to A. Beveridge, February 18, 1919.

24. On this point, see Herbert Storing, *Toward a More Perfect Union,* ed. Joseph M. Bessette (Washington, D.C.: American Enterprise Institute, 1995), pp. 382–83; and Joseph M. Bessette and Jeffrey Tulis, "The Constitution, Politics, and the Presidency," in Bessette and Tulis, eds., *The Presidency in the Constitutional Order* (Baton Rouge: Louisiana State University Press, 1981), pp. 8–16.

25. Here we might recall the argument made in another context by Publius in *Federalist* 1: "My motives must remain in the depository of my own breast. My arguments will be open to all, and may be judged by all." I am also grateful to Jeffrey Tulis for clarifying my thinking on this point.

26. H. Lodge to T. Roosevelt, February 28, 1912, in *Selections from the Correspondence of Theodore Roosevelt and Henry Cabot Lodge, 1884–1918,* ed. Henry Cabot Lodge, 2 vols. (New York: Scribner's, 1925), 2:423. It is worth noting that while Lodge felt compelled to criticize the Bull Moose on constitutional grounds, he did not do so on partisan grounds. Indeed, Lodge refused to join William Howard Taft in the campaign of the Republican Party against Roosevelt.

27. Lodge to J. Bishop, October 26, 1918, Lodge Papers, Massachusetts Historical Society.

28. "Not Wilson's War, Republicans Say," *New York Times,* October 26, 1918, pp. 1–2; Lodge to J. Bishop, November 16, 1918, Lodge Papers, Massachusetts Historical Society.

29. Lodge to W. Bigelow, November 26, 1918, Lodge Papers, Massachusetts Historical Society.

30. *Congressional Record,* 65th Cong., 3d sess., December 21, 1918, p. 724.

31. Ibid.

32. Ibid.

33. Ibid., pp. 724–28; Lodge to T. Roosevelt, December 23, 1918, *Correspondence,* 2:550.

34. The Round Robin is reprinted in Lodge, *Senate and the League,* p. 119.

35. Henry Cabot Lodge, "The Treaty-Making Powers of the Senate," *A Fighting Frigate and Other Essays* (Freeport, N.Y.: Books for Libraries Press, 1969), pp. 254–55 (my emphasis).

36. Ibid., pp. 219–56; Lodge, *The Senate of the United States* (New York: Charles Scribner's Sons, 1921), pp. 26–28; Holt, *Treaties Defeated by the Senate,* pp. 179–80, 185–87; John A. Garraty, *Henry Cabot Lodge* (New York: Alfred A. Knopf, 1965), p. 356.

37. Wilson, *Constitutional Government,* p. 139.

38. Ibid., pp. 139–40.

39. House diary, January 27, 1918, *PWW,* 46:115–16; House diary, October 13, 1918, ibid., 51:316–17.

40. Two Wilson radiograms to J. Tumulty, February 22, 1919, ibid., 55:225–26.

41. Ibid., 55:268–76, quotation on p. 274. See also Grayson diary, February 26, 1917, ibid., 55:267.

42. C. Eliot to J. Tumulty, July 2, 1919, ibid., 61:373–74; J. Williams to Wilson, July 9, 1919, ibid., 61:411; Wilson to J. Williams, July 15, 1919; ibid., 61:482; W. Wiseman to E. House, July 19, 1919, ibid., 61:561–62. See also Wilson to W. McAdoo, August 5, 1919, printed in editors' note, ibid., 62:185–86. The invitations to and news reports of the meetings are found in ibid., 61:492–93, 515–17, 544–49, 569–70, 593–95, 599–602; 62:29, 43–45, 90–92. See also Kurt Wimer, "Woodrow Wilson Tries Conciliation: An Effort That Failed," *Historian* 25 (August 1963): 419–38.

43. An address in Boston, February 24, 1919, *PWW,* 55:238–45; an address at the Metropolitan Opera House, March 4, 1919, ibid., 55:418.

44. Wilson and his entourage traveled through Indianapolis, St. Louis, Kansas City, Des Moines, Iowa, Omaha, Sioux Falls, S.D., Minneapolis, Bismarck, N.D., Billings, Mont., Spokane, Wash., Tacoma, Wash., Portland, San Francisco, Los Angeles, San Diego, Sacramento, Salt Lake City, Cheyenne, Wyo., Denver, and various points in between before Wilson collapsed on September 26; Bailey, *Great Betrayal,* pp. 102–114.

45. See the memoir of Wilson's physician, Dr. Cary Grayson, *Woodrow Wilson: An Intimate Memoir* (Washington, D.C.: Potomac Books, 1977), pp. 82–100, and Edwin Weinstein, *Woodrow Wilson: A Medical and Psychological Biography* (Princeton: Princeton University Press, 1981), pp. 332–57, for accounts of Wilson's physical demise in 1919.

46. *PWW,* 58:607–40, 64:497–507. See also Krattenmaker, "New Medical Evidence Reshapes View of Wilson's Presidency," p. 7.

47. Wilson, *Constitutional Government,* p. 78.

48. Wilson's comments were recorded by his brother-in-law; *PWW,* 67:605.

49. Ibid., 64:199–202.

50. Another problem was that in several states the governors would have to make interim appointments to serve out the length of the resigned senators' terms; in still other states it was not clear how soon the elections could be held. Attorney General A. Mitchell Palmer pointed out these difficulties to the president's wife, who had asked him to investigate the scheme's feasibility; ibid., 64:214–15.

51. Ibid., 64:257–58.

52. Ibid., 64:267–69 (Lansing's emphasis).

53. G. Hitchcock to E. Wilson, with enclosure, November 18, 1919, ibid., 64:58–60; Ashurst diary, November 19, 1919, ibid., 64:62–64; a statement, December 12, 1919, ibid., 64:187; J. Tumulty to E. Wilson, December 16, 1919, ibid., 64:190; a memorandum by Robert Lansing, December 16, 1919, ibid., 64:192–94; E. Wilson to G. Hitchcock, December 19, 1919, ibid., 64:206; W. Bryan to H. Ashurst, November 23, 1919, reprinted in Henry Fountain Ashurst, *A Many-Colored Toga: The Diary of Henry Fountain Ashurst,* ed. George Sparks (Tucson: University of Arizona Press, 1962), p. 116–17; Ashurst diary, January 7, 1920, *PWW,* 64:252.

54. W. McAdoo to C. Glass, December 13, 1919, McAdoo Papers, Library of Congress; R. Woolley to E. House, June 17, 1919, Baker Papers, Library of Congress; David Burner, *The Politics of Provincialism: The Democratic Party in Transition* (New York: Alfred Knopf, 1967), pp. 52–53. This discussion is adapted from Daniel Stid, "Woodrow Wilson and the Problem of Party Government," *Polity* 26 (Summer 1994): 576.

55. F. Lane to G. Lane, January 30, 1919, in *The Letters of Franklin Knight Lane,* ed. Anne Wintermute Lane and Louise Herrick (New York: Houghton Mifflin, 1922), p. 307; "The Future of the Democratic Party," *New Republic,* July 7, 1919, p. 164; William Hard, "The President Relapses," *New Republic,* December 14, 1918, pp. 184–86; "The President on Trial," *Nation,* September 6, 1919, pp. 326–27.

56. A memorandum by Stockton Axson, ca. August 1919, *PWW,* 67:607; McCormick diary, July 1–3, 1919, ibid., 61:366; quotations from memorandum by Robert Lansing, September 1, 1919, ibid., 62:612. See also a special message to Congress, May 20, 1919, ibid., 59:291–92.

57. J. Tumulty to Wilson, June 4, 1919, ibid., 60:154. For Tumulty's recommendations on how to bring about this realignment, see J. Tumulty to Wilson, January 30, 1919, ibid., 54:390–93; J. Tumulty to Wilson, June 4, 1919, ibid., 60:145–53; Wilson to J. Tumulty, June 17, 1919, ibid., 60:644.

58. Address to a joint session of Congress, August 8, 1919, ibid., 62:210–12; in his meeting with the Senate Foreign Relations Committee on August 19, 1919, Wilson reiterated this argument, ibid., 62:340–41. Before he went before the Senate committee, Wilson requested that several of his department heads send him information on how the delayed ratification was hurting the economy in their sectors. See, e.g., C. Glass to Wilson, with enclosure, August 13, 1919, ibid., 62:266–67; D. Houston to Wilson, August 13, 1919, ibid., 62:268–70; R. Lansing to Wilson, August 15, 1919, ibid., 62:322–23.

59. Wilson to G. Hitchcock, January 26, 1920, ibid., 64:329; Wilson to G. Hitchcock, March 8, 1920, ibid., 65:67–71.

60. Daniels diary, April 20, 1920, ibid., 65:212.

61. John Chalmers Vinson, *Referendum for Isolation: The Defeat of Article 10 of the League of Nations Covenant* (Athens: University of Georgia Press, 1961); *New Republic,* November 10, 1920, pp. 254–55.

CONCLUSION

1. Charles O. Jones, *The Presidency in a Separated System* (Washington, D.C.: Brookings Institution, 1994), pp. 1–12; James Sundquist, "Needed: A Political Theory for the New Era of Coalition Government in the United States," *Political Science Quarterly* 103 (1988) 4:613–35, quotation on p. 635. See also Austin Ranney, *The Doctrine of Responsible Party Government* (Urbana: University of Illinois Press, 1954).

2. The speeches of Lodge and Harding are reprinted in the *New York Times,* July 23, 1920, p. 4. See also Andrew Sinclair, *The Available Man: The Life Behind the Masks of Warren Gamaliel Harding* (New York: Macmillan, 1965), pp. 151–53.

3. Wilfred Binkley, *President and Congress,* 3d ed. (New York: Random House, 1962), pp. 265–73.

4. See, e.g., Edwin Corwin, *The Presidency: Office and Powers, 1787–1957* (New York: New York University Press, 1957), pp. 305–17; James Sundquist, *Decline and Resurgence of Congress* (Washington D.C.: Brookings Institution, 1981), pp. 30–35; Binkley, *President and Congress,* pp. 228–64, 289–336.

5. Harold Hongju Koh, *The National Security Constitution* (New Haven: Yale University Press, 1990), pp. 89–99; Louis Fisher, *Presidential War Power* (Lawrence: University Press of Kansas, 1995), pp. 45–69.

6. Corwin, *The Presidency,* pp. 306–8, 314–15, 515; Binkley, *President and Congress,* pp. 294–98; Lindsay Rogers, "Reorganization: Post-Mortem Notes," *Political Science Quarterly* 53 (June 1938): 170; Sidney M. Milkis, *The President and the Parties* (New York: Oxford University Press, 1993), part 1. See also Theodore Lowi, *The Personal President* (Ithaca, N.Y.: Cornell University Press, 1986), pp. 44–66; James MacGregor Burns, *Presidential Government: The Crucible of Leadership* (New York: Avon, 1967), pp. 117–25.

7. See, e.g., Corwin, *The Presidency,* pp. 331–39; E. E. Schattschneider, *Party Government* (New York: Holt, Rinehart, 1942), pp. 206–10.

8. William Yandell Elliot, *The Need for Constitutional Reform* (New York: Whittlesey House, 1935); Henry Hazlitt, *A New Constitution Now* (New York: Whittlesey House, 1942); Thomas K. Finletter, *Can Representative Government Do the Job?* (New York: Reynal and Hitchcock, 1945); Corwin, *The Presidency,* pp. 335–39.

9. *American Political Science Review* 44 (September 1950): supplement.

10. Ibid.

11. Austin Ranney, "'Toward a More Responsible Two-Party System': A Commentary," *American Political Science Review* 45 (June 1951): 492–99; Evron Kirkpatrick, "'Toward a More Responsible Two-Party System': Political Science, Policy Science, or Pseudo Science?" *American Political Science Review* 65 (September 1971): 965–79.

12. James Q. Wilson, "Political Parties and the Separation of Powers," in *The Separation of Powers—Does It Still Work?* ed. Robert Goldwin and Art Kaufman (Washington, D.C.: American Enterprise Institute, 1986), pp. 31–36.

13. James Ceaser, *Presidential Selection: Theory and Development* (Princeton: Princeton University Press, 1979); Nelson Polsby, *The Consequences of Party Reform* (New York: Oxford University Press, 1983).

14. Morris Fiorina, "The Reagan Years: Turning to the Right or Groping Toward the Middle?" in *The Resurgence of Conservatism in Anglo-American Democracies,* ed. Barry Cooper, et al. (Durham, N.C.: Duke University Press, 1988), pp. 430–59; James Sundquist, "Strengthening the National Parties," in *Elections American Style,* ed. A. James Reichley (Washington, D.C.: Brookings Institution, 1987), pp. 195–221.

15. "A Bicentennial Analysis of the American Political Structure" (Washington, D.C.: Committee on the Constitutional System, 1987). See also Charles Hardin, *Presidential Power and Accountability: Toward a New Constitution* (Chicago: University of Chicago Press, 1974); Lloyd Cutler, "To Form a Government," *Foreign Affairs* 59 (Fall 1980): 126–43; James Sundquist, *Constitutional Reform and Effective Government* (Washington, D.C.: Brookings Institution, 1986); Donald Robinson, *Government for a Third American Century* (Boulder, Colo.: Westview Press, 1989).

16. American Political Science Association, Committee on Political Parties, "Toward a More Responsible Two-Party System," p. 35.

17. Kent Weaver and Bert Rockman, *Do Institutions Matter?* (Washington, D.C.: Brookings Institution, 1993), pp. 445–61. See also Arend Lijphart, *Democracies: Patterns of Majoritarian and Consensus Government in 21 Countries* (New Haven: Yale University Press, 1984).

18. See, for example, Bernard Bailyn, *The Ideological Origins of the American Revolution* (Cambridge: Harvard University Press, 1967), pp. 55–93; Samuel Huntington, *American Politics: The Promise of Disharmony* (Cambridge, Mass.: Belknap Press, 1981), pp. 14–15; Ranney, *Party Government,* pp. 160–62; and James Sterling Young and Richard L. Riley, "Party Government and Political Culture," paper presented at the annual meeting of the American Political Science Association, San Francisco, California, September 1990.

19. On this point, see Don K. Price, *America's Unwritten Constitution: Science, Religion, and Political Responsibility* (Baton Rouge: Louisiana State University Press, 1983), p. 73.

20. For incisive discussions of the political and cultural obstacles facing the Committee on the Constitutional System by two of its most thoughtful spokespersons, see Sundquist, *Constitutional Reform,* pp. 242–52, and the comments by Donald Robinson in two conferences cosponsored by the committee, the proceedings of

which have been published in *Beyond Gridlock? Prospects for Governance in the Clinton Years*, ed. James Sundquist (Washington, D.C.: Brookings Institution, 1993), pp. 55–59, and *Back to Gridlock? Governance in the Clinton Years*, ed. James Sundquist (Washington, D.C., Brookings Institution, 1995), pp. 88–93.

21. Sundquist, *Beyond Gridlock?* pp. 58–59; Sundquist, *Back to Gridlock?* p. 89.

22. Arthur M. Schlesinger Jr., *The Cycles of American History* (Boston: Houghton Mifflin, 1986), pp. 307–8; "Reclaiming Britain's Constitution," *Economist*, October 14, 1995, p. 18; "Britain's Constitution: The Case for Reform," *Economist*, October 14, 1995, pp. 25–28.

23. See Cutler, "To Form a Government," pp. 126–28; Philip Cerny, "Political Entropy and American Decline," *Millennium* 18 (1989) 1:47–63; J. William Fulbright, "American Foreign Policy in the 20th Century Under an 18th Century Constitution," *Cornell Law Quarterly* 47 (Fall 1961) 1:1–13.

24. Michel Debre, "The Constitution of 1958, Its Raison D'etre and How It Evolved," in *The Impact of the Fifth Republic on France*, ed. William Andrews and Stanley Hoffman (Albany: State University of New York Press, 1981), pp. 6–7.

25. Cutler, "To Form a Government," p. 127.

26. David Epstein, *The Political Theory of the Federalist* (Chicago: University of Chicago Press, 1984), pp. 176–79.

27. On this point, see Schlesinger, *Cycles of American History*, pp. 309–11.

28. See note 45 in Chapter 7.

29. Ralph Ketcham, *Presidents Above Party: The First American Presidency, 1789–1829* (Chapel Hill: University of North Carolina Press, 1984), pp. 231–35. On the tradeoffs, see also George A. Curran, "Woodrow Wilson's Theory and Practice Regarding the Relations of the President and Congress" (Ph.D. diss., Fordham University, 1948), pp. 189–92.

30. Milkis emphasizes the importance of government through administration in *The President and the Parties*, while Lowi focuses on the president's plebiscitary appeals to the masses in *The Personal President*. Both scholars, however, see the New Deal as the critical juncture in the demise of parties.

31. Alexander Hamilton, John Jay, and James Madison, *The Federalist* (New York: Random House, 1937), p. 458.

32. On this point, see Barbara Sinclair, *Legislators, Leaders, and Lawmaking: The U.S. House of Representatives in the Post Reform Era* (Baltimore: Johns Hopkins University Press, 1995), chap. 1.

33. John H. Aldrich and David W. Rohde, "A Tale of Two Speakers: A Comparison of Policy Making in the 100th and 104th Congress," paper delivered at the annual meeting of the American Political Science Association, August 29–September 1, 1996, San Francisco, p. 2.

34. Kenneth Shepsle, "The Changing Textbook Congress," in John Chubb and Paul Peterson, eds, *Can the Government Govern?* (Washington, D.C.: Brookings Institution, 1989), pp. 238–66; David Rohde, *Parties and Leaders in the Postreform House* (Chicago: University of Chicago Press, 1991); Barbara Sinclair, "The Speaker as

Party Leader," in *The Speaker: Leadership in the U.S. House of Representatives,* ed. Ronald M. Peters Jr. (Washington, D.C.: Congressional Quarterly Press, 1995), pp. 40–60.

35. See William Connelly and John Pitney, *Congress' Permanent Minority? Republicans in the U.S. House* (Lanham, Md.: Rowman and Littlefield, 1994); Ronald M. Peters Jr., "A Republican Speakership," in Peters, ed., *The Speaker,* pp. 263–82; Daniel Stid, "Transformational Leadership in Congress?" paper presented at the annual meeting of the American Political Science Association, August 29–September 1, 1996, San Francisco.

36. Lawrence Dodd and Bruce Oppenheimer, "Congress and the Emerging Order: Conditional Party Government or Constructive Partisanship," in *Congress Reconsidered,* eds. Dodd and Oppenheimer, 6th ed. (Washington, D.C.: Congressional Quarterly Press, 1997), pp. 390–413.

37. Wilson, *Congressional Government* (Boston: Houghton Mifflin, 1885), pp. 332–33.

✤ Index